NAPLEX® MATH REVIEW

David Heckman, PharmD

Copyright ©2021 by David Heckman, PharmD

NAPLEX® Math Review

ISBN-13: 978-1942682042

Copyright © 2021 by David Heckman, PharmD
All rights reserved. This book is protected by copyright. No portion of this book may be reproduced in any form, including photocopying, without the author's written permission.

The author does not assume and hereby disclaims any liability to any party for losses, damages, and/or failures caused by error or omission, regardless of whether such error or omission resulted from negligence, oversight, accident, or any other cause.

This publication does not contain actual exam content.

NAPLEX® and NABP® are federally registered trademarks of the National Association of Boards of Pharmacy (NABP®). The National Association of Boards of Pharmacy (NABP®) does not endorse, authorize, or sponsor this or any other study guide.

Published by Heckman Media

Printed in the United States of America

TABLE *of* CONTENTS

Ideal Body Weight 7-9
Adjusted Body Weight 11-15
Body Surface Area 17-22
Creatinine Clearance 24-31
Corrected Calcium 33-35

Pediatric Dosing Equations
    Clark's Rule 37-42
    Young's Rule 37-42
    Pediatric Body Surface Area (BSA) Dosing 37-42

Percent Concentration
    Weight/Weight 43-46
    Volume/Volume 47-49
    Weight/Volume 51-58

Ratio Strength 59-64
Parts Per Million 65-69
Milliequivalents 70-76
Millimolarity 77-80
Milliosmolarity 82-88
Simple Dilution 89-92
Alligation Medial 93-96
Alligation Alternate 97-104

Prescription Balances
    Percent Error 105-107
    Sensitivity Requirement 105-107
    Minimum Weighable Quantity 105-107

Henderson-Hasselbalch 108-114

Parenteral Nutrition
    Calorie Requirement 115-128
    Protein Requirement 115-128
    Fluid Requirement 115-128
    Nitrogen Balance 115-128

Infusion Flow Rate/Drip Rate 129-132
Dissociation Factor 133-134
Sodium Chloride Equivalents 135-140
Temperature Conversion 141-144
Quantity/Day-Supply 145-148
Density 149-151
Specific Gravity 153-155

Biostatistics
    Absolute Risk Reduction 156-165
    Number Needed to Treat 156-165
    Relative Risk 156-165
    Relative Risk Reduction 156-165

Tips for Success 167
Must-Know Conversion Factors 169-171
Must-Know Sig Codes 173

START HERE

→

IDEAL BODY WEIGHT (IBW)

EQUATIONS TO MEMORIZE
IBW (male) = 50 kg + 2.3 kg for each inch of height over 5 feet
IBW (female) = 45.5 kg + 2.3 kg for each inch of height over 5 feet

PREPARING for POTENTIAL PITFALLS
IBW is based purely on a patient's **GENDER & HEIGHT**
Information other than gender and height is irrelevant, with the exception of amputations.
IBW should be reduced by a factor that corresponds with the specific amputation; however, because only about 1 in 190 Americans have an amputation, we do not recommend memorizing these factors.

MUST-KNOW CONVERSION FACTORS
1 foot = 12 inches   1 inch = 2.54 centimeters
2.2 pounds = 1 kilogram

1. OW is a 73-year-old female with a weight of 148 pounds and a height of 5 ft. 5 in. What is OW's ideal body weight in kilograms? *57 kg*

2. GJ is a 65-year-old male with a weight of 178 pounds and a height of 6ft. 2 in. What is OW's ideal body weight in kilograms? *82.2 kg*

3. AK is a 62-year-old woman with a weight of 81 kilograms and a height of 1.72 meters. What is AK's ideal body weight in kilograms? *63.23 kg*

4. JP is a 91-year-old man with a weight of 94 kilograms and a height of 183 centimeters. What is JP's ideal body weight in kilograms? *77.6*

5. AM is a 25-year-old female with a creatinine clearance of 99 mL/min and a height of 5 ft. 2 inches. What is AM's ideal body weight in kilograms? *50.1 kg*

6. CD is a 30-year-old male with a body surface area of 1.81 m² and a height of 5 ft. 9 in. What is CD's ideal body weight in kilograms? *70.7*

7. CG is a 75-year-old woman with a weight of 44 kg and a height of 160 cm. What is CG's ideal body weight in kilograms? *52.4 kg*

SOLUTIONS for IDEAL BODY WEIGHT PROBLEMS

1. OW is a 73-year-old female with a weight of 148 pounds and a height of 5 ft. 5 in. What is OW's ideal body weight?

    SOLUTION: Apply the equation to estimate the ideal body weight for a female patient.

    IBW (female) = 45.5 kg + (2.3 kg for each inch of height over 5 feet) = 45.5 kg + (2.3 kg x 5) = 57 kg

    NOTE: Actual weight is irrelevant. IBW is based on a patient's gender and height.

2. GJ is a 65-year-old male with a weight of 178 pounds and a height of 6ft. 2 in. What is OW's ideal body weight?

    SOLUTION: Apply the equation to estimate the ideal body weight for a male patient.

    IBW (male) = 50 kg + (2.3 kg for each inch of height over 5 feet) = 50 kg + (2.3 kg x 14) = 82.2 kg

    NOTE: Actual weight is irrelevant. IBW is based on a patient's gender and height.

3. AK is a 62-year-old woman with a weight of 81 kilograms and a height of 1.72 meters. What is AK's ideal body weight?

    STEP 1: Convert units of height to inches.

    $$1.72 \text{ m} \times \frac{100 \text{ cm}}{\text{m}} \times \frac{\text{in}}{2.54 \text{ cm}} = 67.7 \text{ in}$$

    STEP 2: Apply the equation to estimate the ideal body weight for a female patient.

    IBW (female) = 45.5 kg + (2.3 kg for each inch of height over 5 feet) = 45.5 kg + (2.3 kg x 7.7) = 63.2 kg

    NOTE: 5 feet = 60 inches

4. JP is a 91-year-old man with a weight of 94 kilograms and a height of 183 centimeters. What is JP's ideal body weight?

    STEP 1: Convert units of height to inches.

    $$183 \text{ cm} \times \frac{\text{in}}{2.54 \text{ cm}} = 72 \text{ in}$$

    STEP 2: Apply the equation to estimate the ideal body weight for a male patient.

    IBW (male) = 50 kg + (2.3 kg for each inch of height over 5 feet) = 50 kg + (2.3 kg x 12) = 77.6 kg

    NOTE: 5 feet = 60 inches

5. AM is a 25-year-old female with a creatinine clearance of 99 mL/min and a height of 5 ft. 2 inches. What is AM's ideal body weight?

    SOLUTION: Apply the equation to estimate the ideal body weight for a female patient.

    IBW (female) = 45.5 kg + (2.3 kg for each inch of height over 5 feet) = 45.5 kg + (2.3 kg x 2) = 50.1 kg

    NOTE: CrCl is irrelevant. IBW is based on a patient's gender and height.

6. CD is a 30-year-old male with a body surface area of 1.81 m² and a height of 5 ft. 9 in. What is CD's ideal body weight?

    SOLUTION: Apply the equation to estimate the ideal body weight for a male patient.

    IBW (male) = 50 kg + (2.3 kg for each inch of height over 5 feet) = 50 kg + (2.3 kg x 9) = 70.7 kg

    NOTE: BSA is irrelevant. IBW is based on a patient's gender and height.

7. CG is a 75-year-old woman with a weight of 44 kg and a height of 160 cm. What is CG's ideal body weight?

    STEP 1: Convert units of height to inches.

    $$160 \text{ cm} \times \frac{\text{in}}{2.54 \text{ cm}} = 63 \text{ in}$$

    STEP 2: Apply the equation to estimate the ideal body weight for a female patient.

    IBW (female) = 45.5 kg + (2.3 kg for each inch of height over 5 feet) = 45.5 kg + (2.3 kg x 3) = 52.4 kg

    NOTE: 5 feet = 60 inches

REFERENCES
1. Devine BJ. Gentamicin therapy. *Drug Intell Clin Pharm*. 1974; 8:650–655.
2. Ziegler-Graham K, MacKenzie EJ, Ephraim PL, Travison TG, Brookmeyer R. Estimating the Prevalence of Limb Loss in the United States: 2005 to 2050. *Archives of Physical Medicine and Rehabilitation* 2008;89(3):422-9.

ADJUSTED BODY WEIGHT (ABW)

EQUATION TO MEMORIZE
ABW = IBW + 0.4(TBW – IBW)

NOTE: Calculation of ABW is only warranted if the patient's total body weight (TBW) is > 30% over IBW.

PREPARING *for* POTENTIAL PITFALLS
Always begin by calculating IBW, then check if TBW is > 30% over IBW.
Only calculate ABW if the patient is obese (TBW > 30% over IBW)

1. HJ is a male that weighs 97 kg and has a height of 5 ft. 3 in. What is HJ's adjusted body weight in kilograms?

2. LS is a female that weighs 64 kg and has a height of 5 ft. 1 in. What is LS's adjusted body weight in kilograms?

3. SG is a 170-pound male with a creatinine clearance of 100 mL/min, a body temperature of 100.1°F, and a height of 6 ft. 0 in. What is SG's adjusted body weight in kilograms?

4. BB is a 192-pound female with a height of 5 ft. 5 in., a creatinine clearance of 115 mL/min, and a serum potassium level of 4.0 mEq/L. What is BB's adjusted body weight in kilograms?

5. LT is a 176-pound male that is 162.5 cm tall. What is LT's adjusted body weight in kilograms?

6. TP is a 312-pound female that is 172.5 cm tall. What is TP's adjusted body weight in kilograms?

7. MP is a 293-pound man that is 6ft. 4in. tall. What is MP's adjusted body weight in kilograms?

SOLUTIONS *for* ADJUSTED BODY WEIGHT PROBLEMS

1. HJ is a male that weighs 97 kg and is 5 ft. 3 in tall. What is HJ's adjusted body weight?

    STEP 1: Apply the equation to calculate the ideal body weight for a male patient.

    IBW (male) = 50 kg + (2.3 kg for each inch of height over 5 feet) = 50 kg + (2.3 kg x 3) = 56.9 kg

    STEP 2: Determine whether TBW > 30% over IBW.

    $$\frac{TBW - IBW}{IBW} = \frac{97 \text{ kg} - 56.9 \text{ kg}}{56.9 \text{ kg}} = \frac{40.1 \text{ kg}}{56.9 \text{ kg}} = 0.705$$

    > Weight adjustment is only necessary for obese patients (TBW > 30% over IBW)

    TRANSLATION: The patient's total body weight (TBW) is 70.5% over IBW; therefore, the patient is obese.

    STEP 3: Given that the patient is obese, apply the equation to calculate the patient's adjusted body weight.

    ABW = IBW + 0.4(TBW − IBW)

    = 56.9 kg + 0.4(97 kg − 56.9 kg) = 56.9 kg + 0.4(40.1 kg) = 72.9 kg

2. LS is a female that weighs 64 kg and is 5 ft. 1 in tall. What is LS's adjusted body weight?

    STEP 1: Apply the equation to calculate the ideal body weight for a female patient.

    IBW (female) = 45.5 kg + (2.3 kg for each inch of height over 5 feet) = 45.5 kg + (2.3 kg x 1) = 47.8 kg

    STEP 2: Determine whether TBW > 30% over IBW.

    $$\frac{TBW - IBW}{IBW} = \frac{64 \text{ kg} - 47.8 \text{ kg}}{47.8 \text{ kg}} = \frac{16.2 \text{ kg}}{47.8 \text{ kg}} = 0.339$$

    TRANSLATION: The patient's total body weight (TBW) is 33.9% over IBW; therefore, the patient is obese.

    STEP 3: Given that the patient is obese, apply the equation to calculate the patient's adjusted body weight.

    ABW = IBW + 0.4(TBW − IBW)

    = 47.8 kg + 0.4(64 kg − 47.8 kg) = 47.8 kg + 0.4(16.2 kg) = 54.3 kg

3. SG is a 170-pound male with a creatinine clearance of 100 mL/min, a body temperature of 100.1°F, and a height of 6 ft. 0 in. What is SG's adjusted body weight?

    STEP 1: Apply the equation to calculate the ideal body weight for a male patient.

    $$\text{IBW (male)} = 50 \text{ kg} + (2.3 \text{ kg for each inch of height over 5 feet}) = 50 \text{ kg} + (2.3 \text{ kg} \times 12) = 77.6 \text{ kg}$$

    STEP 2: Convert patient's weight from pounds to kilograms.

    $$170 \text{ lb} \times \frac{\text{kg}}{2.2 \text{ lb}} = 77.3 \text{ kg}$$

    STEP 3: Determine whether TBW > 30% over IBW.

    $$\frac{\text{TBW} - \text{IBW}}{\text{IBW}} = \frac{77.3 \text{ kg} - 77.6 \text{ kg}}{77.6 \text{ kg}} = \frac{-0.3 \text{ kg}}{77.6 \text{ kg}} = -0.004$$

    TRANSLATION: The patient's total body weight (TBW) is 0.4% below IBW; therefore, the patient is not obese.

    > Adjusted body weight should **not** be calculated unless the patient is obese.

4. BB is a 192-pound female with a height of 5 ft. 5 in., a creatinine clearance of 115 mL/min, and a serum potassium level of 4.0 mEq/L. What is BB's adjusted body weight?

    STEP 1: Apply equation to estimate ideal body weight for a female patient.

    $$\text{IBW (female)} = 45.5 \text{ kg} + (2.3 \text{ kg for each inch of height over 5 feet}) = 45.5 \text{ kg} + (2.3 \text{ kg} \times 5) = 57 \text{ kg}$$

    STEP 2: Convert total body weight from units of pounds to kilograms.

    $$192 \text{ lb} \times \frac{\text{kg}}{2.2 \text{ lb}} = 87.3 \text{ kg}$$

    STEP 3: Determine whether TBW > 30% over IBW.

    $$\frac{\text{TBW} - \text{IBW}}{\text{IBW}} = \frac{87.3 \text{ kg} - 57 \text{ kg}}{57 \text{ kg}} = \frac{30.3 \text{ kg}}{57 \text{ kg}} = 0.532$$

    TRANSLATION: The patient's total body weight (TBW) is 53.2% over IBW; therefore, the patient is obese.

    STEP 4: Given that the patient is obese, apply the equation to calculate the patient's adjusted body weight.

    $$\text{ABW} = \text{IBW} + 0.4(\text{TBW} - \text{IBW})$$

    $$= 57 \text{ kg} + 0.4(87.3 \text{ kg} - 57 \text{ kg}) = 57 \text{ kg} + 0.4(30.3 \text{ kg}) = 69.1 \text{ kg}$$

5. LT is a 176-pound male that is 162.5 cm tall. What is LT's adjusted body weight?

    STEP 1: Convert units of height to inches.

    $$162.5 \text{ cm} \times \frac{\text{in}}{2.54 \text{ cm}} = 64 \text{ in}$$

    STEP 2: Apply the equation to calculate the ideal body weight for a male patient.

    IBW (male) = 50 kg + (2.3 kg for each inch of height over 5 feet) = 50 kg + (2.3 kg x 4) = 59.2 kg

    NOTE: 5 feet = 60 inches

    STEP 3: Convert total body weight from units of pounds to kilograms.

    $$176 \text{ lb} \times \frac{\text{kg}}{2.2 \text{ lb}} = 80 \text{ kg}$$

    STEP 4: Determine whether TBW > 30% over IBW.

    $$\frac{\text{TBW} - \text{IBW}}{\text{IBW}} = \frac{80 \text{ kg} - 59.2 \text{ kg}}{59.2 \text{ kg}} = \frac{20.8 \text{ kg}}{59.2 \text{ kg}} = 0.351$$

    TRANSLATION: The patient's total body weight (TBW) is 35.1% over IBW; therefore, the patient is obese.

    STEP 5: Given that the patient is obese, apply the equation to calculate the patient's adjusted body weight.

    ABW = IBW + 0.4(TBW − IBW)

    = 59.2 kg + 0.4(80 kg − 59.2 kg) = 59.2 kg + 0.4(20.8 kg) = 67.5 kg

6. TP is a 312-pound female that is 172.5 cm tall. What is TP's adjusted body weight?

    STEP 1: Convert units of height to inches.

    $$172.5 \text{ cm} \times \frac{\text{in}}{2.54 \text{ cm}} = 67.9 \text{ in}$$

    STEP 2: Apply equation to estimate ideal body weight for a female patient.

    IBW (female) = 45.5 kg + (2.3 kg for each inch of height over 5 feet) = 45.5 kg + (2.3 kg x 7.9) = 63.7 kg

    NOTE: 5 feet = 60 inches

    STEP 3: Convert units of weight from pounds to kilograms.

    $$312 \text{ lb} \times \frac{\text{kg}}{2.2 \text{ lb}} = 141.8 \text{ kg}$$

    STEP 4: Determine whether TBW > 30% over IBW.

    $$\frac{\text{TBW} - \text{IBW}}{\text{IBW}} = \frac{141.8 \text{ kg} - 63.7 \text{ kg}}{63.7 \text{ kg}} = \frac{78.1 \text{ kg}}{63.7 \text{ kg}} = 1.23$$

    TRANSLATION: The patient's total body weight (TBW) is 123% higher than IBW; therefore, the patient is obese.

    STEP 5: Given that the patient is obese, apply the equation to calculate the patient's adjusted body weight.

    ABW = IBW + 0.4(TBW − IBW) = 63.7 kg + 0.4(141.8 kg − 63.7 kg) = 63.7 kg + 0.4(78.1 kg) = 94.9 kg

7. ML is a 293-pound man that is 6ft. 4in. tall. What is MP's adjusted body weight?

   STEP 1: Apply equation to estimate ideal body weight for a male patient.

   $$\text{IBW (male)} = 50 \text{ kg} + (2.3 \text{ kg for each inch of height over 5 feet}) = 50 \text{ kg} + (2.3 \text{ kg} \times 16) = 86.8 \text{ kg}$$

   STEP 2: Convert units of weight from pounds to kilograms.

   $$293 \text{ lb} \times \frac{\text{kg}}{2.2 \text{ lb}} = 133.2 \text{ kg}$$

   STEP 3: Determine whether TBW > 30% over IBW.

   $$\frac{\text{TBW} - \text{IBW}}{\text{IBW}} = \frac{133.2 \text{ kg} - 86.8 \text{ kg}}{86.8 \text{ kg}} = \frac{46.4 \text{ kg}}{86.8 \text{ kg}} = 0.535$$

   TRANSLATION: The patient's total body weight (TBW) is 53.5% higher than IBW; therefore, the patient is obese.

   STEP 4: Given that the patient is obese, apply the equation to calculate the patient's adjusted body weight.

   $$\text{ABW} = \text{IBW} + 0.4(\text{TBW} - \text{IBW})$$

   $$= 86.8 \text{ kg} + 0.4(133.2 \text{ kg} - 86.8 \text{ kg}) = 86.8 \text{ kg} + 0.4(46.4 \text{ kg}) = 105.4 \text{ kg}$$

REFERENCES
1. Pai, M. P. and Bearden, D. T. (2007), Antimicrobial Dosing Considerations in Obese Adult Patients. Pharmacotherapy: The Journal of Human Pharmacology and Drug Therapy, 27: 1081-1091.

BODY SURFACE AREA (BSA)

THE MOSTELLER FORMULA

$$\text{BSA (m}^2\text{)} = \sqrt{\frac{\text{height (cm) x weight (kg)}}{3{,}600}}$$

★ When using a calculator, remember to execute all calculations inside the square root sign before applying the square root function.

COMMON APPLICATIONS
Cancer chemotherapeutic agents are commonly dosed according to the patient's BSA.

MUST-KNOW VALUES & CONVERSION FACTORS
1 inch = 2.54 centimeters; 2.2 pounds = 1 kilogram
The average adult BSA is 1.73 m^2

1) What is the body surface area of a patient that is 5 ft and 4 in tall and weighs 110 pounds?

2) What is the body surface area of a patient that is 6 ft 1 in tall and weighs 220 pounds?

3) What is the body surface area of a patient that is 152 cm tall and weighs 67 kilograms?

4) What is the body surface area of a patient that is 171 cm tall and weighs 81 kilograms?

5) What is the body surface area of a patient that is 1.63 meters tall and weighs 99 kilograms?

6) What is the body surface area of a patient that is 1.96 meters tall and weighs 105 kilograms?

7) What is the body surface area of a patient that is 5 ft 11 in tall and weighs 205 pounds?

8) A patient receives doxorubicin 50 mg/m^2 once on day 1 of a 21-day cycle for acute myeloid leukemia. How many milligrams will the patient receive in three cycles if he is 6 ft 1 in tall and weighs 225 pounds?

9) A patient receives paclitaxel 135 mg/m^2 once on day 1 of a 21-day cycle for non-small cell lung cancer. How many milligrams will the patient receive in one dose if she is 1.60 meters tall and weighs 79 kilograms?

10) A patient receives vinblastine 6 mg/m^2 once on days 1 and 15 of a 28-day cycle for Hodgkin lymphoma. How many milligrams will the patient receive in one cycle if he is 171 cm tall and weighs 82 kilograms?

11) LH is receiving Adrucil® (fluorouracil) 500 mg/m^2 on days 1, 8, 15, 22, 29, and 36 of a 56-day cycle for colon cancer. If LH is 5ft 5 in tall and weighs 105 pounds, how many milligrams will LH receive per dose?

12) AP is receiving Taxotere® (docetaxel) 80 mg/m^2 on day 1 of a 21-day cycle for metastatic breast cancer. If AP is 6ft 0 in tall and weighs 178 pounds, how many milligrams of docetaxel will she receive per cycle?

13) TK is receiving mitomycin 20 mg/m^2 once on day 1 of a 42-day cycle as part of a multidrug regimen for stomach cancer. If TK is 155 cm tall and weighs 55 kilograms, how many milligrams of mitomycin will she receive on day 1 of the cycle?

14) LM is receiving Platinol® (cisplatin) 20 mg/m^2 once on days 1, 2, 3, 4, and 5 of a 21-day cycle for metastatic testicular cancer. If LM is 1.80 meters tall and weighs 85 kilograms, how many milligrams of cisplatin will he receive during one cycle?

SOLUTIONS for BODY SURFACE AREA PROBLEMS

1) What is the body surface area of a patient that is 5 ft and 4 in tall and weighs 110 pounds?

   STEP 1: Convert units of height to centimeters and weight to kilograms.

   HEIGHT
   $$64 \text{ in} \times \frac{2.54 \text{ cm}}{\text{in}} = 162.6 \text{ cm}$$

   WEIGHT
   $$110 \text{ lb} \times \frac{\text{kg}}{2.2 \text{ lb}} = 50 \text{ kg}$$

   STEP 2: Apply equation to calculate body surface area.

   $$BSA = \sqrt{\frac{\text{height (cm)} \times \text{weight (kg)}}{3{,}600}} = \sqrt{\frac{162.6 \text{ cm} \times 50 \text{ kg}}{3{,}600}} = \sqrt{2.26} = 1.50 \text{ m}^2$$

2) What is the body surface area of a patient that is 6 ft 1 in tall and weighs 220 pounds?

   STEP 1: Convert units of height to centimeters and weight to kilograms.

   HEIGHT
   $$73 \text{ in} \times \frac{2.54 \text{ cm}}{\text{in}} = 185.4 \text{ cm}$$

   WEIGHT
   $$220 \text{ lb} \times \frac{\text{kg}}{2.2 \text{ lb}} = 100 \text{ kg}$$

   STEP 2: Apply equation to calculate body surface area.

   $$BSA = \sqrt{\frac{\text{height (cm)} \times \text{weight (kg)}}{3{,}600}} = \sqrt{\frac{185 \text{ cm} \times 100 \text{ kg}}{3{,}600}} = \sqrt{5.14} = 2.27 \text{ m}^2$$

3) What is the body surface area of a patient that is 152 cm tall and weighs 67 kilograms?

   SOLUTION: Apply equation to calculate body surface area.

   $$BSA = \sqrt{\frac{\text{height (cm)} \times \text{weight (kg)}}{3{,}600}} = \sqrt{\frac{152 \text{ cm} \times 67 \text{ kg}}{3{,}600}} = \sqrt{2.83} = 1.68 \text{ m}^2$$

4) What is the body surface area of a patient that is 171 cm tall and weighs 81 kilograms?

   SOLUTION: Apply equation to calculate body surface area.

   $$BSA = \sqrt{\frac{\text{height (cm)} \times \text{weight (kg)}}{3{,}600}} = \sqrt{\frac{171 \text{ cm} \times 81 \text{ kg}}{3{,}600}} = \sqrt{3.85} = 1.96 \text{ m}^2$$

5) What is the body surface area of a patient that is 1.63 meters tall and weighs 99 kilograms?

   STEP 1: Convert units of height to centimeters.

   HEIGHT

   $$1.63 \text{ m} \times \frac{100 \text{ cm}}{\text{m}} = 163 \text{ cm}$$

   STEP 2: Apply equation to calculate body surface area.

   $$\text{BSA} = \sqrt{\frac{\text{height (cm)} \times \text{weight (kg)}}{3{,}600}} = \sqrt{\frac{163 \text{ cm} \times 99 \text{ kg}}{3{,}600}} = \sqrt{4.48} = 2.12 \text{ m}^2$$

6) What is the body surface area of a patient that is 1.96 meters tall and weighs 105 kilograms?

   STEP 1: Convert units of height to centimeters.

   HEIGHT

   $$1.96 \text{ m} \times \frac{100 \text{ cm}}{\text{m}} = 196 \text{ cm}$$

   STEP 2: Apply equation to calculate body surface area.

   $$\text{BSA} = \sqrt{\frac{\text{height (cm)} \times \text{weight (kg)}}{3{,}600}} = \sqrt{\frac{196 \text{ cm} \times 105 \text{ kg}}{3{,}600}} = \sqrt{5.72} = 2.39 \text{ m}^2$$

7) What is the body surface area of a patient that is 5 ft 11 in tall and weighs 205 pounds?

   STEP 1: Convert units of height to centimeters and weight to kilograms.

   HEIGHT

   $$71 \text{ in} \times \frac{2.54 \text{ cm}}{\text{in}} = 180.3 \text{ cm}$$

   WEIGHT

   $$205 \text{ lb} \times \frac{\text{kg}}{2.2 \text{ lb}} = 93.2 \text{ kg}$$

   STEP 2: Apply equation to calculate body surface area.

   $$\text{BSA} = \sqrt{\frac{\text{height (cm)} \times \text{weight (kg)}}{3{,}600}} = \sqrt{\frac{180.3 \text{ cm} \times 93.2 \text{ kg}}{3{,}600}} = \sqrt{4.67} = 2.16 \text{ m}^2$$

8) A patient receives doxorubicin 50 mg/m² once on day 1 of a 21-day cycle for acute myeloid leukemia. How many milligrams will the patient receive in three cycles if he is 6 ft 1 in tall and weighs 225 pounds?

STEP 1: Convert units of height to centimeters and weight to kilograms.

HEIGHT

$$73 \text{ in} \times \frac{2.54 \text{ cm}}{\text{in}} = 185.4 \text{ cm}$$

WEIGHT

$$225 \text{ lb} \times \frac{\text{kg}}{2.2 \text{ lb}} = 102.3 \text{ kg}$$

STEP 2: Apply equation to calculate body surface area.

$$BSA = \sqrt{\frac{\text{height (cm)} \times \text{weight (kg)}}{3{,}600}} = \sqrt{\frac{185.4 \text{ cm} \times 102.3 \text{ kg}}{3{,}600}} = \sqrt{5.27} = 2.295 \text{ m}^2$$

STEP 3: Calculate the number of milligrams in three cycles.

$$\frac{50 \text{ mg}}{\text{m}^2 \cdot \text{cycle}} \times 2.295 \text{ m}^2 \times 3 \text{ cycles} = 344 \text{ mg}$$

9) A patient receives paclitaxel 135 mg/m² once on day 1 of a 21-day cycle for non-small cell lung cancer. How many milligrams will the patient receive in one dose if she is 1.60 meters tall and weighs 79 kilograms?

STEP 1: Convert units of height to centimeters.

HEIGHT

$$1.60 \text{ m} \times \frac{100 \text{ cm}}{\text{m}} = 160 \text{ cm}$$

STEP 2: Apply equation to calculate body surface area.

$$BSA = \sqrt{\frac{\text{height (cm)} \times \text{weight (kg)}}{3{,}600}} = \sqrt{\frac{160 \text{ cm} \times 79 \text{ kg}}{3{,}600}} = \sqrt{3.51} = 1.874 \text{ m}^2$$

STEP 3: Calculate the number of milligrams per dose

$$\frac{135 \text{ mg}}{\text{m}^2} \times 1.874 \text{ m}^2 = 253 \text{ mg}$$

10) A patient receives vinblastine 6 mg/m² once on days 1 and 15 of a 28-day cycle for Hodgkin lymphoma. How many milligrams will the patient receive in one cycle if he is 171 cm tall and weighs 82 kilograms?

STEP 1: Apply equation to calculate body surface area.

$$BSA = \sqrt{\frac{\text{height (cm)} \times \text{weight (kg)}}{3{,}600}} = \sqrt{\frac{171 \text{ cm} \times 82 \text{ kg}}{3{,}600}} = \sqrt{3.895} = 1.974 \text{ m}^2$$

STEP 2: Calculate the number of milligrams per cycle.

$$\frac{6 \text{ mg}}{\text{m}^2 \cdot \text{dose}} \times 1.974 \text{ m}^2 \times \frac{2 \text{ doses}}{\text{cycle}} = 23.7 \text{ mg/cycle}$$

11) LH is receiving Adrucil® (fluorouracil) 500 mg/m² on days 1, 8, 15, 22, 29, and 36 of a 56-day cycle for colon cancer. If LH is 5ft 5 in tall and weighs 105 pounds, how many milligrams will LH receive per dose?

   STEP 1: Convert units of height to centimeters and weight to kilograms.

   HEIGHT
   $$65 \text{ in} \times \frac{2.54 \text{ cm}}{\text{in}} = 165.1 \text{ cm}$$

   WEIGHT
   $$105 \text{ lb} \times \frac{\text{kg}}{2.2 \text{ lb}} = 47.73 \text{ kg}$$

   STEP 2: Apply equation to calculate body surface area.

   $$\text{BSA} = \sqrt{\frac{\text{height (cm)} \times \text{weight (kg)}}{3{,}600}} = \sqrt{\frac{165.1 \text{ cm} \times 47.73 \text{ kg}}{3{,}600}} = \sqrt{2.19} = 1.48 \text{ m}^2$$

   STEP 3: Calculate the dose.

   $$\frac{500 \text{ mg}}{\text{m}^2 \cdot \text{dose}} \times 1.48 \text{ m}^2 = 740 \text{ mg/dose}$$

12) AP is receiving Taxotere® (docetaxel) 80 mg/m² on day 1 of a 21-day cycle for metastatic breast cancer. If AP is 6ft 0 in tall and weighs 178 pounds, how many milligrams of docetaxel will she receive per cycle?

   STEP 1: Convert units of height to centimeters and weight to kilograms.

   HEIGHT
   $$72 \text{ in} \times \frac{2.54 \text{ cm}}{\text{in}} = 182.9 \text{ cm}$$

   WEIGHT
   $$178 \text{ lb} \times \frac{\text{kg}}{2.2 \text{ lb}} = 80.9 \text{ kg}$$

   STEP 2: Apply equation to calculate body surface area.

   $$\text{BSA} = \sqrt{\frac{\text{height (cm)} \times \text{weight (kg)}}{3{,}600}} = \sqrt{\frac{182.9 \text{ cm} \times 80.9 \text{ kg}}{3{,}600}} = \sqrt{4.11} = 2.03 \text{ m}^2$$

   STEP 3: Calculate the number of milligrams per cycle.

   $$\frac{80 \text{ mg}}{\text{m}^2 \cdot \text{dose}} \times 2.03 \text{ m}^2 \times \frac{1 \text{ dose}}{\text{cycle}} = 162 \text{ mg/cycle}$$

13) TK is receiving mitomycin 20 mg/m² once on day 1 of a 42-day cycle as part of a multidrug regimen for stomach cancer. If TK is 155 cm tall and weighs 55 kilograms, how many milligrams of mitomycin will TK receive on day 1 of the cycle?

   STEP 1: Apply equation to calculate body surface area.

   $$\text{BSA} = \sqrt{\frac{\text{height (cm)} \times \text{weight (kg)}}{3{,}600}} = \sqrt{\frac{155 \text{ cm} \times 55 \text{ kg}}{3{,}600}} = \sqrt{2.37} = 1.54 \text{ m}^2$$

   STEP 2: Calculate the dose.

   $$\frac{20 \text{ mg}}{\text{m}^2} \times 1.54 \text{ m}^2 = 30.8 \text{ mg}$$

14) LM is receiving Platinol® (cisplatin) 20 mg/m² once on days 1, 2, 3, 4, and 5 of a 21-day cycle for metastatic testicular cancer. If LM is 1.80 meters tall and weighs 85 kilograms, how many milligrams of cisplatin will he receive during one cycle?

STEP 1: Convert units of height to centimeters.

HEIGHT

$$1.80 \text{ m} \times \frac{100 \text{ cm}}{\text{m}} = 180 \text{ cm}$$

STEP 2: Apply equation to calculate body surface area.

$$\text{BSA} = \sqrt{\frac{\text{height (cm)} \times \text{weight (kg)}}{3{,}600}} = \sqrt{\frac{180 \text{ cm} \times 85 \text{ kg}}{3{,}600}} = \sqrt{4.25} = 2.06 \text{ m}^2$$

STEP 3: Calculate the number of milligrams per cycle.

$$\frac{20 \text{ mg}}{\text{m}^2 \cdot \text{dose}} \times 2.06 \text{ m}^2 \times \frac{5 \text{ doses}}{\text{cycle}} = \boxed{206 \text{ mg/cycle}}$$

REFERENCE
1. Mosteller RD. (1987). Simplified calculation of body surface area. N Engl J Med, 317, 1098.

CREATININE CLEARANCE (CrCl)

COCKCROFT-GAULT EQUATION

$$CrCl = \frac{(140 - Age) \times Weight}{72 \times S_{Cr}} \times 0.85, \text{ if female}$$

NOTE: Always remember to multiply by 0.85 for female patients.
Numerous equations can estimate creatinine clearance; however, the Cockcroft-Gault equation is by far the most popular.

APPROPRIATE WEIGHT FOR THE COCKCROFT-GAULT EQUATION

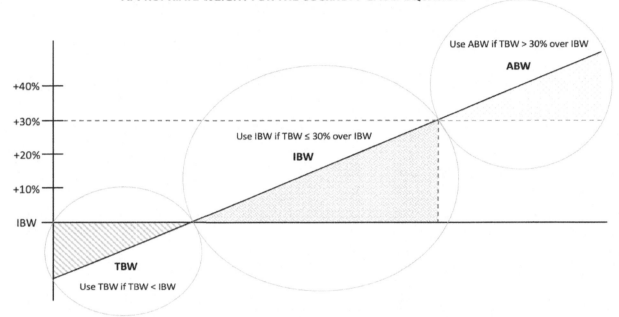

Weight in the Cockcroft-Gault equation can be total body weight (TBW), ideal body weight (IBW), or adjusted body weight (ABW). Originally, in 1976, TBW (or "actual body weight") was used. Now, unless specified otherwise, TBW should be used if the patient's TBW is below IBW, IBW if the patient's TBW is less than or equal to 30% over IBW, or ABW if the patient's TBW is more than 30% over IBW (see image above).

CRITICAL THINKING

Why not use actual body weight (TBW) when calculating CrCl for obese patients? As expected of a compound that is renally excreted, creatinine is highly polar. By definition, water-soluble (hydrophilic/lipophobic) compounds distribute poorly into fat tissue.

DO NOT ROUND SERUM CREATININE

For elderly patients with a SCr < 1 or 0.8 mg/dL, many pharmacists have been taught to round up to 1 mg/dL; however, current evidence suggests that this practice leads to an overestimation of renal function/elimination rate. As a consequence of rounding up, patients may receive higher doses than necessary, which increases the likelihood of toxicity. For this reason, it is likely best to avoid rounding up on the NAPLEX®; however, in practice, institutional protocols may require rounding.

STAGES OF CHRONIC KIDNEY DISEASE

Moderate Renal Impairment	30 – 59 mL/min
Severe Renal Impairment	15 – 29 mL/min
Renal Failure	< 15 mL/min (or dialysis)

CREATININE CLEARANCE (CrCl)

1) FS is a 79-year-old male that weighs 165 pounds. According to the Cockcroft-Gault equation, if his serum creatinine is 1.8 mg/dL, what is his creatinine clearance?

2) RS is a 62-year-old female that weighs 110 pounds. Her serum creatinine is 1.4 mg/dL. What is RS's creatinine clearance according to the Cockcroft-Gault equation?

3) BN is a 50-year-old man that weighs 115 kilograms and is 6 ft 0 in tall. His serum creatinine is 1.6 mg/dL. What is BN's creatinine clearance according to the Cockcroft-Gault equation?

4) TW is a 64-year-old woman that is 63 kilograms and 5' 5" tall. Her serum creatinine is 0.9 mg/dL. What is TW's creatinine clearance according to the Cockcroft-Gault equation?

5) VB is a 42-year-old male that weighs 54 kilograms and is 5 ft 7 in tall. His serum creatinine is 1.1 mg/dL. What is VB's creatinine clearance according to the Cockcroft-Gault equation?

6) TM is a 99-year-old female with a weight of 59 kilograms and a height of 175 centimeters. Her serum creatinine is 0.7 mg/dL. What is TM's estimated creatinine clearance according to the Cockcroft-Gault equation?

7) GB is an 83-year-old male that weighs 112 kilograms and is 168 centimeters tall. His serum creatinine is 4.7 mg/dL. What is GB's creatinine clearance according to the Cockcroft-Gault equation?

8) LK is a 71-year-old female with hospital-acquired pneumonia. LK's physician orders Levaquin® (levofloxacin) with instructions to take 750 mg by mouth daily for 6 days. The dose must be adjusted for renal function according to the hospital pharmacy protocol (see below). Given a weight of 68 kilograms, a height of 178 centimeters, and a serum creatinine level of 3.5 mg/dL, which dose and frequency of levofloxacin should LK receive?

    Renal Dosing Protocol for Levaquin® (levofloxacin)
    CrCl 20-49 mL/min: 750 mg by mouth on days 1, 3 and 5
    CrCl 10-19 mL/min: 750 mg on day 1, then 500 mg on days 3 and 5
    CrCl is < 10 mL/min: consult physician

9) HP is a 77-year-old male with herpes simplex encephalitis. The physician orders acyclovir 750 mg intravenously every 8 hours. The dose must be adjusted for renal function according to the hospital pharmacy protocol (see below). Given a weight of 198 pounds, a height of 6 ft 3 in, and a serum creatinine level of 4.0 mg/dL, how should the order be modified?

    Renal Dosing Protocol for Zovirax® (acyclovir)
    CrCl 25-50 mL/min: change the dosing frequency to 12 hours
    CrCl 10-24 mL/min: change the dosing frequency to 24 hours
    CrCl < 10 mL/min: decrease the dose by 50% and change the dosing frequency to 24 hours

10) JW is a 64-year-old female with type II diabetes mellitus. JW's physician orders sitagliptin 100 mg by mouth once daily. Sitagliptin is eliminated predominantly by renal excretion, and the dose must be adjusted for renal function according to the hospital pharmacy protocol (see below). Given a weight of 70 kilograms, height of 5 ft 4 in, and serum creatinine level of 2.8 mg/dL, which dose of sitagliptin should JW receive?

    Renal Dosing Protocol for Januvia® (sitagliptin)
    CrCl ≥ 45 mL/min: 100 mg by mouth once daily
    CrCl 30-44 mL/min: 50 mg by mouth once daily
    CrCl < 30 mL/min: 25 mg by mouth once daily

SOLUTIONS for CrCl PROBLEMS

1) FS is a 79-year-old male that weighs 165 pounds. According to the Cockcroft-Gault equation, if his serum creatinine is 1.8 mg/dL, what is his creatinine clearance?

   STEP 1: Convert the weight from pounds to kilograms.

   $$165 \text{ lb} \times \frac{\text{kg}}{2.2 \text{ lb}} = 75 \text{ kg}$$

   STEP 2: Estimate creatinine clearance using the Cockcroft-Gault Equation.

   $$\text{CrCl} = \frac{(140 - \text{Age}) \times \text{Weight}}{72 \times S_{Cr}} = \frac{(140 - 79) \times 75}{72 \times 1.8} = 35.3 \text{ mL/min}$$

   NOTE: When IBW cannot be determined (e.g., when the patient height is unknown), use TBW to estimate CrCl.

2) RS is a 62-year-old female that weighs 110 pounds. Her serum creatinine is 1.4 mg/dL. What is RS's creatinine clearance according to the Cockcroft-Gault equation?

   STEP 1: Convert the weight from pounds to kilograms.

   $$110 \text{ lb} \times \frac{\text{kg}}{2.2 \text{ lb}} = 50 \text{ kg}$$

   STEP 2: Estimate creatinine clearance using the Cockcroft-Gault Equation. Don't forget to multiply by 0.85 for females.

   $$\text{CrCl} = \frac{(140 - \text{Age}) \times \text{Weight}}{72 \times S_{Cr}} \times 0.85 = \frac{(140 - 62) \times 50}{72 \times 1.4} \times 0.85 = 32.9 \text{ mL/min}$$

   NOTE: When IBW cannot be determined (e.g., when the patient height is unknown), use TBW to estimate CrCl.

3) BN is a 50-year-old man that weighs 115 kilograms and is 6 ft 0 in tall. His serum creatinine is 1.6 mg/dL. What is BN's creatinine clearance according to the Cockcroft-Gault equation?

   STEP 1: Calculate ideal body weight.

   IBW (male) = 50 kg + (2.3 kg for each inch of height over 5 feet) = 50 kg + (2.3 kg x 12) = 77.6 kg

   STEP 2: Determine whether total body weight (TBW) is > 30% over IBW.

   $$\frac{\text{TBW} - \text{IBW}}{\text{IBW}} = \frac{115 \text{ kg} - 77.6 \text{ kg}}{77.6 \text{ kg}} = 0.482 = 48.2\%$$

   TRANSLATION: The patient's TBW is 48.2% over IBW; therefore, the patient is obese.

   STEP 3: Apply equation to calculate patient's adjusted body weight (ABW).

   $$\text{ABW} = \text{IBW} + 0.4(\text{TBW} - \text{IBW})$$

   = 77.6 kg + 0.4(115 kg – 77.6 kg) = 77.6 kg + 0.4(37.4 kg) = 92.6 kg

   STEP 4: Estimate creatinine clearance using the Cockcroft-Gault Equation.

   $$\text{CrCl} = \frac{(140 - \text{Age}) \times \text{Weight}}{72 \times S_{Cr}} = \frac{(140 - 50) \times 92.6}{72 \times 1.6} = 72.3 \text{ mL/min}$$

4) TW is a 64-year-old woman that is 63 kilograms and 5' 5" tall. Her serum creatinine is 0.9 mg/dL. What is TW's creatinine clearance according to the Cockcroft-Gault equation?

STEP 1: Calculate ideal body weight.

$$\text{IBW (female)} = 45.5 \text{ kg} + (2.3 \text{ kg for each inch of height over 5 feet}) = 45.5 \text{ kg} + (2.3 \text{ kg} \times 5) = 57 \text{ kg}$$

NOTE: 5 feet = 60 inches.

STEP 2: Determine whether total body weight (TBW) is > 30% over IBW.

$$\frac{\text{TBW} - \text{IBW}}{\text{IBW}} = \frac{63 \text{ kg} - 57 \text{ kg}}{57 \text{ kg}} = 0.105 = 10.5\%$$

TRANSLATION: The patient's TBW is 10.5% over IBW; therefore, the patient is not obese.

STEP 3: Estimate creatinine clearance using the Cockcroft-Gault Equation. Don't forget to multiply by 0.85 for females.

$$\text{CrCl} = \frac{(140 - \text{Age}) \times \text{Weight}}{72 \times S_{Cr}} \times 0.85 = \frac{(140 - 64) \times 57}{72 \times 0.9} \times 0.85 = 56.8 \text{ mL/min}$$

NOTE: Use IBW to estimate CrCl since TBW < 30% over IBW.

5) VB is a 42-year-old male that weighs 54 kilograms and is 5 ft 7 in tall. His serum creatinine is 1.1 mg/dL. What is VB's creatinine clearance according to the Cockcroft-Gault equation?

STEP 1: Calculate ideal body weight.

$$\text{IBW (male)} = 50 \text{ kg} + (2.3 \text{ kg for each inch of height over 5 feet}) = 50 \text{ kg} + (2.3 \text{ kg} \times 7) = 66.1 \text{ kg}$$

STEP 2: Determine whether total body weight (TBW) is > 30% over IBW.

$$\frac{\text{TBW} - \text{IBW}}{\text{IBW}} = \frac{54 \text{ kg} - 66.1 \text{ kg}}{66.1 \text{ kg}} = -0.183 = -18.3\%$$

TRANSLATION: The patient's total body weight (TBW) is 18.3% below IBW; therefore, the patient is not obese.

STEP 3: Estimate creatinine clearance using the Cockcroft-Gault Equation.

$$\text{CrCl} = \frac{(140 - \text{Age}) \times \text{Weight}}{72 \times S_{Cr}} = \frac{(140 - 42) \times 54}{72 \times 1.1} = 66.8 \text{ mL/min}$$

NOTE: Use TBW to estimate CrCl since TBW < IBW.

6) TM is a 99-year-old female with a weight of 59 kilograms and a height of 175 centimeters. Her serum creatinine is 0.7 mg/dL. What is TM's estimated creatinine clearance according to the Cockcroft-Gault equation?

STEP 1: Convert the height from centimeters to inches.

$$175 \text{ cm} \times \frac{\text{in}}{2.54 \text{ cm}} = 68.9 \text{ in}$$

STEP 2: Calculate ideal body weight.

IBW (female) = 45.5 kg + (2.3 kg for each inch of height over 5 feet) = 45.5 kg + (2.3 kg x 8.9) = 66 kg

NOTE: 5 feet = 60 inches.

STEP 3: Determine whether total body weight (TBW) is > 30% above IBW.

$$\frac{\text{TBW} - \text{IBW}}{\text{IBW}} = \frac{59 \text{ kg} - 66 \text{ kg}}{66 \text{ kg}} = -0.106 = -10.6\%$$

TRANSLATION: The patient's TBW is 10.6% below IBW; therefore, the patient is not obese.

STEP 4: Estimate creatinine clearance using the Cockcroft-Gault Equation. Don't forget to multiply by 0.85 for females.

$$\text{CrCl} = \frac{(140 - \text{Age}) \times \text{Weight}}{72 \times S_{Cr}} \times 0.85 = \frac{(140 - 99) \times 59}{72 \times 0.7} \times 0.85 = 40.8 \text{ mL/min}$$

NOTE: Use TBW to estimate CrCl since TBW < IBW.

7) GB is an 83-year-old male that weighs 112 kilograms and is 168 centimeters tall. His serum creatinine is 4.7 mg/dL. What is GB's creatinine clearance according to the Cockcroft-Gault equation?

STEP 1: Convert the height from centimeters to inches.

$$168 \text{ cm} \times \frac{\text{in}}{2.54 \text{ cm}} = 66.14 \text{ in}$$

STEP 2: Calculate ideal body weight.

IBW (male) = 50 kg + (2.3 kg for each inch of height over 5 feet) = 50 kg + (2.3 kg x 6.14) = 64.1 kg

NOTE: 5 feet = 60 inches.

STEP 3: Determine whether total body weight (TBW) is > 30% above IBW.

$$\frac{\text{TBW} - \text{IBW}}{\text{IBW}} = \frac{112 \text{ kg} - 64.1 \text{ kg}}{64.1 \text{ kg}} = 0.747 = 74.7\%$$

TRANSLATION: The patient's TBW is 74.7% over IBW; therefore, the patient is obese.

STEP 4: Apply equation to calculate patient's adjusted body weight (ABW).

$$\text{ABW} = \text{IBW} + 0.4(\text{TBW} - \text{IBW})$$

$$= 64.1 \text{ kg} + 0.4(112 \text{ kg} - 64.1 \text{ kg}) = 64.1 \text{ kg} + 0.4(47.9 \text{ kg}) = 83.3 \text{ kg}$$

STEP 5: Estimate creatinine clearance using the Cockcroft-Gault Equation.

$$\text{CrCl} = \frac{(140 - \text{Age}) \times \text{Weight}}{72 \times S_{Cr}} = \frac{(140 - 83) \times 83.3}{72 \times 4.7} = 14 \text{ mL/min}$$

8) LK is a 71-year-old female with hospital-acquired pneumonia. LK's physician orders Levaquin® (levofloxacin) with instructions to take 750 mg by mouth daily for 6 days. The dose must be adjusted for renal function according to the hospital pharmacy protocol (see below). Given a weight of 68 kilograms, a height of 178 centimeters, and a serum creatinine level of 3.5 mg/dL, which dose and frequency of levofloxacin should LK receive?

<u>Renal Dosing Protocol for Levaquin® (levofloxacin)</u>
CrCl 20-49 mL/min: 750 mg by mouth on days 1, 3 and 5
CrCl 10-19 mL/min: 750 mg on day 1, then 500 mg on days 3 and 5
CrCl is < 10 mL/min: consult physician

STEP 1: Convert the height from centimeters to inches.

$$178 \text{ cm} \times \frac{\text{in}}{2.54 \text{ cm}} = 70.1 \text{ in}$$

STEP 2: Calculate ideal body weight.

$$\text{IBW (female)} = 45.5 \text{ kg} + (2.3 \text{ kg for each inch of height over 5 feet}) = 45.5 \text{ kg} + (2.3 \text{ kg} \times 10.1) = 68.7 \text{ kg}$$

NOTE: 5 feet = 60 inches.

STEP 3: Determine whether total body weight (TBW) is > 30% above IBW.

$$\frac{\text{TBW} - \text{IBW}}{\text{IBW}} = \frac{68 \text{ kg} - 68.7 \text{ kg}}{68.7 \text{ kg}} = -0.01 = -1\%$$

TRANSLATION: The patient's TBW is 1% below IBW; therefore, the patient is not obese.

STEP 4: Estimate creatinine clearance using the Cockcroft-Gault Equation. Don't forget to multiply by 0.85 for females.

$$\text{CrCl} = \frac{(140 - \text{Age}) \times \text{Weight}}{72 \times S_{Cr}} \times 0.85 = \frac{(140 - 71) \times 68}{72 \times 3.5} \times 0.85 = 15.8 \text{ mL/min}$$

NOTE: Use TBW to estimate CrCl since TBW < IBW.

STEP 5: Indicate the appropriate dose and frequency based on the estimated CrCl.

CrCl 10-19 mL/min ∴ Levofloxacin 750 mg by mouth on day 1, then 500 mg on days 3 and 5

9) HP is a 77-year-old male with herpes simplex encephalitis. The physician orders acyclovir 750 mg intravenously every 8 hours. The dose must be adjusted for renal function according to the hospital pharmacy protocol (see below). Given a weight of 198 pounds, a height of 6 ft 3 in, and a serum creatinine level of 4.0 mg/dL, how should the order be modified?

Renal Dosing Protocol for Zovirax® (acyclovir)
CrCl 25-50 mL/min: change the dosing frequency to 12 hours
CrCl 10-24 mL/min: change the dosing frequency to 24 hours
CrCl < 10 mL/min: decrease the dose by 50% and change the dosing frequency to 24 hours

STEP 1: Convert the weight from pounds to kilograms.

$$198 \text{ lb} \times \frac{\text{kg}}{2.2 \text{ lb}} = 90 \text{ kg}$$

STEP 2: Calculate ideal body weight.

$$\text{IBW (male)} = 50 \text{ kg} + (2.3 \text{ kg for each inch of height over 5 feet}) = 50 \text{ kg} + (2.3 \text{ kg} \times 15) = 84.5 \text{ kg}$$

NOTE: 5 feet = 60 inches.

STEP 3: Determine whether total body weight (TBW) is > 30% over IBW.

$$\frac{\text{TBW} - \text{IBW}}{\text{IBW}} = \frac{90 \text{ kg} - 84.5 \text{ kg}}{84.5 \text{ kg}} = 0.065 = 6.5\%$$

TRANSLATION: The patient's TBW is 6.5% over IBW; therefore, the patient is not obese.

STEP 4: Estimate creatinine clearance using the Cockcroft-Gault Equation.

$$\text{CrCl} = \frac{(140 - \text{Age}) \times \text{Weight}}{72 \times S_{Cr}} = \frac{(140 - 77) \times 84.5}{72 \times 4} = 18.5 \text{ mL/min}$$

NOTE: Use IBW to estimate CrCl since TBW < 30% over IBW.

STEP 5: Indicate the appropriate modification based on the estimated CrCl.

CrCl 10-24 mL/min ∴ change the dosing frequency to 24 hours

10) JW is a 64-year-old female with type II diabetes mellitus. JW's physician orders sitagliptin 100 mg by mouth once daily. Sitagliptin is eliminated predominantly by renal excretion, and the dose must be adjusted for renal function according to the hospital pharmacy protocol (see below). Given a weight of 70 kilograms, height of 5 ft 4 in, and serum creatinine level of 2.8 mg/dL, which dose of sitagliptin should JW receive?

<u>Renal Dosing Protocol for Januvia® (sitagliptin)</u>
CrCl ≥ 45 mL/min: 100 mg by mouth once daily
CrCl 30-44 mL/min: 50 mg by mouth once daily
CrCl < 30 mL/min: 25 mg by mouth once daily
ESRD/HD/PD: 25 mg by mouth once daily

STEP 1: Calculate ideal body weight.

$$\text{IBW (female)} = 45.5 \text{ kg} + (2.3 \text{ kg for each inch of height over 5 feet}) = 45.5 \text{ kg} + (2.3 \text{ kg} \times 4) = 54.7 \text{ kg}$$

NOTE: 5 feet = 60 inches.

STEP 2: Determine whether total body weight (TBW) is > 30% above IBW.

$$\frac{\text{TBW} - \text{IBW}}{\text{IBW}} = \frac{70 \text{ kg} - 54.7 \text{ kg}}{54.7 \text{ kg}} = 0.28 = 28\%$$

TRANSLATION: The patient's TBW is 28% over IBW; therefore, the patient is not obese.

STEP 3: Estimate creatinine clearance using the Cockcroft-Gault Equation. Don't forget to multiply by 0.85 for females.

$$\text{CrCl} = \frac{(140 - \text{Age}) \times \text{Weight}}{72 \times S_{Cr}} \times 0.85 = \frac{(140 - 64) \times 54.7}{72 \times 2.8} \times 0.85 = 17.5 \text{ mL/min}$$

NOTE: Use IBW to estimate CrCl since TBW < 30% over IBW.

STEP 4: Select the appropriate dose based on the estimated CrCl.

$$\text{CrCl} < 30 \text{ mL/min} \therefore \text{Sitagliptin 25 mg by mouth once daily}$$

REFERENCES
1. Winter MA, Guhr KN, Berg GM. Impact of various body weights and serum creatinine concentrations on the bias and accuracy of the Cockcroft-Gault equation. *Pharmacotherapy*. 2012;32(7):604-612.
2. Goucher, Edward, et al. "Hydrophilic stationary phases: A practical approach for the co-analysis of compounds with varying polarity in biological matrices." *Journal of separation science* 33.6-7 (2010): 955-965.
3. Nguyen, Timothy, Yanique Foster, and Shpres Cekaj. "Older adult kidney function assessment and rounding creatinine led to medication dosing error." *American journal of therapeutics* 25.4 (2018): e439-e446.
4. Levey, Andrew S., et al. "National Kidney Foundation practice guidelines for chronic kidney disease: evaluation, classification, and stratification." *Annals of internal medicine* 139.2 (2003): 137-147.
5. Cockcroft DW, Gault MH. Prediction of creatinine clearance from serum creatinine. Nephron. 1976; 16:31.

CORRECTED CALCIUM

CALCULATE CORRECTED CALCIUM WHEN SERUM ALBUMIN < 3.5 MG/DL

Calcium ions have a strong affinity for protein in the bloodstream. Protein-bound calcium is physiologically inactive. Labs may measure, specifically, the concentration of ionized calcium in the blood. However, a lab may measure the total serum calcium concentration. If serum albumin is less than 3.5 g/dL, the total serum calcium concentration must be adjusted to reflect the ionized calcium concentration. If the adjustment is not applied, then a low concentration of total calcium will give the impression that ionized calcium is also low. A low concentration of protein-bound calcium does not necessarily mean a low concentration of free (ionized) calcium. In fact, for every 1 g/dL decrease in serum albumin, the concentration of protein-bound calcium decreases by about 0.8 mg/dL without affecting the concentration of free calcium ions in the bloodstream.

EQUATION *for* CORRECTED CALCIUM

$$\text{Corrected Calcium (mg/dL)} = \text{Serum Calcium (mg/dL)} + 0.8(4 - \text{Serum Albumin (g/dL)})$$

NOTE: The normal range for serum calcium is approximately 8.5-10.5 mg/dL. The laboratory determines the precise range. Only total serum calcium (ionized + protein-bound) requires correction with low serum albumin. Measurements of ionized calcium, by definition, exclude protein-bound calcium and, therefore, should not be "corrected."

1. PW has a total serum calcium level of 7.9 mg/dL, and his albumin level is 3.0 g/dL. What is the PW's corrected calcium level?

2. KA has a total serum calcium level of 6.4 mg/dL and a serum albumin level of 1.7 g/dL. What is the KA's corrected calcium level?

3. TM has a total serum calcium level of 5.9 mg/dL and a serum albumin level of 7.6 g/L. What is the TM's corrected calcium level?

4. BL has a serum calcium level of 4.7 mg/dL and a serum albumin level of 21 g/L. What is the BL's corrected calcium level?

5. RR has an ionized calcium level of 4.81 mg/dL and a serum albumin level of 2.4 g/dL. What is RR's corrected calcium level?

6. DL has a total serum calcium level of 9.81 mg/dL and a serum albumin level of 4.4 g/dL. What is DL's corrected calcium level?

SOLUTIONS for CORRECTED CALCIUM PROBLEMS

1. PW has a total serum calcium level of 7.9 mg/dL, and his albumin level is 3.0 g/dL. What is the PW's corrected calcium level?

    SOLUTION: Apply the equation to calculate corrected calcium.

    Corrected Calcium = Serum Calcium + 0.8(4 − Serum Albumin)
    = 7.9 mg/dL + 0.8(4 − 3)
    = 7.9 mg/dL + 0.8(1)
    = 7.9 mg/dL + 0.8
    = 8.7 mg/dL

2. KA has a total serum calcium level of 6.4 mg/dL and a serum albumin level of 1.7 g/dL. What is the KA's corrected calcium level?

    SOLUTION: Apply the equation to calculate corrected calcium.

    Corrected Calcium = Serum Calcium + 0.8(4 − Serum Albumin)
    = 6.4 mg/dL + 0.8(4 − 1.7)
    = 6.4 mg/dL + 0.8(2.3)
    = 6.4 mg/dL + 1.84
    = 8.2 mg/dL

3. TM has a total serum calcium level of 5.9 mg/dL and a serum albumin level of 7.6 g/L. What is the TM's corrected calcium level?

    STEP 1: Convert units of concentration for albumin from g/L to g/dL.

    $$\frac{7.6 \text{ g}}{\text{L}} \times \frac{\text{L}}{10 \text{ dL}} = 0.76 \text{ g/dL}$$

    STEP 2: Apply equation to calculate corrected calcium.

    Corrected Calcium = Serum Calcium + 0.8(4 − Serum Albumin)
    = 5.9 mg/dL + 0.8(4 − 0.76)
    = 5.9 mg/dL + 0.8(3.24)
    = 5.9 mg/dL + 2.59
    = 8.5 mg/dL

4. BL has a serum calcium level of 4.7 mg/dL and a serum albumin level of 21 g/L. What is the BL's corrected calcium level?

    STEP 1: Convert units of concentration for albumin from g/L to g/dL.

    $$\frac{21 \text{ g}}{\text{L}} \times \frac{\text{L}}{10 \text{ dL}} = 2.1 \text{ g/dL}$$

    STEP 2: Apply equation to calculate corrected calcium.

    Corrected Calcium = Serum Calcium + 0.8(4 − Serum Albumin)
    = 4.7 mg/dL + 0.8(4 − 2.1)
    = 4.7 mg/dL + 0.8(1.9)
    = 4.7 mg/dL + 1.52
    = 6.2 mg/dL

5. RR has an ionized calcium level of 4.81 mg/dL and a serum albumin level of 2.4 g/dL. What is RR's corrected calcium level?

    SOLUTION: Not applicable. Calculation of corrected calcium is only necessary for measurements of total serum calcium. Although RR does have hypoalbuminemia, measurements of ionized calcium, by definition, exclude protein-bound calcium. Therefore, ionized calcium concentrations are unaffected by serum albumin concentrations.

6. DL has a total serum calcium level of 9.81 mg/dL and a serum albumin level of 4.4 g/dL. What is DL's corrected calcium level?

    SOLUTION: Not applicable. Calculation of corrected calcium only applies in cases of hypoalbuminemia (serum albumin concentration of less than 3.5 g/dL).

REFERENCES
1. Payne RB, Little AJ, Williams RB, Milner JR. Interpretation of Serum Calcium in Patients with Abnormal Serum Proteins. British Medical Journal. 1973;4(5893):643-646.

PEDIATRIC DOSING EQUATIONS

CLARK'S RULE[1]

$$\text{Child Dose} = \frac{\text{Weight (lb)}}{150 \text{ lb}} \times \text{Adult Dose}$$

YOUNG'S RULE[2]

$$\text{Child Dose} = \frac{\text{Age}}{(\text{Age} + 12)} \times \text{Adult Dose}$$

BODY SURFACE AREA (BSA) DOSING[3]

$$\text{Child Dose} = \frac{\text{BSA}}{1.73 \text{ m}^2} \times \text{Adult Dose}$$

150 POUNDS
THE AVERAGE STANDARD ADULT WEIGHT[1]

1.73 m^2
THE AVERAGE STANDARD ADULT BSA[4]

1. KM is a 7-year-old female that is 3' 11" tall and weighs 55.0 pounds. She is about to receive a medication for which the normal adult dose is 750 mg. What is the appropriate dose for KM according to Clark's rule, Young's rule, and pediatric BSA dosing?

2. MS is a 3-year-old male that is 3 ft 1 in tall and weighs 32.0 pounds. He is about to receive a medication for which the normal adult dose is 10 mg. What is the appropriate dose for this patient according to Clark's rule, Young's rule, and pediatric BSA dosing?

3. LR, a 22-month-old female, is 32 inches tall and weighs 25 pounds. She is about to receive a medication for which the normal adult dose is 1 gram. What is the appropriate dose in milligrams for LR according to Clark's rule, Young's rule, and pediatric BSA dosing?

4. KH, a 14-month-old male, is 31 inches tall and weighs 24 pounds. He is about to receive a medication for which the normal adult dose is 250 mg. What is the appropriate dose for KH according to Clark's rule, Young's rule, and pediatric BSA dosing?

5. LC is an 11-year-old female with a height of 147 centimeters and a weight of 37 kilograms. Her pediatrician wants to prescribe a medication for which no pediatric dosing information is available. If the normal adult dose is 75 micrograms, how many micrograms should LC receive according to Clark's rule, Young's rule, and pediatric BSA dosing?

6. KW is a 10-year-old male with a height of 136 centimeters and a weight of 32 kilograms. His pediatrician prescribes a medication for which no pediatric dosing information is available. If the normal adult dose is 1.2 grams, how many milligrams should KW receive according to Clark's rule, Young's rule, and pediatric BSA dosing? Round each answer to the nearest 10 milligrams.

7. MO is a 10-month-old female that is 71 centimeters tall and weighs 8.8 kilograms. Her pediatrician prescribed medication with an adult dose of 500 mg. How many micrograms should MO receive according to Clark's rule, Young's rule, and pediatric BSA dosing?

8. TW is a 6-month-old male that is 66 centimeters tall and weighs 7.6 kilograms. His pediatrician prescribed medication with an adult dose of 900 mg. What is the appropriate dose for TW according to Clark's rule, Young's rule, and pediatric BSA dosing?

9. KS is a 6-year-old male that is 3' 5" tall and weighs 49 pounds. He is about to receive a medication for which the normal adult dose is 20 mg. What is the appropriate dose for KS according to Clark's rule, Young's rule, and pediatric BSA dosing?

10. MT, a 5-year-old female, is 26 inches tall and weighs 16 pounds. Her pediatrician prescribes a medication for which the normal adult dose is 10 mg/kg. The package insert indicates the appropriate dose for patients between 2 to 12 years old is 4 mg/kg. What is the appropriate dose for MT?

MUST-KNOW CONVERSION FACTORS
1 inch = 2.54 centimeters
2.2 pounds = 1 kilogram

SOLUTIONS for PEDIATRIC DOSING PROBLEMS

1. KM is a 7-year-old female that is 3' 11" tall and weighs 55.0 pounds. She is about to receive a medication for which the normal adult dose is 750 mg. What is the appropriate dose for KM according to Clark's rule, Young's rule, and pediatric BSA dosing?

CLARK'S RULE

$$\text{Child Dose} = \frac{\text{Weight (lb)}}{150 \text{ lb}} \times \text{Adult Dose}$$

$$\therefore \text{Child Dose} = \frac{55.0 \text{ lb}}{150 \text{ lb}} \times 750 \text{ mg} = 275 \text{ mg}$$

YOUNG'S RULE

$$\text{Child Dose} = \frac{\text{Age}}{(\text{Age} + 12)} \times \text{Adult Dose}$$

$$\therefore \text{Child Dose} = \frac{7}{(7 + 12)} \times 750 \text{ mg} = 276 \text{ mg}$$

BODY SURFACE AREA (BSA)

$$\text{Child Dose} = \frac{\text{BSA}}{1.73 \text{ m}^2} \times \text{Adult Dose}$$

$$\therefore \text{Child Dose} = \sqrt{\frac{47 \text{ in} \times \frac{2.54 \text{ cm}}{\text{in}} \times 55.0 \text{ lb} \times \frac{\text{kg}}{2.2 \text{ lb}}}{3,600}} \div 1.73 \text{ m}^2 \times 750 \text{ mg} = 395 \text{ mg}$$

2. MS is a 3-year-old male that is 3 ft 1 in tall and weighs 32.0 pounds. He is about to receive a medication for which the normal adult dose is 10 mg. What is the appropriate dose for this patient according to Clark's rule, Young's rule, and pediatric BSA dosing?

CLARK'S RULE

$$\text{Child Dose} = \frac{\text{Weight (lb)}}{150 \text{ lb}} \times \text{Adult Dose}$$

$$\therefore \text{Child Dose} = \frac{32.0 \text{ lb}}{150 \text{ lb}} \times 10 \text{ mg} = 2.1 \text{ mg}$$

YOUNG'S RULE

$$\text{Child Dose} = \frac{\text{Age}}{(\text{Age} + 12)} \times \text{Adult Dose}$$

$$\therefore \text{Child Dose} = \frac{3}{(3 + 12)} \times 10 \text{ mg} = 2 \text{ mg}$$

BODY SURFACE AREA (BSA)

$$\text{Child Dose} = \frac{\text{BSA}}{1.73 \text{ m}^2} \times \text{Adult Dose}$$

$$\therefore \text{Child Dose} = \sqrt{\frac{37 \text{ in} \times \frac{2.54 \text{ cm}}{\text{in}} \times 32.0 \text{ lb} \times \frac{\text{kg}}{2.2 \text{ lb}}}{3,600}} \div 1.73 \text{ m}^2 \times 10 \text{ mg} = 3.6 \text{ mg}$$

3. LR, a 22-month-old female, is 32 inches tall and weighs 25 pounds. She is about to receive a medication for which the normal adult dose is 1 gram. What is the appropriate dose in milligrams for LR according to Clark's rule, Young's rule, and pediatric BSA dosing?

CLARK'S RULE

$$\text{Child Dose} = \frac{\text{Weight (lb)}}{150 \text{ lb}} \times \text{Adult Dose}$$

$$= \frac{25 \text{ lb}}{150 \text{ lb}} \times 1{,}000 \text{ mg} = 167 \text{ mg}$$

YOUNG'S RULE

$$\text{Child Dose} = \frac{\text{Age}}{(\text{Age} + 12)} \times \text{Adult Dose}$$

$$= \frac{2}{(2 + 12)} \times 1{,}000 \text{ mg} = 143 \text{ mg}$$

NOTE: If the patient's age is expressed in terms of months, then convert the age to the nearest year when using Young's rule.

BODY SURFACE AREA (BSA)

$$\text{Child Dose} = \frac{\text{BSA}}{1.73 \text{ m}^2} \times \text{Adult Dose}$$

$$\therefore \text{Child Dose} = \sqrt{\frac{32 \text{ in} \times \frac{2.54 \text{ cm}}{\text{in}} \times 25 \text{ lb} \times \frac{\text{kg}}{2.2 \text{ lb}}}{3{,}600}} \div 1.73 \text{ m}^2 \times 1 \text{ gram} \times \frac{1{,}000 \text{ mg}}{\text{gram}} = 293 \text{ mg}$$

4. KH, a 14-month-old male, is 31 inches tall and weighs 24 pounds. He is about to receive a medication for which the normal adult dose is 250 mg. What is the appropriate dose for KH according to Clark's rule, Young's rule, and pediatric BSA dosing?

CLARK'S RULE

$$\text{Child Dose} = \frac{\text{Weight (lb)}}{150 \text{ lb}} \times \text{Adult Dose}$$

$$= \frac{24 \text{ lb}}{150 \text{ lb}} \times 250 \text{ mg} = 40 \text{ mg}$$

YOUNG'S RULE

$$\text{Child Dose} = \frac{\text{Age}}{(\text{Age} + 12)} \times \text{Adult Dose}$$

$$= \frac{1}{(1 + 12)} \times 250 \text{ mg} = 19 \text{ mg}$$

NOTE: If the patient's age is expressed in terms of months, then convert the age to the nearest year when using Young's rule.

BODY SURFACE AREA (BSA)

$$\text{Child Dose} = \frac{\text{BSA}}{1.73 \text{ m}^2} \times \text{Adult Dose}$$

$$\therefore \text{Child Dose} = \sqrt{\frac{31 \text{ in} \times \frac{2.54 \text{ cm}}{\text{in}} \times 24 \text{ lb} \times \frac{\text{kg}}{2.2 \text{ lb}}}{3{,}600}} \div 1.73 \text{ m}^2 \times 250 \text{ mg} = 71 \text{ mg}$$

5. LC is an 11-year-old female with a height of 147 centimeters and a weight of 37 kilograms. Her pediatrician wants to prescribe a medication for which no pediatric dosing information is available. If the normal adult dose is 75 micrograms, how many micrograms should LC receive according to Clark's rule, Young's rule, and pediatric BSA dosing?

CLARK'S RULE

$$\text{Child Dose} = \frac{\text{Weight (lb)}}{150 \text{ lb}} \times \text{Adult Dose}$$

$$= \frac{37 \text{ kg}}{150 \text{ lb}} \times \frac{2.2 \text{ lb}}{\text{kg}} \times 75 \text{ mcg} = 41 \text{ mcg}$$

YOUNG'S RULE

$$\text{Child Dose} = \frac{\text{Age}}{(\text{Age} + 12)} \times \text{Adult Dose}$$

$$= \frac{11}{(11 + 12)} \times 75 \text{ mcg} = 36 \text{ mcg}$$

NOTE: The patient's weight must be converted to pounds for Clark's rule.

BODY SURFACE AREA (BSA)

$$\text{Child Dose} = \frac{\text{BSA}}{1.73 \text{ m}^2} \times \text{Adult Dose}$$

$$\therefore \text{Child Dose} = \sqrt{\frac{147 \text{ cm} \times 37 \text{ kg}}{3{,}600}} \div 1.73 \text{ m}^2 \times 75 \text{ mcg} = 53 \text{ mcg}$$

6. KW is a 10-year-old male with a height of 136 centimeters and a weight of 32 kilograms. His pediatrician prescribes a medication for which no pediatric dosing information is available. If the normal adult dose is 1.2 grams, how many milligrams should KW receive according to Clark's rule, Young's rule, and pediatric BSA dosing? Round each answer to the nearest 10 milligrams.

CLARK'S RULE

$$\text{Child Dose} = \frac{\text{Weight (lb)}}{150 \text{ lb}} \times \text{Adult Dose}$$

$$= \frac{32 \text{ kg}}{150 \text{ lb}} \times \frac{2.2 \text{ lb}}{\text{kg}} \times 1{,}200 \text{ mg} = 563.2 \text{ mg} \therefore 560 \text{ mg}$$

YOUNG'S RULE

$$\text{Child Dose} = \frac{\text{Age}}{(\text{Age} + 12)} \times \text{Adult Dose}$$

$$= \frac{10}{(10 + 12)} \times 1{,}200 \text{ mg} = 545.5 \text{ mg} \therefore 550 \text{ mg}$$

NOTE: The patient's weight must be converted to pounds for Clark's rule.

BODY SURFACE AREA (BSA)

$$\text{Child Dose} = \frac{\text{BSA}}{1.73 \text{ m}^2} \times \text{Adult Dose}$$

$$\therefore \text{Child Dose} = \sqrt{\frac{136 \text{ cm} \times 32 \text{ kg}}{3{,}600}} \div 1.73 \text{ m}^2 \times 1.2 \text{ grams} \times \frac{1{,}000 \text{ mg}}{\text{gram}} = 763 \text{ mcg} \therefore 760 \text{ mg}$$

7. MO is a 10-month-old female that is 71 centimeters tall and weighs 8.8 kilograms. Her pediatrician prescribed medication with an adult dose of 500 mg. How many micrograms should MO receive according to Clark's rule, Young's rule, and pediatric BSA dosing?

CLARK'S RULE

$$\text{Child Dose} = \frac{\text{Weight (lb)}}{150 \text{ lb}} \times \text{Adult Dose}$$

$$= \frac{8.8 \text{ kg}}{150 \text{ lb}} \times \frac{2.2 \text{ lb}}{\text{kg}} \times 500 \text{ mg} \times \frac{1{,}000 \text{ mcg}}{\text{mg}} = 65{,}000 \text{ mcg}$$

YOUNG'S RULE

$$\text{Child Dose} = \frac{\text{Age}}{(\text{Age} + 12)} \times \text{Adult Dose}$$

$$= \frac{1}{(1 + 12)} \times 500 \text{ mg} \times \frac{1{,}000 \text{ mcg}}{\text{mg}} = 38{,}000 \text{ mcg}$$

BODY SURFACE AREA (BSA)

$$\text{Child Dose} = \frac{\text{BSA}}{1.73 \text{ m}^2} \times \text{Adult Dose}$$

$$\therefore \text{Child Dose} = \sqrt{\frac{71 \text{ cm} \times 8.8 \text{ kg}}{3{,}600}} \div 1.73 \text{ m}^2 \times 500 \text{ mg} \times \frac{1{,}000 \text{ mcg}}{\text{mg}} = 120{,}000 \text{ mcg}$$

8. TW is a 6-month-old male that is 66 centimeters tall and weighs 7.6 kilograms. His pediatrician prescribed medication with an adult dose of 900 mg. What is the appropriate dose for TW according to Clark's rule, Young's rule, and pediatric BSA dosing?

CLARK'S RULE

$$\text{Child Dose} = \frac{\text{Weight (lb)}}{150 \text{ lb}} \times \text{Adult Dose}$$

$$= \frac{7.6 \text{ kg}}{150 \text{ lb}} \times \frac{2.2 \text{ lb}}{\text{kg}} \times 900 \text{ mg} = 100 \text{ mg}$$

YOUNG'S RULE

$$\text{Child Dose} = \frac{\text{Age}}{(\text{Age} + 12)} \times \text{Adult Dose}$$

$$= \frac{1}{(1 + 12)} \times 900 \text{ mg} = 69 \text{ mg}$$

BODY SURFACE AREA (BSA)

$$\text{Child Dose} = \frac{\text{BSA}}{1.73 \text{ m}^2} \times \text{Adult Dose}$$

$$\therefore \text{Child Dose} = \sqrt{\frac{66 \text{ cm} \times 7.6 \text{ kg}}{3{,}600}} \div 1.73 \text{ m}^2 \times 900 \text{ mg} = 194 \text{ mg}$$

9. KS is a 6-year-old male that is 3' 5" tall and weighs 49 pounds. He is about to receive a medication for which the normal adult dose is 20 mg. What is the appropriate dose for KS according to Clark's rule, Young's rule, and pediatric BSA dosing?

CLARK'S RULE

$$\text{Child Dose} = \frac{\text{Weight (lb)}}{150 \text{ lb}} \times \text{Adult Dose}$$

$$= \frac{49 \text{ lb}}{150 \text{ lb}} \times 20 \text{ mg} = 6.5 \text{ mg}$$

YOUNG'S RULE

$$\text{Child Dose} = \frac{\text{Age}}{(\text{Age} + 12)} \times \text{Adult Dose}$$

$$= \frac{6}{(6 + 12)} \times 20 \text{ mg} = 6.7 \text{ mg}$$

BODY SURFACE AREA (BSA)

$$\text{Child Dose} = \frac{\text{BSA}}{1.73 \text{ m}^2} \times \text{Adult Dose}$$

$$\therefore \text{Child Dose} = \sqrt{\frac{41 \text{ in} \times \frac{2.54 \text{ cm}}{\text{in}} \times 49 \text{ lb} \times \frac{\text{kg}}{2.2 \text{ lb}}}{3{,}600}} \div 1.73 \text{ m}^2 \times 20 \text{ mg} = 9.3 \text{ mg}$$

10. MT, a 5-year-old female, is 26 inches tall and weighs 16 pounds. Her pediatrician prescribes a medication for which the normal adult dose is 10 mg/kg. The package insert indicates the appropriate dose for patients between 2 to 12 years old is 4 mg/kg. What is the appropriate dose for MT?

SOLUTION: Use the information from the package insert to calculate the appropriate dose based on the patient's age and weight.

$$16 \text{ lb} \times \frac{\text{kg}}{2.2 \text{ lb}} \times \frac{4 \text{ mg}}{\text{kg}} = 29 \text{ mg}$$

NOTE: Clark's Rule, Young's Rule, and BSA dosing should be reserved for situations when a pediatric dose is otherwise unavailable.

REFERENCES
1. Delgado, B. J., & Bajaj, T. (2019). Clark's Rule. In StatPearls [Internet]. StatPearls Publishing.
2. Wade CI, Martinez T. Youngs Rule. In: StatPearls. StatPearls Publishing, Treasure Island (FL); 2020.
3. Prince SJ. International Journal of Pharmaceutical Compounding; Edmond Vol. 9, Iss. 1, (Jan/Feb 2005):57.
4. Heaf, J. G. (2007). The origin of the 1.73-m² body surface area normalization: problems and implications. Clinical Physiology and Functional Imaging, 27(3), 135-137.

PERCENT CONCENTRATION WEIGHT/WEIGHT

DEFINITION *of* PERCENT CONCENTRATION WEIGHT/WEIGHT

Percent weight/weight (% w/w) can be defined as the grams of active ingredient per 100 grams of the formulation.

1. How many milligrams of testosterone are present in a single 5-gram packet of AndroGel® (testosterone) 1% (w/w) transdermal gel?

2. How many grams of benzocaine are present in a standard 28-gram tube of Boil Ease® (benzocaine) 20% (w/w) topical ointment?

3. A 42.5-gram tube of Premarin® (conjugated estrogens) vaginal cream contains 0.625 mg of conjugated estrogens per gram of cream. What is the strength of the cream in terms of percent (w/w)?

4. How many milligrams of pure hydrocortisone powder would be required to prepare a 30-gram tube of hydrocortisone 3% (w/w) cream?

5. How many milligrams of tretinoin would be present in a 40-gram tube of Renova® (tretinoin) 0.02% (w/w) topical cream?

6. How many micrograms of betamethasone should be present in a 30-gram tube of Diprosone® (betamethasone) 0.05% (w/w) topical ointment?

7. How many grams of pure triamcinolone acetonide powder would be needed to make a one-pound jar of triamcinolone acetonide 0.75% (w/w) topical ointment?

8. Four grams of mupirocin are diluted with a polyethylene glycol ointment base to a final mass of 200 grams. Calculate the percent (w/w) concentration of the final product.

SOLUTIONS *for* % W/W PROBLEMS

1. How many milligrams of testosterone are present in a single 5-gram packet of AndroGel® (testosterone) 1% (w/w) transdermal gel?

   STEP 1: Express the strength in terms of mass based on the definition of percent concentration (w/w).

   $$\text{Testosterone 1\% (w/w) gel} = 1 \text{ g } of \text{ testosterone}/100 \text{ g } of \text{ gel}$$

   STEP 2: Perform dimensional analysis.

   $$\frac{1 \text{ g } of \text{ testosterone}}{100 \text{ g } of \text{ gel}} = \frac{\text{UNKNOWN}}{5 \text{ g } of \text{ gel}} \therefore \text{UNKNOWN} = \frac{1 \text{ g } of \text{ testosterone}}{100 \text{ g } of \text{ gel}} \times 5 \text{ g } of \text{ gel} = 0.05 \text{ g } of \text{ testosterone}$$

   STEP 3: Convert units from grams to milligrams to answer the question correctly.

   $$0.05 \text{ g } of \text{ testosterone} \times \frac{1{,}000 \text{ mg}}{\text{g}} = 50 \text{ mg } of \text{ testosterone}$$

2. How many grams of benzocaine are present in a standard 28-gram tube of Boil Ease® (benzocaine) 20% (w/w) topical ointment?

   STEP 1: Express the strength in terms of mass based on the definition of percent concentration (w/w).

   $$\text{Benzocaine 20\% (w/w)} = 20 \text{ g } of \text{ benzocaine}/100 \text{ g } of \text{ ointment}$$

   STEP 2: Perform dimensional analysis.

   $$\frac{20 \text{ g } of \text{ benzocaine}}{100 \text{ g } of \text{ ointment}} = \frac{\text{UNKNOWN}}{28 \text{ g } of \text{ ointment}} \therefore \text{UNKNOWN} = \frac{20 \text{ g } of \text{ benzocaine}}{100 \text{ g } of \text{ ointment}} \times 28 \text{ g } of \text{ ointment} = 5.6 \text{ g } of \text{ benzocaine}$$

3. A 42.5-gram tube of Premarin® (conjugated estrogens) vaginal cream contains 0.625 mg of conjugated estrogens per gram of cream. What is the strength of the cream in terms of percent (w/w)?

   STEP 1: Convert units of mass for the active ingredient from milligrams to grams.

   $$\frac{0.625 \text{ mg } of \text{ conjugated estrogens}}{1 \text{ g } of \text{ vaginal cream}} \times \frac{1 \text{ g}}{1{,}000 \text{ mg}} = \frac{0.000625 \text{ g } of \text{ conjugated estrogens}}{1 \text{ g } of \text{ vaginal cream}}$$

   STEP 2: Perform dimensional analysis.

   $$\frac{0.000625 \text{ g } of \text{ conjugated estrogens}}{1 \text{ g } of \text{ vaginal cream}} = \frac{\text{UNKNOWN}}{100 \text{ g } of \text{ vaginal cream}} \therefore \text{UNKNOWN} = \frac{0.000625 \text{ g } of \text{ conjugated estrogens}}{1 \text{ g } of \text{ vaginal cream}} \times 100 \text{ g } of \text{ vaginal cream}$$

   $$= 0.0625 \text{ g } of \text{ conjugated estrogens}$$

   STEP 3: Express the strength in terms of percent concentration (w/w).

   $$\frac{0.0625 \text{ g } of \text{ conjugated estrogens}}{100 \text{ g } of \text{ vaginal cream}} = \text{conjugated estrogens 0.0625\% (w/w) vaginal cream}$$

4. How many milligrams of pure hydrocortisone powder would be required to prepare a 30-gram tube of hydrocortisone 3% (w/w) cream?

   STEP 1: Express the strength in terms of mass based on the definition of percent concentration (w/w).

   $$\text{Hydrocortisone 3\% (w/w)} = 3 \text{ g of hydrocortisone}/100 \text{ g of cream}$$

   STEP 2: Perform dimensional analysis.

   $$\frac{3 \text{ g of hydrocortisone}}{100 \text{ g of cream}} = \frac{\text{UNKNOWN}}{30 \text{ g of cream}} \therefore \text{UNKNOWN} = \frac{3 \text{ g of hydrocortisone}}{100 \text{ g of cream}} \times 30 \text{ g of cream} = 0.9 \text{ g of hydrocortisone}$$

   STEP 3: Convert units from grams to milligrams to answer the question correctly.

   $$0.9 \text{ g of cream} \times \frac{1{,}000 \text{ mg}}{\text{g}} = 900 \text{ mg of hydrocortisone}$$

5. How many milligrams of tretinoin would be present in a 40-gram tube of Renova® (tretinoin) 0.02% (w/w) topical cream?

   STEP 1: Express the strength in terms of mass based on the definition of percent concentration (w/w).

   $$\text{Tretinoin 0.02\% (w/w)} = 0.02 \text{ g of tretinoin}/100 \text{ g of cream}$$

   STEP 2: Perform dimensional analysis.

   $$\frac{0.02 \text{ g of tretinoin}}{100 \text{ g of cream}} = \frac{\text{UNKNOWN}}{40 \text{ g of cream}} \therefore \text{UNKNOWN} = \frac{0.02 \text{ g of tretinoin}}{100 \text{ g of cream}} \times 40 \text{ g of cream} = 0.008 \text{ g of tretinoin}$$

   STEP 3: Convert units from grams to milligrams to answer the question correctly.

   $$0.008 \text{ g of tretinoin} \times \frac{1{,}000 \text{ mg}}{\text{g}} = 8 \text{ mg of tretinoin}$$

6. How many micrograms of betamethasone should be present in a 30-gram tube of Diprosone® (betamethasone) 0.05% (w/w) topical ointment?

   STEP 1: Express the strength in terms of mass based on the definition of percent concentration (w/w).

   $$\text{Betamethasone 0.05\% (w/w)} = 0.05 \text{ g of betamethasone}/100 \text{ g of ointment}$$

   STEP 2: Perform dimensional analysis.

   $$\frac{0.05 \text{ g of betamethasone}}{100 \text{ g of ointment}} = \frac{\text{UNKNOWN}}{30 \text{ g of ointment}} \therefore \text{UNKNOWN} = \frac{0.05 \text{ g of betamethasone}}{100 \text{ g of ointment}} \times 30 \text{ g of ointment} = 0.015 \text{ g of betamethasone}$$

   STEP 3: Convert units from grams to micrograms to answer the question correctly.

   $$0.015 \text{ g of betamethasone} \times \frac{1{,}000{,}000 \text{ mcg}}{\text{g}} = 15{,}000 \text{ mcg of betamethasone}$$

7. How many grams of pure triamcinolone acetonide powder would be needed to make a one-pound jar of triamcinolone acetonide 0.75% (w/w) topical ointment?

   STEP 1: Express the strength in terms of mass based on the definition of percent concentration (w/w).

   $$\text{Triamcinolone acetonide } 0.75\% \text{ (w/w)} = 0.75 \text{ g } of \text{ triamcinolone acetonide}/100 \text{ g } of \text{ ointment}$$

   STEP 2: Convert units of mass from pounds to grams.

   $$1 \text{ pound } of \text{ ointment} \times \frac{454 \text{ g}}{\text{pound}} = 454 \text{ g } of \text{ ointment}$$

   STEP 3: Perform dimensional analysis.

   $$\frac{0.75 \text{ g } of \text{ triamcinolone acetonide}}{100 \text{ g } of \text{ ointment}} = \frac{\text{UNKNOWN}}{454 \text{ g } of \text{ ointment}}$$

   $$\therefore \text{UNKNOWN} = \frac{0.75 \text{ g } of \text{ triamcinolone acetonide}}{100 \text{ g } of \text{ ointment}} \times 454 \text{ g } of \text{ ointment} = 3.4 \text{ g } of \text{ triamcinolone acetonide}$$

8. Four grams of mupirocin are diluted with a polyethylene glycol ointment base to a final mass of 200 grams. Calculate the percent (w/w) concentration of the final product.

   Since we know how many grams of mupirocin are present in 200 grams of ointment, simply multiply by ½ to determine the amount present in 100 grams. Then express the strength in terms of percentage based on the definition of percent concentration (w/w).

   STEP 1: Perform dimensional analysis to determine the mass of mupirocin in 100 grams of ointment.

   $$\frac{4 \text{ g } of \text{ mupirocin}}{200 \text{ g } of \text{ ointment}} = \frac{\text{UNKNOWN}}{100 \text{ g } of \text{ ointment}} \quad \therefore \text{UNKNOWN} = \frac{4 \text{ g } of \text{ mupirocin}}{200 \text{ g } of \text{ ointment}} \times 100 \text{ g } of \text{ ointment} = 2 \text{ g } of \text{ mupirocin}$$

   STEP 2: Now, knowing the mass of the active ingredient that is present in 100 grams of the formulation, express the strength in terms of percent concentration (w/w).

   $$\text{mupirocin 2\% (w/w) ointment}$$

PERCENT CONCENTRATION VOLUME/VOLUME

DEFINITION *of* PERCENT CONCENTRATION VOLUME/VOLUME

Percent volume/volume (% v/v) can be defined as the milliliters of active ingredient per 100 milliliters of the formulation.

1. Cheratussin® AC (codeine and guaifenesin) liquid contains alcohol as an excipient. If the concentration of alcohol in Cheratussin® AC is 3.8% (v/v), how many milliliters of alcohol are present in a 473-mL bottle?

2. What is the percent concentration (v/v) of tea tree oil if a 15-mL bottle of emulsion contains 0.75-mL of pure tea tree oil?

3. If prednisolone 15 mg/5 mL syrup contains alcohol 5% (v/v), how many milliliters of alcohol are present in one teaspoonful?

4. Another manufacturer produces prednisolone sodium phosphate oral solution, which provides the same amount of active ingredient per unit of volume as the prednisolone 15 mg/5 mL syrup. If a 237-mL bottle of prednisolone sodium phosphate oral solution contains 4.74 milliliters of alcohol, what is the percent concentration (v/v) of alcohol?

5. According to USP Chapter 797, the preferred disinfectant for sterile compounding equipment is 70% (v/v) isopropyl alcohol solution. What volume (in milliliters) of pure isopropyl alcohol is present in a one-pint bottle?

6. Suppose a topical wound irrigation solution is compounded by combining 180 milliliters of ethyl alcohol with 50 milligrams of antibiotic powder and sterile water to bring the final volume to 250 milliliters. What is the percent concentration (v/v) of ethanol?

7. One version of calamine topical suspension contains calamine 8% (w/v), zinc oxide 8% (w/v), and liquefied phenol 1% (v/v). How many liters of liquefied phenol would be needed to manufacture a 500-gallon batch?

SOLUTIONS for % V/V PROBLEMS

1. Cheratussin® AC (codeine and guaifenesin) liquid contains alcohol as an excipient. If the concentration of alcohol in Cheratussin® AC is 3.8% (v/v), how many milliliters of alcohol are present in a 473-mL bottle?

   STEP 1: Express the strength in terms of volume based on the definition of percent concentration (v/v).

   $$\text{Alcohol 3.8\% (v/v)} = 3.8 \text{ mL } of \text{ alcohol}/100 \text{ mL } of \text{ liquid}$$

   STEP 2: Perform dimensional analysis.

   $$\frac{3.8 \text{ mL } of \text{ alcohol}}{100 \text{ mL } of \text{ liquid}} = \frac{\text{UNKNOWN}}{473 \text{ mL } of \text{ liquid}} \therefore \text{UNKNOWN} = \frac{3.8 \text{ mL } of \text{ alcohol}}{100 \text{ mL } of \text{ liquid}} \times 473 \text{ mL } of \text{ liquid} = 18 \text{ mL } of \text{ alcohol}$$

2. What is the percent concentration (v/v) of tea tree oil if a 15-mL bottle of emulsion contains 0.75-mL of pure tea tree oil?

   STEP 1: Perform dimensional analysis to determine the volume of tea tree oil that would be present in 100 mL of emulsion.

   $$\frac{0.75 \text{ mL } of \text{ tea tree oil}}{15 \text{ mL } of \text{ emulsion}} = \frac{\text{UNKNOWN}}{100 \text{ mL } of \text{ emulsion}} \therefore \text{UNKNOWN} = \frac{0.75 \text{ mL } of \text{ tea tree oil}}{15 \text{ mL } of \text{ emulsion}} \times 100 \text{ mL } of \text{ emulsion} = 5 \text{ mL } of \text{ tea tree oil}$$

   STEP 2: Express the strength in terms of percent concentration (v/v).

   $$5 \text{ mL } of \text{ tea tree oil}/100 \text{ mL } of \text{ emulsion} = \text{tea tree oil 5\% (v/v) emulsion}$$

3. If prednisolone 15 mg/5 mL syrup contains alcohol 5% (v/v), how many milliliters of alcohol are present in one teaspoonful?

   STEP 1: Express the strength in terms of volume based on the definition of percent concentration (v/v).

   $$\text{Alcohol 5\% (v/v)} = 5 \text{ mL } of \text{ alcohol}/100 \text{ mL } of \text{ syrup}$$

   STEP 2: Perform dimensional analysis.

   $$\frac{5 \text{ mL } of \text{ alcohol}}{100 \text{ mL } of \text{ syrup}} = \frac{\text{UNKNOWN}}{5 \text{ mL } of \text{ syrup}} \therefore \text{UNKNOWN} = \frac{5 \text{ mL } of \text{ alcohol}}{100 \text{ mL } of \text{ syrup}} \times 5 \text{ mL } of \text{ liquid} = 0.25 \text{ mL } of \text{ alcohol}$$

   NOTE: 1 teaspoon = 5 milliliters

4. Another manufacturer produces prednisolone sodium phosphate oral solution, which provides the same amount of active ingredient per unit of volume as the prednisolone 15 mg/5 mL syrup. If a 237-mL bottle of prednisolone sodium phosphate oral solution contains 4.74 milliliters of alcohol, what is the percent concentration (v/v) of alcohol?

   STEP 1: Perform dimensional analysis.

   $$\frac{4.74 \text{ mL } of \text{ alcohol}}{237 \text{ mL } of \text{ solution}} = \frac{\text{UNKNOWN}}{100 \text{ mL } of \text{ solution}} \therefore \text{UNKNOWN} = \frac{4.74 \text{ mL } of \text{ alcohol}}{237 \text{ mL } of \text{ solution}} \times 100 \text{ mL } of \text{ solution} = 2 \text{ mL } of \text{ alcohol}$$

   STEP 2: Express the strength in terms of percent concentration (v/v).

   $$2 \text{ mL } of \text{ alcohol}/100 \text{ mL } of \text{ solution} = \text{alcohol 2\% (v/v) solution}$$

5. According to USP Chapter 797, the preferred disinfectant for sterile compounding equipment is 70% (v/v) isopropyl alcohol solution. What volume (in milliliters) of pure isopropyl alcohol is present in a one-pint bottle?

    STEP 1: Express the strength in terms of volume based on the definition of percent concentration (v/v).

    Isopropyl alcohol 70% (v/v) = 70 mL *of* isopropyl alcohol/100 mL *of* solution

    STEP 2: Convert one pint to units of milliliters.

    $$1 \text{ pint} \times \frac{16 \text{ fluid ounces}}{\text{pint}} \times \frac{29.57 \text{ milliliters}}{\text{fluid ounce}} = 473 \text{ milliliters}$$

    STEP 2: Perform dimensional analysis.

    $$\frac{70 \text{ mL } of \text{ isopropyl alcohol}}{100 \text{ mL } of \text{ solution}} = \frac{\text{UNKNOWN}}{473 \text{ mL } of \text{ solution}}$$

    $$\therefore \text{UNKNOWN} = \frac{70 \text{ mL } of \text{ isopropyl alcohol}}{100 \text{ mL } of \text{ solution}} \times 473 \text{ mL } of \text{ solution} = 331 \text{ mL } of \text{ isopropyl alcohol}$$

6. Suppose a topical wound irrigation solution is compounded by combining 180 milliliters of ethyl alcohol with 50 milligrams of antibiotic powder and sterile water to bring the final volume to 250 milliliters. What is the percent concentration (v/v) of ethanol?

    STEP 1: Perform dimensional analysis.

    $$\frac{180 \text{ mL } of \text{ ethanol}}{250 \text{mL } of \text{ solution}} = \frac{\text{UNKNOWN}}{100 \text{ mL } of \text{ solution}} \quad \therefore \text{UNKNOWN} = \frac{180 \text{ mL } of \text{ ethanol}}{250 \text{ mL } of \text{ solution}} \times 100 \text{ mL } of \text{ solution} = 72 \text{ mL } of \text{ ethanol}$$

    STEP 2: Express the strength in terms of percent concentration (v/v).

    72 mL *of* ethanol/100 mL *of* solution = ethanol 72% (v/v) solution

7. One version of calamine topical suspension contains calamine 8% (w/v), zinc oxide 8% (w/v), and liquefied phenol 1% (v/v). How many liters of liquefied phenol would be needed to manufacture a 500-gallon batch?

    STEP 1: Express the strength in terms of volume based on the definition of percent concentration (v/v).

    Liquefied phenol 1% (v/v) = 1 mL *of* liquefied phenol/100 mL *of* suspension

    STEP 2: Convert volume to milliliters.

    $$500 \text{ gallons} \times \frac{128 \text{ fluid ounces}}{\text{gallon}} \times \frac{29.57 \text{ milliliters}}{\text{fluid ounce}} = 1{,}892{,}480 \text{ milliliters}$$

    STEP 3: Perform dimensional analysis.

    $$\frac{1 \text{ mL } of \text{ liquefied phenol}}{100 \text{ mL } of \text{ suspension}} = \frac{\text{UNKNOWN}}{1{,}892{,}480 \text{ mL } of \text{ suspension}}$$

    $$\therefore \text{UNKNOWN} = \frac{1 \text{ mL } of \text{ liquefied phenol}}{100 \text{ mL } of \text{ suspension}} \times 1{,}892{,}480 \text{ mL } of \text{ suspension} = 18{,}924.8 \text{ mL } of \text{ liquefied phenol}$$

    STEP 4: Convert units from milliliters to liters to answer the question correctly.

    $$18{,}924.8 \text{ mL } of \text{ liquefied phenol} \times \frac{L}{1{,}000 \text{ mL}} = 18.9248 \text{ L } of \text{ liquefied phenol}$$

PERCENT CONCENTRATION WEIGHT/VOLUME

DEFINITION of PERCENT CONCENTRATION WEIGHT/WEIGHT

Percent weight/volume (% w/v) can be defined as the grams of active ingredient per 100 milliliters of the formulation.

---

1. What is the percent concentration (w/v) of a 2,500,000-microgram solution of clindamycin dissolved in 250 milliliters of water?

2. What is the percent concentration (w/v) of a 473-mL oral solution that contains 567.6 mg of chlorhexidine gluconate?

3. A 6-month-old female receives one-half dropperful of sodium fluoride 0.11% (w/v) oral drops. If one dropperful equals one milliliter, how many milligrams of sodium fluoride did she receive?

4. Clobetasol propionate topical solution is commercially available in a 50-mL bottle. If each milliliter contains 0.5 mg of clobetasol propionate, what is the strength (% w/v) of the solution?

5. Antipyrine-benzocaine otic solution contains benzocaine 1.4% (w/v) and antipyrine 5.4% (w/v) in an anhydrous glycerin base. How many milligrams of each active ingredient is contained in one 15-mL bottle?

6. How many grams of sodium chloride are present in one liter of sodium chloride 0.9% (w/v) solution?

7. How many bags of 250-mL sterile sodium citrate 4% (w/v) solution can be produced from 1 kilogram of sodium citrate?

8. How many liters of dextrose 5% (w/v) solution can be produced with 500 grams of dextrose?

9. What mass (in milligrams) of fluocinolone is present in 60 milliliters of fluocinolone 0.01% (w/v) topical oil?

10. Diphenhydramine oral solution contains 12.5 milligrams of diphenhydramine per teaspoon. What is the percent concentration (w/v)?

11. What is the mass (in milligrams) of tobramycin in 15 milliliters of Tobrex® (tobramycin) 0.3% (w/v) ophthalmic solution?

12. If a 4-mL vial of norepinephrine 4 mg/4mL injection solution is diluted to a final volume of 50 milliliters using dextrose 5% (w/v) in water, then what is the concentration (% w/v) of norepinephrine after dilution?

13. What concentration (%w/v) of ketoconazole would be produced by compounding the formula below?
    Ketoconazole Topical Solution[1]:
    Ketoconazole   1 gram
    Dimethyl sulfoxide   5 milliliters
    Polyethylene glycol 300 qs   100 milliliters

14. What concentration (% w/v) of promethazine hydrochloride would be produced by compounding the formula below?
    Promethazine Hydrochloride Nasal Spray[2]:
    Promethazine HCl   12.5 grams
    Disodium edetate   10 grams
    Calcium chloride   4 milligrams
    Sodium metabisulfite   25 milligrams
    Phenol   500 milligrams
    Acetic acid/sodium acetate   qs   pH 4–5.5
    Sterile water   qs   100 mL

15. Compounding the formula below would produce what concentration (% w/v) of clobetasol propionate?
    Zinc Pyrithione and Clobetasol Lotion[3]:
    Zinc pyrithione   200 milligrams
    Clobetasol propionate   50 milligrams
    Isopropyl alcohol 91%   20 milliliters
    Isopropyl myristate   80 milliliters

SOLUTIONS for % W/V PROBLEMS

1. What is the percent concentration (w/v) of a 2,500,000-microgram solution of clindamycin dissolved in 250 milliliters of water?

   STEP 1: Convert mass from micrograms to grams.

   $$2{,}500{,}000 \text{ mcg } of \text{ clindamycin} \times \frac{g}{1{,}000{,}000 \text{ mcg}} = 2.5 \text{ g } of \text{ clindamycin}$$

   STEP 2: Set up a proportion and solve for the unknown.

   $$\frac{2.5 \text{ g } of \text{ clindamycin}}{250 \text{ mL } of \text{ solution}} = \frac{\text{UNKNOWN}}{100 \text{ mL } of \text{ solution}} \therefore \text{UNKNOWN} = \frac{2.5 \text{ g } of \text{ clindamycin}}{250 \text{ mL } of \text{ solution}} \times 100 \text{ mL } of \text{ solution} = 1 \text{ g } of \text{ clindamycin}$$

   STEP 3: Express the strength in terms of percent concentration (w/v).

   $$\frac{1 \text{ g } of \text{ clindamycin}}{100 \text{ mL } of \text{ solution}} = \text{clindamycin 1\% (w/v) solution}$$

2. What is the percent concentration (w/v) of a 473-mL oral solution that contains 567.6 mg of chlorhexidine gluconate?

   STEP 1: Convert mass from milligrams to grams.

   $$567.6 \text{ mg } of \text{ chlorhexidine gluconate} \times \frac{g}{1{,}000 \text{ mg}} = 0.5676 \text{ g } of \text{ chlorhexidine gluconate}$$

   STEP 2: Perform dimensional analysis.

   $$\frac{0.5676 \text{ g } of \text{ chlorhexidine gluconate}}{473 \text{ mL } of \text{ oral solution}} = \frac{\text{UNKNOWN}}{100 \text{ mL } of \text{ oral solution}}$$

   $$\therefore \text{UNKNOWN} = \frac{0.5676 \text{ g } of \text{ chlorhexidine gluconate}}{473 \text{ mL } of \text{ oral solution}} \times 100 \text{ mL } of \text{ oral solution}$$

   $$= 0.12 \text{ g } of \text{ chlorhexidine gluconate}$$

   STEP 3: Express the strength in terms of percent concentration (w/v).

   $$\frac{0.12 \text{ g } of \text{ chlorhexidine gluconate}}{100 \text{ mL } of \text{ solution}} = \text{chlorhexidine gluconate 0.12\% (w/v) oral solution}$$

3. A 6-month-old female receives one-half dropperful of sodium fluoride 0.11% (w/v) oral drops. If one dropperful equals one milliliter, how many milligrams of sodium fluoride did she receive?

   STEP 1: Express the strength in terms of mass and volume based on the definition of percent concentration (w/v).

   $$\text{sodium fluoride 0.11\% (w/v) oral drops} = \frac{0.11 \text{ g } of \text{ sodium fluoride}}{100 \text{ mL } of \text{ oral drops}}$$

   STEP 2: Perform dimensional analysis.

   $$\frac{0.11 \text{ g } of \text{ sodium fluoride}}{100 \text{ mL } of \text{ oral drops}} = \frac{\text{UNKNOWN}}{0.5 \text{ mL } of \text{ oral drops}}$$

   $$\therefore \text{UNKNOWN} = \frac{0.11 \text{ g } of \text{ sodium fluoride}}{100 \text{ mL } of \text{ oral drops}} \times 0.5 \text{ mL } of \text{ oral drops} = 0.00055 \text{ g } of \text{ sodium fluoride}$$

   STEP 3: Convert mass from grams to milligrams to answer the question correctly.

   $$0.00055 \text{ g } of \text{ sodium fluoride} \times \frac{1{,}000 \text{ mg}}{\text{g}} = 0.55 \text{ mg } of \text{ sodium fluoride}$$

4. Clobetasol propionate topical solution is commercially available in a 50-mL bottle. If each milliliter contains 0.5 mg of clobetasol propionate, what is the strength (% w/v) of the solution?

   STEP 1: Convert mass from milligrams to grams.

   $$0.5 \text{ mg } of \text{ clobetasol propionate} \times \frac{\text{g}}{1{,}000 \text{ mg}} = 0.0005 \text{ g } of \text{ clobetasol propionate}$$

   STEP 2: Perform dimensional analysis.

   $$\frac{0.0005 \text{ g } of \text{ clobetasol propionate}}{1 \text{ mL } of \text{ topical solution}} = \frac{\text{UNKNOWN}}{100 \text{ mL } of \text{ topical solution}}$$

   $$\therefore \text{UNKNOWN} = \frac{0.0005 \text{ g } of \text{ clobetasol propionate}}{1 \text{ mL } of \text{ topical solution}} \times 100 \text{ mL } of \text{ topical solution} = 0.05 \text{ g } of \text{ clobetasol propionate}$$

   STEP 3: Express the strength in terms of percent concentration (w/v).

   $$\frac{0.05 \text{ g } of \text{ clobetasol propionate}}{100 \text{ mL } of \text{ solution}} = \text{clobetasol propionate 0.05\% (w/v) topical solution}$$

5. Antipyrine-benzocaine otic solution contains benzocaine 1.4% (w/v) and antipyrine 5.4% (w/v) in an anhydrous glycerin base. How many milligrams of each active ingredient is contained in one 15-mL bottle?

   PART I: BENZOCAINE

   STEP 1: Express the strength in terms of mass and volume based on the definition of percent concentration (w/v).

   $$\text{benzocaine 1.4\% (w/v) otic solution} = \frac{1.4 \text{ g } of \text{ benzocaine}}{100 \text{ mL } of \text{ otic solution}}$$

   STEP 2: Perform dimensional analysis.

   $$\frac{1.4 \text{ g } of \text{ benzocaine}}{100 \text{ mL } of \text{ otic solution}} = \frac{\text{UNKNOWN}}{15 \text{ mL } of \text{ otic solution}} \therefore \text{UNKNOWN} = \frac{1.4 \text{ g } of \text{ benzocaine}}{100 \text{ mL } of \text{ otic solution}} \times 15 \text{ mL } of \text{ otic solution} = 0.21 \text{ g } of \text{ benzocaine}$$

   STEP 3: Convert mass from grams to milligrams to answer the question correctly.

   $$0.21 \text{ g } of \text{ benzocaine} \times \frac{1{,}000 \text{ mg}}{\text{g}} = 210 \text{ mg } of \text{ benzocaine}$$

   PART II: ANTIPYRINE

   STEP 1: Express the strength in terms of mass and volume based on the definition of percent concentration (w/v).

   $$\text{antipyrine 5.4\% (w/v) otic solution} = \frac{5.4 \text{ g } of \text{ antipyrine}}{100 \text{ mL } of \text{ otic solution}}$$

   STEP 2: Perform dimensional analysis.

   $$\frac{5.4 \text{ g } of \text{ antipyrine}}{100 \text{ mL } of \text{ otic solution}} = \frac{\text{UNKNOWN}}{15 \text{ mL } of \text{ otic solution}} \therefore \text{UNKNOWN} = \frac{5.4 \text{ g } of \text{ antipyrine}}{100 \text{ mL } of \text{ otic solution}} \times 15 \text{ mL } of \text{ otic solution} = 0.81 \text{ g } of \text{ antipyrine}$$

   STEP 3: Convert mass from grams to milligrams to answer the question correctly.

   $$0.81 \text{ g } of \text{ benzocaine} \times \frac{1{,}000 \text{ mg}}{\text{g}} = 810 \text{ mg } of \text{ antipyrine}$$

6. How many grams of sodium chloride are present in one liter of sodium chloride 0.9% (w/v) solution?

   STEP 1: Express the strength in terms of mass and volume based on the definition of percent concentration (w/v).

   $$\text{sodium chloride 0.9\% (w/v) solution} = \frac{0.9 \text{ g } of \text{ sodium chloride}}{100 \text{ mL } of \text{ solution}}$$

   STEP 2: Convert volume from liters to milliliters.

   $$1 \text{ L } of \text{ solution} \times \frac{1{,}000 \text{ mL}}{\text{L}} = 1{,}000 \text{ mL } of \text{ solution}$$

   STEP 3: Perform dimensional analysis.

   $$\frac{0.9 \text{ g } of \text{ sodium chloride}}{100 \text{ mL } of \text{ solution}} = \frac{\text{UNKNOWN}}{1{,}000 \text{ mL } of \text{ solution}} \therefore \text{UNKNOWN} = \frac{0.9 \text{ g } of \text{ sodium chloride}}{100 \text{ mL } of \text{ solution}} \times 1{,}000 \text{ mL } of \text{ solution} = 9 \text{ g } of \text{ sodium chloride}$$

7. How many bags of 250-mL sterile sodium citrate 4% (w/v) solution can be produced from 1 kilogram of sodium citrate?

   STEP 1: Express the strength in terms of mass and volume based on the definition of percent concentration (w/v).

   $$\text{sodium citrate 4\% (w/v) solution} = \frac{4 \text{ g of sodium citrate}}{100 \text{ mL of solution}}$$

   STEP 2: Perform dimensional analysis to determine the mass of sodium citrate needed to make one 250-mL bag of solution.

   $$\frac{4 \text{ g of sodium citrate}}{100 \text{ mL of solution}} = \frac{\text{UNKNOWN}}{250 \text{ mL of solution}} \therefore \text{UNKNOWN} = \frac{4 \text{ g of sodium citrate}}{100 \text{ mL of solution}} \times 250 \text{ mL of solution} = 10 \text{ g of sodium citrate}$$

   STEP 3: Convert the given mass of sodium citrate from kilograms to grams.

   $$1 \text{ kg of sodium citrate} \times \frac{1{,}000 \text{ g}}{\text{kg}} = 1{,}000 \text{ g of sodium citrate}$$

   STEP 4: Perform dimensional analysis to determine how many bags can be made from the given mass of sodium citrate.

   $$\frac{10 \text{ g of sodium citrate}}{1 \text{ bag of solution}} = \frac{1{,}000 \text{ g of sodium citrate}}{\text{UNKNOWN}}$$

   $$\therefore \text{UNKNOWN} = 1{,}000 \text{ g of sodium citrate} \times \frac{1 \text{ bag of solution}}{10 \text{ g of sodium citrate}} = 100 \text{ bags of solution}$$

8. How many liters of dextrose 5% (w/v) solution can be produced with 500 grams of dextrose?

   STEP 1: Express the strength in terms of mass and volume based on the definition of percent concentration (w/v).

   $$\text{dextrose 5\% (w/v) solution} = \frac{5 \text{ g of dextrose}}{100 \text{ mL of solution}}$$

   STEP 2: Perform dimensional analysis.

   $$\frac{5 \text{ g of dextrose}}{100 \text{ mL of solution}} = \frac{500 \text{ g of dextrose}}{\text{UNKNOWN}} \therefore \text{UNKNOWN} = 500 \text{ g of dextrose} \times \frac{100 \text{ mL of solution}}{5 \text{ g of dextrose}} = 10{,}000 \text{ mL of solution}$$

   STEP 3: Convert volume from milliliters to liters to answer the question correctly.

   $$10{,}000 \text{ mL of solution} \times \frac{\text{L}}{1{,}000 \text{ mL}} = 10 \text{ L of solution}$$

9. What mass (in milligrams) of fluocinolone is present in 60 milliliters of fluocinolone 0.01% (w/v) topical oil?

   STEP 1: Express the strength in terms of mass and volume based on the definition of percent concentration (w/v).

   $$\text{fluocinolone 0.01\% (w/v) topical oil} = \frac{0.01 \text{ g of fluocinolone}}{100 \text{ mL of topical oil}}$$

   STEP 2: Perform dimensional analysis.

   $$\frac{0.01 \text{ g of fluocinolone}}{100 \text{ mL of oil}} = \frac{\text{UNKNOWN}}{60 \text{ mL of oil}} \therefore \text{UNKNOWN} = \frac{0.01 \text{ g of fluocinolone}}{100 \text{ mL of oil}} \times 60 \text{ mL of oil} = 0.006 \text{ g of fluocinolone}$$

   STEP 3: Convert mass from grams to milligrams to answer the question correctly.

   $$0.006 \text{ g of fluocinolone} \times \frac{1{,}000 \text{ mg}}{\text{g}} = 6 \text{ mg of fluocinolone}$$

10. Diphenhydramine oral solution contains 12.5 milligrams of diphenhydramine per teaspoon. What is the percent concentration (w/v)?

    STEP 1: Convert units of mass from milligrams to grams and volume from teaspoons to milliliters.

    $$\frac{12.5 \text{ mg } of \text{ diphenhydramine}}{\text{teaspoon } of \text{ oral solution}} \times \frac{g}{1{,}000 \text{ mg}} \times \frac{\text{teaspoon}}{5 \text{ mL}} = \frac{0.0025 \text{ g } of \text{ diphenhydramine}}{1 \text{ mL } of \text{ oral solution}}$$

    STEP 2: Perform dimensional analysis to determine how many grams of diphenhydramine are present in 100 mL of solution.

    $$\frac{0.0025 \text{ g } of \text{ diphenhydramine}}{1 \text{ mL } of \text{ oral solution}} = \frac{\text{UNKNOWN}}{100 \text{ mL } of \text{ oral solution}} \therefore \text{UNKNOWN} = \frac{0.0125 \text{ g } of \text{ diphenhydramine}}{5 \text{ mL } of \text{ oral solution}} \times 100 \text{ mL } of \text{ oral solution}$$

    $$= 0.25 \text{ g } of \text{ diphenhydramine}$$

    STEP 3: Express the strength in terms of percent concentration (w/v).

    $$\frac{0.25 \text{ g } of \text{ diphenhydramine}}{100 \text{ mL } of \text{ oral solution}} = \text{diphenhydramine } 0.25\% \text{ (w/v) oral solution}$$

11. What is the mass (in milligrams) of tobramycin in 15 milliliters of Tobrex® (tobramycin) 0.3% (w/v) ophthalmic solution?

    STEP 1: Perform dimensional analysis to determine how many grams of tobramycin are present in 15 mL of solution.

    $$\frac{0.3 \text{ g } of \text{ tobramycin}}{100 \text{ mL } of \text{ solution}} = \frac{\text{UNKNOWN}}{15 \text{ mL } of \text{ solution}} \therefore \text{UNKNOWN} = \frac{0.3 \text{ g } of \text{ tobramycin}}{100 \text{ mL } of \text{ solution}} \times 15 \text{ mL } of \text{ solution} = 0.045 \text{ g } of \text{ tobramycin}$$

    STEP 2: Convert mass from grams to milligrams to answer the question correctly.

    $$0.045 \text{ g } of \text{ tobramycin} \times \frac{1{,}000 \text{ mg}}{g} = 45 \text{ mg } of \text{ tobramycin}$$

12. If a 4-mL vial of norepinephrine 4 mg/4mL injection solution is diluted to a final volume of 50 milliliters using dextrose 5% (w/v) in water, then what is the concentration (% w/v) of norepinephrine after dilution?

    STEP 1: Convert mass from milligrams to grams.

    $$4 \text{ mg } of \text{ norepinephrine} \times \frac{g}{1{,}000 \text{ mg}} = 0.004 \text{ g } of \text{ norepinephrine}$$

    STEP 2: Perform dimensional analysis.

    $$\frac{0.004 \text{ g } of \text{ norepinephrine}}{50 \text{ mL } of \text{ injection solution}} = \frac{\text{UNKNOWN}}{100 \text{ mL } of \text{ injection solution}} \therefore \text{UNKNOWN} = \frac{0.004 \text{ g } of \text{ norepinephrine}}{50 \text{ mL } of \text{ injection solution}} \times 100 \text{ mL } of \text{ injection solution}$$

    $$= 0.008 \text{ g } of \text{ norepinephrine}$$

    STEP 3: Express the strength in terms of percent concentration (w/v).

    $$\frac{0.008 \text{ g } of \text{ norepinephrine}}{100 \text{ mL } of \text{ injection solution}} = \text{norepinephrine } 0.008\% \text{ (w/v) injection solution}$$

13. What concentration (% w/v) of ketoconazole would be produced by compounding the formula below?
    Ketoconazole Topical Solution[1]:
    Ketoconazole   1 gram
    Dimethyl sulfoxide   5 milliliters
    Polyethylene glycol 300 qs 100 milliliters

    STEP 1: Express the concentration of ketoconazole in terms of mass and volume from the information provided.

    $$\frac{1 \text{ g of ketoconazole}}{100 \text{ mL of solution}}$$

    Note: The recipe calls for "polyethylene glycol 300 qs 100 milliliters," which means the compounder will add enough polyethylene glycol during the final step of the process to bring the total volume of the solution to 100 milliliters.

    STEP 2: Express the strength in terms of percent concentration (w/v).

    $$\frac{1 \text{ g of ketoconazole}}{100 \text{ mL of solution}} = \text{ketoconazole 1\% (w/v) topical solution}$$

14. What concentration (% w/v) of promethazine hydrochloride would be produced by compounding the formula below?
    Promethazine Hydrochloride Nasal Spray[2]:
    Promethazine HCl   12.5 grams
    Disodium edetate   10 grams
    Calcium chloride   4 milligrams
    Sodium metabisulfite   25 milligrams
    Phenol   500 milligrams
    Acetic acid/sodium acetate   qs   pH 4–5.5
    Sterile water   qs   100 mL

    STEP 1: Express the concentration of promethazine hydrochloride in terms of mass and volume.

    $$\frac{12.5 \text{ g of promethazine hydrochloride}}{100 \text{ mL of nasal spray}}$$

    Note: The recipe calls for "sterile water qs 100 milliliters," which means the compounder will add enough sterile water during the final step of the process to bring the final volume of the solution to 100 milliliters.

    STEP 2: Express the strength in terms of percent concentration (w/v).

    $$\frac{12.5 \text{ g of promethazine hydrochloride}}{100 \text{ mL of nasal spray}} = \text{promethazine hydrochloride 12.5\% (w/v) nasal spray}$$

15. Compounding the formula below would produce what concentration (% w/v) of clobetasol propionate?

    Zinc Pyrithione and Clobetasol Lotion[3]:
Zinc pyrithione	200 milligrams
Clobetasol propionate	50 milligrams
Isopropyl alcohol 91%	20 milliliters
Isopropyl myristate	80 milliliters

    STEP 1: Determine the total volume of the formulation.

    $$20 \text{ mL } of \text{ isopropyl alcohol 91\%} + 80 \text{ mL } of \text{ isopropyl myristate} = 100 \text{ mL } of \text{ total volume}$$

    Note: The influence of the solid ingredients (200 mg of zinc pyrithione and 50 mg of clobetasol propionate) on the total volume would be negligible.

    STEP 2: Convert the units of mass for clobetasol propionate from milligrams to grams.

    $$50 \text{ mg } of \text{ clobetasol propionate} \times \frac{g}{1,000 \text{ mg}} = 0.05 \text{ g } of \text{ clobetasol propionate}$$

    STEP 3: Express the concentration of clobetasol propionate in terms of mass and volume.

    $$\frac{0.05 \text{ g } of \text{ clobetasol propionate}}{100 \text{ mL } of \text{ lotion}}$$

    STEP 4: Express the strength in terms of percent concentration (w/v).

    $$\frac{0.05 \text{ g } of \text{ clobetasol propionate}}{100 \text{ mL } of \text{ lotion}} = \text{clobetasol propionate 0.05\% (w/v) lotion}$$

REFERENCES

1. Allen, LV. Compounding for superficial fungal infections. *Secundum Artem*. (n.d.);11(4) (available at https://www.perrigo.com).
2. Allen, LV. Compounding for gastrointestinal disorders. *Secundum Artem*. (n.d.);13(2) (available at https://www.perrigo.com).
3. Allen, LV. Compounding for patients with psoriasis. *Secundum Artem*. (n.d.);9(4) (available at https://www.perrigo.com).
4. Tobrex [package insert]. Fort Worth, TX: Alcon Laboratories, Inc; 2012.
5. Chlorhexidine gluconate [package insert]. Zanesville, OH: Cardinal Health; 2017.

RATIO STRENGTH

UNDERSTANDING RATIO STRENGTH

The first number of the ratio (usually the number one) represents the mass or volume of active ingredient. The second number represents the mass or volume of the overall formulation. Ratio strength is proportional to other measures of concentration quantifying the active ingredient in relation to the overall formulation.

COMMON CONCENTRATIONS EXPRESSED AS A RATIO

1:1 = 1 gram per mL = 1 g/mL

1:1,000 = 1 x 10^{-3} grams per mL = 1 mg/mL

1:1,000,000 = 1 x 10^{-6} grams per mL = 1 mcg/mL

SELECT EXAMPLES
testosterone 1% (w/w) gel = testosterone 1:100 gel
ethyl alcohol 2% (v/v) solution = ethyl alcohol 1:50 solution
clobetasol 0.05% (w/v) lotion = clobetasol 1:2,000 lotion

1. What is the mass (in milligrams) of epinephrine in an unopened 50-mL multi-dose vial of lidocaine hydrochloride 0.5% (w/v) with epinephrine 1:200,000 injection solution?

2. What is the ratio strength of a 100-mL intravenous solution that contains 8 milligrams of norepinephrine?

3. What is the mass (in milligrams) of epinephrine in one 0.3-mL EpiPen® auto-injector that contains epinephrine 1:1,000 solution?

4. What is the ratio strength of calcitriol 1 mcg/mL oral solution?

5. What is the ratio strength of Travatan® Z (travoprost) 0.004% (w/v) ophthalmic solution?

6. How many milliliters of lidocaine 1:200 stock solution would be required to compound 50 milliliters of lidocaine 0.25% (w/v) solution?

7. What is the ratio strength of coal tar in the following formula for coal tar ointment?
   Crude coal tar   15 grams
   Polysorbate 80   90 grams
   White petrolatum   195 grams

8. What is the ratio strength of a solution created by dissolving one 300-mg capsule of clindamycin in one liter of purified water?

9. What is the ratio strength of a wound care solution that is created by combining 24 milliliters of sodium hypochlorite 5.25% (w/v) solution with 984 milliliters of sterile water for irrigation?

10. What is the ratio strength of gentamicin in the following formula for gentamicin otic solution?
    Gentamicin   100 milligrams
    Glycerin   ad   100 milliliters

11. What is the ratio strength of morphine sulfate in the following formula for morphine sulfate 8 mg troches (24-count)?
    Morphine sulfate   192 milligrams
    Aspartame   400 milligrams
    Citric acid monohydrate   500 milligrams
    Silica gel   600 milligrams
    Acacia   350 milligrams
    Polyethylene glycol 1500   21,958 milligrams

SOLUTIONS *for* RATIO STRENGTH PROBLEMS

1. What is the mass (in milligrams) of epinephrine in an unopened 50-mL multi-dose vial of lidocaine hydrochloride 0.5% (w/v) with epinephrine 1:200,000 injection solution?

   STEP 1: Set up a proportion and solve for the unknown.

   $$\frac{1 \text{ g of epinephrine}}{200{,}000 \text{ mL of solution}} = \frac{\text{UNKNOWN}}{50 \text{ mL of solution}} \therefore \text{UNKNOWN} = \frac{1 \text{ g of epinephrine}}{200{,}000 \text{ mL of solution}} \times 50 \text{ mL of solution} = 0.00025 \text{ g of epinephrine}$$

   STEP 2: Convert mass from grams to milligrams to answer the question correctly.

   $$0.00025 \text{ g of epinephrine} \times \frac{1{,}000 \text{ mg}}{\text{g}} = 0.25 \text{ mg of epinephrine}$$

2. What is the ratio strength of a 100-mL intravenous solution that contains 8 milligrams of norepinephrine?

   STEP 1: Convert mass from milligrams to grams.

   $$8 \text{ mg of norepinephrine} \times \frac{\text{g}}{1{,}000 \text{ mg}} = 0.008 \text{ g of norepinephrine}$$

   STEP 2: Set up a proportion and solve for the unknown.

   $$\frac{0.008 \text{ g of norepinephrine}}{100 \text{ mL of solution}} = \frac{1 \text{ g of norepinephrine}}{\text{UNKNOWN}} \therefore \text{UNKNOWN} = \frac{100 \text{ mL of solution}}{0.008 \text{ g of norepinephrine}} \times 1 \text{ g of norepinephrine}$$

   $$= 12{,}500 \text{ mL of solution}$$

   STEP 3: Express as ratio strength.

   $$\frac{1 \text{ g of norepinephrine}}{12{,}500 \text{ mL of solution}} = \text{norepinephrine 1:12,500 solution}$$

3. What is the mass (in milligrams) of epinephrine in one 0.3-mL EpiPen® auto-injector that contains epinephrine 1:1,000 solution?

   STEP 1: Set up a proportion and solve for the unknown.

   $$\frac{1 \text{ g of epinephrine}}{1{,}000 \text{ mL of solution}} = \frac{\text{UNKNOWN}}{0.3 \text{ mL of solution}} \therefore \text{UNKNOWN} = \frac{1 \text{ g of epinephrine}}{1{,}000 \text{ mL of solution}} \times 0.3 \text{ mL of solution} = 0.0003 \text{ g of epinephrine}$$

   STEP 2: Convert mass from grams to milligrams to answer the question correctly.

   $$0.0003 \text{ g of epinephrine} \times \frac{1{,}000 \text{ mg}}{\text{g}} = 0.3 \text{ mg of epinephrine}$$

4. What is the ratio strength of calcitriol 1 mcg/mL oral solution?

   STEP 1: Convert units of mass from micrograms to grams.

   $$1 \text{ mcg of calcitriol} \times \frac{\text{g}}{1{,}000{,}000 \text{ mcg}} = 0.000001 \text{ g of calcitriol}$$

   STEP 2: Set up a proportion and solve for the unknown.

   $$\frac{0.000001 \text{ g of calcitriol}}{1 \text{ mL of solution}} = \frac{1 \text{ g of calcitriol}}{\text{UNKNOWN}} \therefore \text{UNKNOWN} = \frac{1 \text{ mL of solution}}{0.000001 \text{ g of calcitriol}} \times 1 \text{ g of calcitriol}$$

   $$= 1{,}000{,}000 \text{ mL of solution}$$

   STEP 3: Express as ratio strength.

   $$\frac{1 \text{ g of calcitriol}}{1{,}000{,}000 \text{ mL of solution}} = \text{calcitriol } 1{:}1{,}000{,}000 \text{ solution}$$

5. What is the ratio strength of Travatan® Z (travoprost) 0.004% (w/v) ophthalmic solution?

   STEP 1: Set up a proportion and solve for the unknown.

   $$\frac{0.004 \text{ g of travoprost}}{100 \text{ mL of solution}} = \frac{1 \text{ g of travoprost}}{\text{UNKNOWN}} \therefore \text{UNKNOWN} = \frac{100 \text{ mL of solution}}{0.004 \text{ g of travoprost}} \times 1 \text{ g of travoprost} = 25{,}000 \text{ mL of solution}$$

   STEP 2: Express as ratio strength.

   $$\frac{1 \text{ g of travoprost}}{25{,}000 \text{ mL of solution}} = \text{travoprost } 1{:}25{,}000 \text{ solution}$$

6. How many milliliters of lidocaine 1:200 stock solution would be required to compound 50 milliliters of lidocaine 0.25% (w/v) solution?

   STEP 1: Determine mass of lidocaine present in 50 mL of lidocaine 0.25% (w/v) solution.

   $$\frac{0.25 \text{ g of lidocaine}}{100 \text{ mL of solution}} \times 50 \text{ mL of solution} = 0.125 \text{ g of lidocaine}$$

   STEP 2: Perform dimensional analysis to determine the volume of lidocaine 1:200 stock solution containing 0.125 g of lidocaine.

   $$0.125 \text{ g of lidocaine} \times \frac{200 \text{ mL of stock solution}}{1 \text{ g of lidocaine}} = 25 \text{ mL of stock solution}$$

7. What is the ratio strength of coal tar in the following formula for coal tar ointment?
   Crude coal tar   15 grams
   Polysorbate 80   90 grams
   White petrolatum   195 grams

   STEP 1: Express the concentration of the active ingredient as a fraction of the total formulation.

   Total mass of formulation = 15 grams + 90 grams + 195 grams = 300 grams

   $$\frac{\text{mass of coal tar}}{\text{total mass of ointment}} = \frac{15 \text{ grams of coal tar}}{300 \text{ grams of ointment}}$$

   STEP 2: Set up a proportion and solve for the unknown.

   $$\frac{15 \text{ grams of coal tar}}{300 \text{ grams of ointment}} = \frac{1 \text{ g of coal tar}}{\text{UNKNOWN}} \therefore \text{UNKNOWN} = \frac{300 \text{ grams of ointment}}{15 \text{ grams of coal tar}} \times 1 \text{ g of coal tar} = 20 \text{ grams of ointment}$$

   STEP 2: Express as ratio strength.

   $$\frac{1 \text{ g of coal tar}}{20 \text{ grams of ointment}} = \text{coal tar 1:20 ointment}$$

8. What is the ratio strength of a solution created by dissolving one 300-mg capsule of clindamycin in one liter of purified water?

   STEP 1: Express the concentration of the active ingredient as a fraction of the total formulation.

   $$\frac{300 \text{ mg of clindamycin}}{1 \text{ L of solution}}$$

   STEP 2: Convert units of volume from liters to milliliters and mass from milligrams to grams

   $$\frac{300 \text{ mg of clindamycin}}{1 \text{ L of solution}} \times \frac{\text{L}}{1{,}000 \text{ mL}} \times \frac{\text{g}}{1{,}000 \text{ mg}} = \frac{0.0003 \text{ g of clindamycin}}{1 \text{ mL of solution}}$$

   ☆Remember that ratio strength is proportional to other measures of concentration that quantify the active ingredient as a fraction of the overall formulation.

   STEP 3: Set up a proportion and solve for the unknown.

   $$\frac{0.0003 \text{ g of clindamycin}}{1 \text{ mL of solution}} = \frac{1 \text{ g of clindamycin}}{\text{UNKNOWN}} \therefore \text{UNKNOWN} = \frac{1 \text{ mL of solution}}{0.0003 \text{ g of clindamycin}} \times 1 \text{ g of clindamycin} = 3{,}333 \text{ mL of solution}$$

   STEP 4: Express as ratio strength.

   $$\frac{1 \text{ g of clindamycin}}{3{,}333 \text{ mL of solution}} = \text{clindamycin 1:3,333 solution}$$

9. What is the ratio strength of a wound care solution composed of 24 milliliters of sodium hypochlorite 5.25% (w/v) solution and 984 milliliters of sterile water for irrigation?

   STEP 1: Calculate the mass of sodium hypochlorite in 24 milliliters of 5.25% (w/v) sodium hypochlorite solution.

   $$\frac{5.25 \text{ grams of sodium hypochlorite}}{100 \text{ mL of solution}} \times 24 \text{ mL of solution} = 1.26 \text{ g of sodium hypochlorite}$$

   STEP 2: Express the concentration of the active ingredient as a fraction of the total formulation.

   Total volume of formulation = 24 milliliters + 984 milliliters = 1,008 milliliters

   $$\frac{\text{mass of sodium hypochlorite}}{\text{total volume of solution}} = \frac{1.26 \text{ g of sodium hypochlorite}}{1,008 \text{ milliliters of solution}}$$

   STEP 3: Set up a proportion and solve for the unknown.

   $$\frac{1.26 \text{ g of sodium hypochlorite}}{1,008 \text{ milliliters of solution}} = \frac{1 \text{ g of sodium hypochlorite}}{\text{UNKNOWN}} \therefore \text{UNKNOWN} = \frac{1,008 \text{ milliliters of solution}}{1.26 \text{ g of sodium hypochlorite}} \times 1 \text{ g of sodium hypochlorite}$$

   $$= 800 \text{ mL of solution}$$

   STEP 4: Express as ratio strength.

   $$\frac{1 \text{ g of sodium hypochlorite}}{800 \text{ mL of solution}} = \text{sodium hypochlorite 1:800 solution}$$

   Note: The strength of this solution is equivalent to quarter-strength Dakin's® solution (sodium hypochlorite 0.125% (w/v) solution).

10. What is the ratio strength of gentamicin in the following formula for gentamicin otic solution?
    Gentamicin   100 milligrams
    Glycerin   ad   100 milliliters

    STEP 1: Convert mass from milligrams to grams.

    $$100 \text{ mg of gentamicin} \times \frac{\text{g}}{1,000 \text{ mg}} = 0.1 \text{ g of gentamicin}$$

    STEP 2: Set up a proportion and solve for the unknown.

    $$\frac{0.1 \text{ g of gentamicin}}{100 \text{ mL of solution}} = \frac{1 \text{ g of gentamicin}}{\text{UNKNOWN}} \therefore \text{UNKNOWN} = \frac{100 \text{ mL of solution}}{0.1 \text{ g of gentamicin}} \times 1 \text{ g of gentamicin} = 1,000 \text{ mL of solution}$$

    STEP 3: Express as ratio strength.

    $$\frac{1 \text{ g of gentamicin}}{1,000 \text{ mL of solution}} = \text{gentamicin 1:1,000 solution}$$

Note: In the context of prescription compounding recipes, the abbreviation "ad" means "up to" and "aa" means "of each."

11. What is the ratio strength of morphine sulfate in the following formula for morphine sulfate 8 mg troches (24-count)?

Morphine sulfate	192 milligrams
Aspartame	400 milligrams
Citric acid monohydrate	500 milligrams
Silica gel	600 milligrams
Acacia	350 milligrams
Polyethylene glycol 1500	21,958 milligrams

STEP 1: Express the concentration of the active ingredient as a fraction of the total formulation.

Total mass *of* formulation = 192 mg + 400 mg + 500 mg + 600 mg + 350 mg + 21,958 mg = 24,000 mg

$$\frac{\text{mass } of \text{ morphine sulfate}}{\text{total mass } of \text{ troches}} = \frac{192 \text{ mg } of \text{ morphine sulfate}}{24,000 \text{ mg } of \text{ troches}}$$

STEP 2: Set up a proportion and solve for the unknown.

$$\frac{192 \text{ mg } of \text{ morphine sulfate}}{24,000 \text{ mg } of \text{ troche}} = \frac{1 \text{ g } of \text{ morphine sulfate}}{\text{UNKNOWN}} \therefore \text{UNKNOWN} = \frac{24,000 \text{ mg } of \text{ troche}}{192 \text{ mg } of \text{ morphine sulfate}} \times 1 \text{ g } of \text{ morphine sulfate}$$

$$= 125 \text{ grams } of \text{ troche}$$

STEP 3: Express as ratio strength.

$$\frac{1 \text{ g } of \text{ morphine sulfate}}{125 \text{ grams } of \text{ troche}} = \text{morphine sulfate 1:125 troche}$$

REFERENCES
1. Lidocaine hydrochloride and epinephrine [package insert]. Lake Forest, IL: Hospira, Inc; 2010.
2. EpiPen [package insert]. Columbia, MD: Meridian Medical Technologies, Inc; 2018.
3. Allen, LV. Compounding for patients with psoriasis. *Secundum Artem*. (n.d.);9(4) (available at https://www.perrigo.com).
4. Dakin's solution [package insert]. Indianapolis, IN: Century Pharmaceuticals, Inc; 2010.
5. Allen, LV. Compounding for otic disorders. *Secundum Artem*. (n.d.);13(1) (available at https://www.perrigo.com).
6. Allen, LV. Compounding for the management of pain. *Secundum Artem*. (n.d.);8(4) (available at https://www.perrigo.com).

PARTS PER MILLION (PPM)

DEFINITION *of* PARTS PER MILLION

"Parts per million" is the number of parts of active ingredient per one million equal parts of the overall formulation. Parts per million is a way of expressing the concentration as a fraction in which the denominator is always 1,000,000.

Like ratio strength, parts per million is proportional to other expressions of concentration that quantify the active ingredient relative to the overall formulation.

SELECT EXAMPLES

testosterone 1% (w/w) gel = 10,000 ppm *of* testosterone
ethyl alcohol 2% (v/v) solution = 20,000 ppm *of* ethyl alcohol
clobetasol 0.05% (w/v) lotion = 500 ppm *of* clobetasol

---

1. If a vial of potassium acetate contains 200 micrograms of aluminum contamination per liter, then what is the concentration of aluminum in terms of parts per million?

2. What is the concentration of ferrous sulfate 0.0005% (w/v) solution in terms of parts per million?

3. How many parts per million of latanoprost are present in Xalatan® (latanoprost) 0.005% ophthalmic solution?

4. What is the ratio strength of a solution that contains 10 ppm of epinephrine?

5. What is the percent concentration (w/v) of a solution that contains norepinephrine 10 parts per million?

6. How many parts per million of fentanyl are present in a vial of fentanyl 50 mcg/mL solution?

7. If a 2,700-milliliter total parenteral admixture contains 40.5 mcg of selenium, then what is the concentration of selenium in terms of parts per million?

8. Suppose an institution has a policy that prohibits the dispensing of parenteral drug products with more than 24 mcg/L of aluminum. Can a product that contains 0.03 parts per million of aluminum be dispensed?

9. If 20 grams of fluoride are added to 5,283 gallons of public water, what is the fluoride concentration in terms of parts per million?

10. If each milliliter of a solution contains 4 micrograms of contamination, what is the concentration of the contaminant in terms of parts per million?

11. How many parts per million of alcohol are present in a phenobarbital elixir that contains alcohol 38% (v/v)?

12. If a fish oil capsule contains 0.01 parts per million of mercury, how many micrograms of mercury are present in a 60-count bottle of one-gram fish oil capsules?

13. If a vaccine contains 100 ppm of thimerosal, how many micrograms of thimerosal are present in one 0.5-mL dose?

SOLUTIONS for PARTS PER MILLION PROBLEMS

1. If a vial of potassium acetate contains 200 micrograms of aluminum contamination per liter, then what is the concentration of aluminum in terms of parts per million?

    STEP 1: Convert units of mass from micrograms to grams and volume from liters to milliliters.

    $$\frac{200 \text{ mcg of aluminum}}{1 \text{ L of solution}} \times \frac{\text{g}}{1{,}000{,}000 \text{ mcg}} \times \frac{\text{L}}{1{,}000 \text{ mL}} = \frac{0.0000002 \text{ g of aluminum}}{1 \text{ mL of solution}}$$

    STEP 2: Set up a proportion and solve for the unknown.

    $$\frac{0.0000002 \text{ g of aluminum}}{1 \text{ mL of solution}} = \frac{\text{UNKNOWN}}{1{,}000{,}000 \text{ parts of solution}} \therefore \text{UNKNOWN} = \frac{0.0000002 \text{ g of aluminum}}{1 \text{ mL of solution}} \times 1{,}000{,}000 \text{ parts of solution}$$

    $$= 0.2 \text{ parts of aluminum}$$

    STEP 3: Express as parts per million.

    $$\frac{0.2 \text{ parts of aluminum}}{1{,}000{,}000 \text{ parts of solution}} = 0.2 \text{ ppm of aluminum}$$

2. What is the concentration of ferrous sulfate 0.0005% (w/v) solution in terms of parts per million?

    STEP 1: Set up a proportion and solve for the unknown.

    $$\frac{0.0005 \text{ g of ferrous sulfate}}{100 \text{ mL of solution}} = \frac{\text{UNKNOWN}}{1{,}000{,}000 \text{ mL of solution}} \therefore \text{UNKNOWN} = \frac{0.0005 \text{ g of ferrous sulfate}}{100 \text{ mL of solution}} \times 1{,}000{,}000 \text{ mL of solution}$$

    $$= 5 \text{ g of ferrous sulfate}$$

    STEP 2: Express as parts per million.

    $$\frac{5 \text{ g of ferrous sulfate}}{1{,}000{,}000 \text{ mL of solution}} = 5 \text{ ppm of ferrous sulfate}$$

3. How many parts per million of latanoprost are present in Xalatan® (latanoprost) 0.005% (w/v) ophthalmic solution?

    STEP 1: Set up a proportion and solve for the unknown.

    $$\frac{0.005 \text{ g of latanoprost}}{100 \text{ mL of solution}} = \frac{\text{UNKNOWN}}{1{,}000{,}000 \text{ mL of solution}} \therefore \text{UNKNOWN} = \frac{0.005 \text{ g of latanoprost}}{100 \text{ mL of solution}} \times 1{,}000{,}000 \text{ mL of solution}$$

    $$= 50 \text{ g of latanoprost}$$

    STEP 2: Express as parts per million.

    $$\frac{50 \text{ g of latanoprost}}{1{,}000{,}000 \text{ mL of solution}} = 50 \text{ ppm of latanoprost}$$

4. What is the ratio strength of a solution that contains 10 ppm of epinephrine?

   STEP 1: Set up a proportion and solve for the unknown.

   $$\frac{10 \text{ g of epinephrine}}{1{,}000{,}000 \text{ mL of solution}} = \frac{1 \text{ g of epinephrine}}{\text{UNKNOWN}} \therefore \text{UNKNOWN} = \frac{1{,}000{,}000 \text{ mL of solution}}{10 \text{ g of epinephrine}} \times 1 \text{ g of epinephrine}$$

   $$= 100{,}000 \text{ mL of solution}$$

   STEP 2: Express as ratio strength.

   $$\frac{1 \text{ g of epinephrine}}{100{,}000 \text{ mL of solution}} = \text{epinephrine 1:100,000 solution}$$

5. What is the percent concentration (w/v) of a solution that contains norepinephrine 10 parts per million?

   STEP 1: Set up a proportion and solve for the unknown.

   $$\frac{10 \text{ g of norepinephrine}}{1{,}000{,}000 \text{ mL of solution}} = \frac{\text{UNKNOWN}}{100 \text{ mL of solution}} \therefore \text{UNKNOWN} = \frac{10 \text{ g of norepinephrine}}{1{,}000{,}000 \text{ mL of solution}} \times 100 \text{ mL of solution} = 0.001 \text{ g of norepinephrine}$$

   STEP 2: Express as percent concentration (w/v).

   $$\frac{0.001 \text{ g of norepinephrine}}{100 \text{ mL of solution}} = \text{norepinephrine 0.001\% (w/v) solution}$$

6. How many parts per million of fentanyl are present in a vial of fentanyl 50 mcg/mL solution?

   STEP 1: Convert units of mass from micrograms to grams.

   $$50 \text{ mcg of fentanyl} \times \frac{\text{g}}{1{,}000{,}000 \text{ mcg}} = 0.00005 \text{ g of fentanyl}$$

   STEP 2: Set up a proportion and solve for the unknown.

   $$\frac{0.00005 \text{ g of fentanyl}}{1 \text{ mL of solution}} = \frac{\text{UNKNOWN}}{1{,}000{,}000 \text{ mL of solution}} \therefore \text{UNKNOWN} = \frac{0.00005 \text{ g of fentanyl}}{1 \text{ mL of solution}} \times 1{,}000{,}000 \text{ mL of solution}$$

   $$= 50 \text{ g of fentanyl}$$

   STEP 3: Express as parts per million.

   $$\frac{50 \text{ g of fentanyl}}{1{,}000{,}000 \text{ mL of solution}} = 50 \text{ ppm of fentanyl}$$

7. If a 2,700-milliliter total parenteral admixture contains 40.5 mcg of selenium, then what is the concentration of selenium in terms of parts per million?

   STEP 1: Convert mass from micrograms to grams.

   $$40.5 \text{ mcg } of \text{ selenium} \times \frac{g}{1,000,000 \text{ mcg}} = 0.0000405 \text{ g } of \text{ selenium}$$

   STEP 2: Set up a proportion and solve for the unknown.

   $$\frac{0.0000405 \text{ g } of \text{ selenium}}{2,700 \text{ mL } of \text{ solution}} = \frac{\text{UNKNOWN}}{1,000,000 \text{ mL } of \text{ solution}} \therefore \text{UNKNOWN} = \frac{0.0000405 \text{ g } of \text{ selenium}}{2,700 \text{ mL } of \text{ solution}} \times 1,000,000 \text{ mL } of \text{ solution}$$

   $$= 0.015 \text{ g } of \text{ selenium}$$

   STEP 3: Express as parts per million.

   $$\frac{0.015 \text{ g } of \text{ selenium}}{1,000,000 \text{ mL } of \text{ solution}} = 0.015 \text{ ppm } of \text{ selenium}$$

8. Suppose an institution has a policy that prohibits the dispensing of parenteral drug products with more than 24 mcg/L of aluminum. Can a product that contains 0.03 parts per million of aluminum be dispensed?

   STEP 1: Convert 0.03 ppm of aluminum to units of mcg/L.

   $$\frac{0.03 \text{ g } of \text{ aluminum}}{1,000,000 \text{ mL } of \text{ solution}} \times \frac{1,000,000 \text{ mcg}}{g} \times \frac{1,000 \text{ mL}}{L} = \frac{30 \text{ mcg } of \text{ aluminum}}{1 \text{ L } of \text{ solution}}$$

   ANSWER: No, because the concentration of aluminum for the product in question exceeds 24 mcg/L.

9. If 20 grams of fluoride are added to 5,283 gallons of public water, what is the fluoride concentration in terms of parts per million?

   STEP 1: Convert units of concentration from grams per gallon to grams per milliliter.

   $$\frac{20 \text{ g } of \text{ fluoride}}{5,283 \text{ gallons } of \text{ water}} \times \frac{\text{gallon}}{128 \text{ fluid ounces}} \times \frac{\text{fluid ounce}}{29.57 \text{ mL}} = \frac{0.000001 \text{ g } of \text{ fluoride}}{1 \text{ mL } of \text{ solution}}$$

   STEP 2: Set up a proportion and solve for the unknown.

   $$\frac{0.000001 \text{ g } of \text{ fluoride}}{1 \text{ mL } of \text{ solution}} = \frac{\text{UNKNOWN}}{1,000,000 \text{ mL } of \text{ solution}} \therefore \text{UNKNOWN} = \frac{0.000001 \text{ g } of \text{ fluoride}}{1 \text{ mL } of \text{ solution}} \times 1,000,000 \text{ mL } of \text{ solution} = 1 \text{ g } of \text{ fluoride}$$

   STEP 3: Express as parts per million.

   $$\frac{1 \text{ g } of \text{ fluoride}}{1,000,000 \text{ mL } of \text{ solution}} = 1 \text{ ppm } of \text{ fluoride}$$

10. If each milliliter of a solution contains 4 micrograms of contamination, what is the concentration of the contaminant in terms of parts per million?

    STEP 1: Convert units of concentration from micrograms per milliliter to grams per milliliter.

    $$\frac{4 \text{ mcg } of \text{ contaminants}}{1 \text{ mL } of \text{ solution}} \times \frac{g}{1,000,000 \text{ mcg}} = \frac{0.000004 \text{ g } of \text{ contaminants}}{1 \text{ mL } of \text{ solution}}$$

    STEP 2: Set up a proportion and solve for the unknown.

    $$\frac{0.000004 \text{ g } of \text{ contaminants}}{1 \text{ mL } of \text{ solution}} = \frac{\text{UNKNOWN}}{1,000,000 \text{ mL } of \text{ solution}} \therefore \text{UNKNOWN} = \frac{0.000004 \text{ g } of \text{ contaminants}}{1 \text{ mL } of \text{ solution}} \times 1,000,000 \text{ mL } of \text{ solution}$$

    $$= 4 \text{ g } of \text{ contaminants}$$

    STEP 3: Express as parts per million.

    $$\frac{4 \text{ g } of \text{ contaminants}}{1,000,000 \text{ mL } of \text{ solution}} = 4 \text{ ppm } of \text{ contaminants}$$

11. How many parts per million of alcohol are present in a phenobarbital elixir that contains alcohol 38% (v/v)?

    STEP 1: Set up a proportion and solve for the unknown.

    $$\frac{38 \text{ mL } of \text{ alcohol}}{100 \text{ mL } of \text{ elixir}} = \frac{\text{UNKNOWN}}{1,000,000 \text{ mL } of \text{ elixir}} \therefore \text{UNKNOWN} = \frac{38 \text{ mL } of \text{ alcohol}}{100 \text{ mL } of \text{ elixir}} \times 1,000,000 \text{ mL } of \text{ elixir} = 380,000 \text{ mL } of \text{ alcohol}$$

    STEP 2: Express as parts per million.

    $$\frac{380,000 \text{ mL } of \text{ alcohol}}{1,000,000 \text{ mL } of \text{ elixir}} = 380,000 \text{ ppm } of \text{ alcohol}$$

12. If a fish oil capsule contains 0.01 parts per million of mercury, how many micrograms of mercury are present in a 60-count bottle of one-gram fish oil capsules?

    STEP 1: Use dimensional analysis to determine the mass of mercury in a 60-count bottle of fish oil.

    $$\frac{0.01 \text{ g } of \text{ mercury}}{1,000,000 \text{ g } of \text{ fish oil}} \times \frac{1 \text{ g } of \text{ fish oil}}{\text{capsule}} \times \frac{60 \text{ capsules}}{\text{bottle}} = \frac{0.0000006 \text{ g } of \text{ mercury}}{\text{bottle}}$$

    STEP 2: Convert mass from grams to micrograms to answer the question correctly.

    $$\frac{0.0000006 \text{ g } of \text{ mercury}}{\text{bottle}} \times \frac{1,000,000 \text{ mcg}}{g} = \frac{0.6 \text{ mcg } of \text{ mercury}}{\text{bottle}}$$

13. If a vaccine contains 100 ppm of thimerosal, how many micrograms of thimerosal are present in one 0.5-mL dose?

    STEP 1: Use dimensional analysis to determine the mass of thimerosal in one 0.5-mL dose of vaccine.

    $$\frac{100 \text{ g } of \text{ thimerosal}}{1,000,000 \text{ mL } of \text{ vaccine}} \times 0.5 \text{ mL } of \text{ vaccine} = 0.00005 \text{ g } of \text{ thimerosal}$$

    STEP 2: Convert mass from grams to micrograms to answer the question correctly.

    $$0.00005 \text{ g } of \text{ thimerosal} \times \frac{1,000,000 \text{ mcg}}{g} = 50 \text{ mcg } of \text{ thimerosal}$$

MILLIEQUIVALENTS

CONVERT *from* MILLIGRAMS TO MILLIEQUIVALENTS*

$$\# \text{ of milliequivalents} = \frac{\# \text{ of milligrams} \times \text{valence}}{\text{molecular (or atomic) weight}}$$

NOTE: The valence is equal to the total charge of cations (or anions) in the compound.

*With medications, we're typically dealing with milliequivalents (one milliequivalent is 1/1,000th of an equivalent).

WEIGHT & VALENCE *of* THE MOST COMMON IONS

ION	VALENCE	ATOMIC OR MOLECULAR WEIGHT
Calcium (Ca^{2+})	2	40 grams/mole
Chloride (Cl^-)	1	35.5 grams/mole
Ferrous Iron (Fe^{2+})	2	56 grams/mole
Ferric Iron (Fe^{3+})	3	56 grams/mole
Lithium (Li^+)	1	7 grams/mole
Magnesium (Mg^{2+})	2	24 grams/mole
Potassium (K^+)	1	39 grams/mole
Sodium (Na^+)	1	23 grams/mole
Zinc (Zn^{2+})	2	65 grams/mole
Acetate ($C_2H_3O_2^{1-}$)	1	59 grams/mole
Bicarbonate (HCO_3^{1-})	1	61 grams/mole
Carbonate (CO_3^{2-})	2	60 grams/mole
Citrate ($C_6H_5O_7^{3-}$)	3	189 grams/mole
Gluconate ($C_6H_{11}O_7^-$)	1	195 grams/mole
Sulfate (SO_4^{2-})	2	96 grams/mole

ATOMIC WEIGHTS *of* THE MOST COMMON ORGANIC ELEMENTS

Carbon (C): 12 grams/mole   Hydrogen (H): 1 gram/mole
Oxygen (O): 16 grams/mole   Nitrogen (N): 14 grams/mole

1. How many milliequivalents of calcium are contained in one Tums® (calcium carbonate) 500 mg chewable tablet? Note: Calcium has an atomic weight of 40 grams/mole and a +2 ionic charge; carbonate has a molecular weight of 60 grams/mole and a -2 ionic charge.

2. How many milliequivalents of lithium are contained in a 300-mg capsule of lithium carbonate? Note: Lithium has an atomic weight of 7 grams/mole and a +1 ionic charge; carbonate has a molecular weight of 60 grams/mole and a -2 ionic charge.

3. How many milliequivalents of calcium are contained in a 667-mg capsule of PhosLo® (calcium acetate). Each atom of calcium is bound to two acetate molecules ($Ca(CH_3COO)_2$), so the molecular weight of the compound is 158 grams/mole.

4. How many milligrams of potassium chloride (KCl) are contained in one 20 mEq tablet of potassium chloride (K-Dur®)? Note: Potassium has an atomic weight of 39 grams/mole and a +1 ionic charge; chlorine has an atomic weight of 35.5 grams/mole and a -1 ionic charge.

5. RW is a 70-year-old female with hypokalemia. Her physician orders a 40-milliequivalent infusion of potassium acetate. How many milligrams of potassium acetate will RW receive? Note: Potassium has an atomic weight of 39 grams/mole and a +1 ionic charge; acetate has a molecular weight of 59 grams/mole and a -1 ionic charge.

6. How many milliequivalents of sodium chloride are contained in a one-liter infusion of normal saline? Note: Sodium has an atomic weight of 23 grams/mole and a +1 ionic charge; chlorine has an atomic weight of 35.5 grams/mole and a -1 ionic charge.

7. How many milliequivalents of sodium bicarbonate are in a 50-mL vial of 7.5% sodium bicarbonate? Note: Sodium has an atomic weight of 23 grams/mole and a +1 ionic charge; bicarbonate has a molecular weight of 61 grams/mole and a -1 ionic charge.

8. Each tablet of RenaPlus™, a potassium supplement for cats and dogs, contains 468 milligrams of potassium gluconate (K(C$_6$H$_{11}$O$_7$)). How many milliequivalents of potassium gluconate are contained in an entire bottle of 100 tablets? Note: Potassium has an atomic weight of 39 grams/mole and a +1 ionic charge; gluconate has a molecular weight of 195 grams/mole and a -1 ionic charge.

9. How many milliequivalents of ferrous iron are contained in a 5-grain ferrous sulfate tablet? Note: Ferrous iron has an atomic weight of 56 grams/mole and a +2 ionic charge; sulfate has a molecular weight of 96 grams/mole and a -2 ionic charge.

10. A physician orders a 16.25-milliequivalent magnesium sulfate infusion. Given that the product is supplied as magnesium sulfate heptahydrate (MgSO$_4$ • 7H$_2$O), how many grams should be dispensed? Note: Magnesium has an atomic weight of 24 grams/mole and a +2 ionic charge; sulfate has a molecular weight of 96 grams/mole and a -2 ionic charge.

11. How many milligrams of sodium are in a 50-mL vial that contains 100 mEq of sodium acetate? Note: Sodium has an atomic weight of 23 grams/mole and a +1 ionic charge; acetate has a molecular weight of 59 grams/mole and a -1 ionic charge.

12. Each milliliter of a 10% calcium chloride injection solution contains 100 milligrams of calcium chloride dihydrate (CaCl2 • 2H2O). How many milliequivalents of calcium are contained in one milliliter of this solution? Note: Calcium has an atomic weight of 40 grams/mole and a +2 ionic charge; chlorine has an atomic weight of 35.5 grams/mole and a -1 ionic charge.

13. Potassium chloride (KCl) is available commercially as a 20 mEq/15mL oral solution. To prevent gastrointestinal irritation, each dose must be diluted prior to administration. What is the concentration in terms of percent weight/volume before dilution? Note: Potassium has a molecular weight of 39 grams/mole and a +1 ionic charge; chlorine has an atomic weight of 35.5 grams/mole and a -1 ionic charge.

14. Magnesium citrate (Mg$_3$(C$_6$H$_5$O$_7$)$_2$)–an osmotic laxative–is available commercially as a 1.745-gram per fluid ounce solution. How many milliequivalents of magnesium are present in a 10-fluid ounce bottle? Note: Magnesium has an atomic weight of 24 grams/mole and a +2 ionic charge; citrate has a molecular weight of 189 grams/mole and a -3 ionic charge.

15. If one 315-milligram tablet of calcium citrate tetrahydrate (Ca$_3$(C$_6$H$_5$O$_7$)$_2$ • 4H$_2$O) contains 66 milligrams of elemental calcium and 250 international units of cholecalciferol, how many milliequivalents of calcium are present in each tablet? Note: Calcium has an atomic weight of 40 grams/mole and a +2 ionic charge. Citrate 189 g/mole -3.

REFERENCES
1. Lithium carbonate [package insert]. Columbus, OH: Roxane Laboratories, Inc; 2016.
2. PhosLo [package insert]. Waltham, MA: Fresenius Medical Care North America; 2018.
3. Calcium chloride injection solution [package insert]. Lake Forest, IL: Hospira, Inc; 2018.
4. Potassium chloride oral solution [package insert]. Greenville, SC: Pharmaceutical Associates Inc; 2014.
5. Magnesium citrate liquid [package insert]. Chesterbrook, PA: AmerisourceBergen; 2016.

SOLUTIONS for MILLIEQUIVALENT PROBLEMS

1. How many milliequivalents of calcium are contained in one Tums® (calcium carbonate) 500 mg chewable tablet? Note: Calcium has an atomic weight of 40 grams/mole and a +2 ionic charge; carbonate has a molecular weight of 60 grams/mole and a -2 ionic charge.

   STEP 1: Determine the total mass (in milligrams) of calcium in one tablet.

   $$\frac{500 \text{ mg of calcium carbonate}}{\text{tablet}} \times \frac{40 \text{ g/mol of Ca}^{2+}}{100 \text{ g/mol of calcium carbonate}} = \frac{200 \text{ mg of Ca}^{2+}}{\text{tablet}}$$

   STEP 2: Enter values into the equation to convert milligrams to milliequivalents.

   $$\text{\# of milliequivalents} = \frac{\text{\# of milligrams} \times \text{valence}}{\text{molecular weight}} = \frac{200 \times 2}{40} = 10 \text{ mEq}$$

2. How many milliequivalents of lithium are contained in a 300-mg capsule of lithium carbonate? Note: Lithium has an atomic weight of 7 grams/mole and a +1 ionic charge; carbonate has a molecular weight of 60 grams/mole and a -2 ionic charge.

   STEP 1: Determine the total mass (in milligrams) of lithium in one capsule.

   $$\frac{300 \text{ mg of lithium carbonate}}{\text{capsule}} \times \frac{14 \text{ g/mol of Li}^{1+}}{74 \text{ g/mol of lithium carbonate}} = \frac{56.8 \text{ mg of Li}^{1+}}{\text{capsule}}$$

   STEP 2: Enter values into the equation to convert milligrams to milliequivalents.

   $$\text{\# of milliequivalents} = \frac{\text{\# of milligrams} \times \text{valence}}{\text{molecular weight}} = \frac{56.8 \times 1}{7} = 8.1 \text{ mEq}$$

3. How many milliequivalents of calcium are contained in a 667-mg capsule of PhosLo® (calcium acetate). Each atom of calcium is bound to two acetate molecules (Ca(CH₃COO)₂), so the molecular weight of the compound is 158 grams/mole.

   STEP 1: Determine the total mass (in milligrams) of calcium in one capsule.

   $$\frac{667 \text{ mg of calcium acetate}}{\text{capsule}} \times \frac{40 \text{ g/mol of Ca}^{2+}}{158 \text{ g/mol of calcium acetate}} = \frac{168.9 \text{ mg of Ca}^{2+}}{\text{capsule}}$$

   STEP 2: Enter values into the equation to convert from milligrams to milliequivalents.

   $$\text{\# of milliequivalents} = \frac{\text{\# of milligrams} \times \text{valence}}{\text{molecular weight}} = \frac{168.9 \times 2}{40} = 8.44 \text{ mEq}$$

4. How many milligrams of potassium chloride (KCl) are contained in one 20 mEq tablet of potassium chloride (K-Dur®)? Note: Potassium has an atomic weight of 39 grams/mole and a +1 ionic charge; chlorine has an atomic weight of 35.5 grams/mole and a -1 ionic charge.

   SOLUTION: Rearrange the equation to convert milliequivalents to milligrams.

   $$\text{\# of milliequivalents} = \frac{\text{\# of milligrams} \times \text{valence}}{\text{molecular weight}}$$

   $$\therefore \text{\# of milligrams} = \frac{\text{\# of milliequivalents} \times \text{molecular weight}}{\text{valence}} = \frac{20 \times (39 + 35.5)}{1} = 1{,}490 \text{ mg}$$

5. RW is a 70-year-old female with hypokalemia. Her physician orders a 40-milliequivalent infusion of potassium acetate. How many milligrams of potassium acetate will RW receive? Note: Potassium has an atomic weight of 39 grams/mole and a +1 ionic charge; acetate has a molecular weight of 59 grams/mole and a -1 ionic charge.

    SOLUTION: Rearrange the equation to convert milliequivalents to milligrams.

    $$\# \text{ of milliequivalents} = \frac{\# \text{ of milligrams} \times \text{valence}}{\text{molecular weight}}$$

    $$\therefore \# \text{ of milligrams} = \frac{\# \text{ of milliequivalents} \times \text{molecular weight}}{\text{valence}} = \frac{40 \times (39 + 59)}{1} = 3{,}920 \text{ mg}$$

6. How many milliequivalents of sodium chloride are contained in a one-liter infusion of normal saline? Note: Sodium has an atomic weight of 23 grams/mole and a +1 ionic charge; chlorine has an atomic weight of 35.5 grams/mole and a -1 ionic charge.

    STEP 1: Multiply the concentration by the volume to determine the mass.

    $$\frac{0.9 \text{ g of sodium chloride}}{100 \text{ mL of solution}} \times 1 \text{ L of solution} \times \frac{1{,}000 \text{ mL}}{1 \text{ L}} = 9 \text{ grams of sodium chloride}$$

    STEP 2: Convert the units of mass from grams to milligrams.

    $$9 \text{ g of sodium chloride} \times \frac{1{,}000 \text{ mg}}{\text{g}} = 9{,}000 \text{ mg of sodium chloride}$$

    STEP 3: Enter values into the equation to convert milligrams to milliequivalents.

    $$\# \text{ of milliequivalents} = \frac{\# \text{ of milligrams} \times \text{valence}}{\text{molecular weight}} = \frac{9{,}000 \times 1}{23 + 35.5} = 154 \text{ mEq}$$

7. How many milliequivalents of sodium bicarbonate are in a 50-mL vial of 7.5% sodium bicarbonate? Note: Sodium has an atomic weight of 23 grams/mole and a +1 ionic charge; bicarbonate has a molecular weight of 61 grams/mole and a -1 ionic charge.

    STEP 1: Multiply the concentration by the volume to determine the mass.

    $$\frac{7.5 \text{ g of sodium bicarbonate}}{100 \text{ mL of solution}} \times 50 \text{ mL of solution} = 3.75 \text{ grams of sodium bicarbonate}$$

    STEP 2: Convert mass from grams to milligrams.

    $$3.75 \text{ grams of sodium bicarbonate} \times \frac{1{,}000 \text{ mg}}{\text{g}} = 3{,}750 \text{ mg of sodium bicarbonate}$$

    STEP 3: Enter values into the equation to convert milligrams to milliequivalents.

    $$\# \text{ of milliequivalents} = \frac{\# \text{ of milligrams} \times \text{valence}}{\text{molecular weight}} = \frac{3{,}750 \times 1}{23 + 61} = 44.6 \text{ mEq}$$

8. Each tablet of RenaPlus™, a potassium supplement for cats and dogs, contains 468 milligrams of potassium gluconate ($K(C_6H_{11}O_7)$). How many milliequivalents of potassium gluconate are contained in an entire bottle of 100 tablets? Note: Potassium has an atomic weight of 39 grams/mole and a +1 ionic charge; gluconate has a molecular weight of 195 grams/mole and a -1 ionic charge.

   STEP 1: Multiply the mass of one tablet by 100 to determine the number of milligrams in one 100-count bottle.

   $$\frac{468 \text{ mg of potassium gluconate}}{\text{tablet}} \times \frac{100 \text{ tablets}}{\text{bottle}} = 46{,}800 \text{ mg of potassium gluconate/bottle}$$

   STEP 2: Enter values into the equation to convert milligrams to milliequivalents.

   $$\text{\# of milliequivalents} = \frac{\text{\# of milligrams} \times \text{valence}}{\text{molecular weight}} = \frac{46{,}800 \times 1}{39 + 195} = 200 \text{ mEq}$$

9. How many milliequivalents of ferrous iron are contained in a 5-grain ferrous sulfate tablet? Note: Ferrous iron has an atomic weight of 56 grams/mole and a +2 ionic charge; sulfate has a molecular weight of 96 grams/mole and a -2 ionic charge.

   STEP 1: Determine the mass (in milligrams) of ferrous iron in one tablet.

   $$5 \text{ grains of ferrous sulfate} \times \frac{64.8 \text{ mg}}{\text{grain}} \times \frac{56 \text{ g/mol of ferrous iron}}{152 \text{ g/mol of ferrous sulfate}} = 119.4 \text{ mg of ferrous iron}$$

   STEP 2: Enter values into the equation to convert milligrams to milliequivalents.

   $$\text{\# of milliequivalents} = \frac{\text{\# of milligrams} \times \text{valence}}{\text{molecular weight}} = \frac{119.4 \times 2}{56} = 4.3 \text{ mEq}$$

10. A physician orders a 16.25-milliequivalent magnesium sulfate infusion. Given that the product is supplied as magnesium sulfate heptahydrate ($MgSO_4 \bullet 7H_2O$), how many grams should be dispensed? Note: Magnesium has an atomic weight of 24 grams/mole and a +2 ionic charge; sulfate has a molecular weight of 96 grams/mole and a -2 ionic charge.

    SOLUTION: Rearrange the equation to convert milliequivalents to milligrams.

    $$\text{\# of milliequivalents} = \frac{\text{\# of milligrams} \times \text{valence}}{\text{molecular weight}}$$

    $$\therefore \text{\# of milligrams} = \frac{\text{\# of milliequivalents} \times \text{molecular weight}}{\text{valence}} = \frac{16.25 \times (24 + 96 + (7 \times 18))}{2} = 1{,}999 \text{ mg} \therefore 2 \text{ grams}$$

    NOTE: The molecular weight of the heptahydrate component is equal to seven times the molecular weight of water (7 x 18) and must be included in the molecular weight calculation for magnesium sulfate heptahydrate.

11. How many milligrams of sodium are in a 50-mL vial that contains 100 mEq of sodium acetate? Note: Sodium has an atomic weight of 23 grams/mole and a +1 ionic charge; acetate has a molecular weight of 59 grams/mole and a -1 ionic charge.

    SOLUTION: Rearrange the equation to convert milliequivalents to milligrams.

    $$\text{\# of milliequivalents} = \frac{\text{\# of milligrams} \times \text{valence}}{\text{molecular weight}}$$

    $$\therefore \text{\# of milligrams} = \frac{\text{\# of milliequivalents} \times \text{molecular weight}}{\text{valence}} = \frac{100 \text{ mEq} \times 23}{1} = 2{,}300 \text{ mg}$$

12. Each milliliter of a 10% calcium chloride injection solution contains 100 milligrams of calcium chloride dihydrate ($CaCl_2 \cdot 2H_2O$). How many milliequivalents of calcium are contained in one milliliter of this solution? Note: Calcium has an atomic weight of 40 grams/mole and a +2 ionic charge; chlorine has an atomic weight of 35.5 grams/mole and a -1 ionic charge.

    STEP 1: Determine the total mass (in milligrams) of calcium in one milliliter of solution.

    $$\frac{100 \text{ mg } of \text{ calcium chloride dihydrate}}{\text{milliliter}} \times \frac{40 \text{ g/mol } of \text{ Ca}^{2+}}{147 \text{ g/mol } of \text{ calcium chloride dihydrate}} = \frac{27.2 \text{ mg } of \text{ Ca}^{2+}}{\text{milliliter}}$$

    NOTE: Dihydrate ($2H_2O$) adds weight to the molecule.

    STEP 2: Enter values into the equation to convert milligrams to milliequivalents.

    $$\# \text{ } of \text{ milliequivalents} = \frac{\# \text{ } of \text{ milligrams} \times \text{valence}}{\text{molecular weight}} = \frac{27.2 \times 2}{40} = 1.36 \text{ mEq } of \text{ Ca}^{2+}$$

13. Potassium chloride (KCl) is available commercially as a 20 mEq/15mL oral solution. To prevent gastrointestinal irritation, each dose must be diluted prior to administration. What is the concentration in terms of percent weight/volume before dilution? Note: Potassium has a molecular weight of 39.1 grams/mole and a +1 ionic charge; chlorine has an atomic weight of 35.5 grams/mole and a -1 ionic charge.

    STEP 1: Rearrange the equation to convert milliequivalents to milligrams.

    $$\# \text{ } of \text{ milliequivalents} = \frac{\# \text{ } of \text{ milligrams} \times \text{valence}}{\text{molecular weight}}$$

    $$\therefore \# \text{ } of \text{ milligrams} = \frac{\# \text{ } of \text{ milliequivalents} \times \text{molecular weight}}{\text{valence}} = \frac{20 \text{ mEq} \times (39.1 + 35.5)}{1} = 1{,}492 \text{ mg}$$

    NOTE: This is the mass of KCl in 15 milliliters of solution before dilution.

    STEP 2: Express concentration in terms of grams per milliliter.

    $$\frac{1{,}492 \text{ mg } of \text{ KCl}}{15 \text{ mL } of \text{ solution}} \times \frac{\text{g}}{1{,}000 \text{ mg}} = \frac{1.492 \text{ g } of \text{ KCl}}{15 \text{ mL } of \text{ solution}}$$

    STEP 3: Set up a proportion and solve for the unknown.

    $$\frac{1.492 \text{ g } of \text{ KCl}}{15 \text{ mL } of \text{ solution}} = \frac{\text{UNKNOWN}}{100 \text{ mL } of \text{ solution}} \therefore \text{UNKNOWN} = \frac{1.492 \text{ g } of \text{ KCl}}{15 \text{ mL } of \text{ solution}} \times 100 \text{ mL } of \text{ solution} = 9.95 \text{ grams } of \text{ KCl}$$

    STEP 4: Express the strength in terms of mass and volume based on the definition of percent concentration (w/v).

    $$\frac{9.95 \text{ grams } of \text{ KCl}}{100 \text{ mL } of \text{ solution}} = \text{KCl 9.95\% (w/v) solution}$$

POTASSIUM DOSES *for* HYPOKALEMIA
Dose for prevention of hypokalemia: 20 mEq/day
Dose for treatment of hypokalemia: 40 – 100 mEq/day

REFERENCE: Potassium chloride oral solution [package insert]. Greenville, SC: Pharmaceutical Associates Inc; 2014.

---

14. Magnesium citrate (Mg$_3$(C$_6$H$_5$O$_7$)$_2$)–an osmotic laxative–is available commercially as a 1.745-gram per fluid ounce solution. How many milliequivalents of magnesium are present in a 10-fluid ounce bottle? Note: Magnesium has an atomic weight of 24 grams/mole and a +2 ionic charge; citrate has a molecular weight of 189 grams/mole and a -3 ionic charge.

    STEP 1: Determine the total mass (in milligrams) of magnesium present in one 10-fluid ounce bottle of magnesium citrate solution.

    $$\frac{1.745 \text{ g of Mg}_3(C_6H_5O_7)_2}{\text{fluid ounce}} \times \frac{10 \text{ fluid ounces}}{\text{bottle}} \times \frac{1{,}000 \text{ mg}}{\text{g}} \times \frac{72 \text{ g/mol of Mg}}{450 \text{ g/mol of Mg}_3(C_6H_5O_7)_2} = \frac{2{,}792 \text{ mg of Mg}}{\text{bottle}}$$

    STEP 2: Enter values into the equation to convert milligrams to milliequivalents.

    $$\# \text{ of milliequivalents} = \frac{\# \text{ of milligrams} \times \text{valence}}{\text{molecular weight}} = \frac{2{,}792 \times 2}{24} = 233 \text{ mEq}$$

15. If one 315-milligram tablet of calcium citrate tetrahydrate (Ca$_3$(C$_6$H$_5$O$_7$)$_2$ • 4H$_2$O) contains 66 milligrams of elemental calcium and 250 international units of cholecalciferol, how many milliequivalents of calcium are present in each tablet? Note: Calcium has an atomic weight of 40 grams/mole and a +2 ionic charge. Citrate 189 g/mole -3.

    SOLUTION: Enter values into the equation to convert milligrams to milliequivalents.

    $$\# \text{ of milliequivalents} = \frac{\# \text{ of milligrams} \times \text{valence}}{\text{molecular weight}} = \frac{66 \times 2}{40 \text{ g/mole}} = 3.3 \text{ mEq}$$

MILLIMOLARITY

CONVERT MILLIGRAMS TO MILLIMOLES

$$\text{\# of millimoles} = \frac{\text{\# of milligrams}}{\text{molecular weight (grams/mole)}}$$

CONVERT MILLIEQUIVALENTS TO MILLIMOLES

$$\text{\# of millimoles} = \frac{\text{\# of milliequivalents}}{\text{valence}}$$

MILLIMOLAR CONCENTRATION (MILLIMOLARITY (mM))

$$\text{millimolarity (mM)} = \frac{\text{millimoles of solute}}{\text{liter of solution}}$$

NOTE: Medications are typically measured in small quantities, such as millimoles (one millimole is 1/1,000th of a mole).

---

1. How many millimoles of sodium chloride are in a 500-mL infusion of one-half normal saline (½NS)? Note: Sodium has an atomic weight of 23 grams/mole and a +1 ionic charge; chlorine has an atomic weight of 35.5 grams/mole and a -1 ionic charge.

2. How many millimoles of calcium are in one 200-milligram dose of calcium chloride dihydrate (CaCl$_2$ • 2H$_2$O)? Note: Calcium has an atomic weight of 40 grams/mole and a +2 ionic charge; chlorine has an atomic weight of 35.5 grams/mole and a -1 ionic charge.

3. How many millimoles of chlorine are contained in a 200-milligram dose of calcium chloride dihydrate?

4. Each milliliter of solution in a 10-milliliter vial of calcium gluconate contains 100 milligrams of calcium gluconate. What is the millimolar concentration of calcium gluconate? Note: Calcium has an atomic weight of 40 grams/mole and a +2 ionic charge; gluconate has a molecular weight of 195 grams/mole and a -1 ionic charge.

5. How many millimoles of calcium are present in a 1,000-milligram/10-milliliter vial of calcium gluconate (Ca(C$_6$H$_{11}$O$_7$)$_2$) solution? Note: Calcium has an atomic weight of 40 grams/mole and a +2 ionic charge; gluconate has a molecular weight of 195 grams/mole and a -1 ionic charge.

6. How many millimoles of gluconate are present in a 1,000-milligram/10-milliliter vial of calcium gluconate (Ca(C$_6$H$_{11}$O$_7$)$_2$) solution? Note: Calcium has an atomic weight of 40 grams/mole and a +2 ionic charge; gluconate has a molecular weight of 195 grams/mole and a -1 ionic charge.

7. What is the millimolar concentration of a 50-milliliter solution that contains 50 milliequivalents of sodium bicarbonate (NaHCO$_3$)?

8. How many millimoles of magnesium sulfate are in a 16.25-milliequivalent infusion? Note: Magnesium has an atomic weight of 24 grams/mole and a +2 ionic charge; sulfate has a molecular weight of 96 grams/mole and a -2 ionic charge.

9. How may millimoles of magnesium citrate (Mg$_3$(C$_6$H$_5$O$_7$)$_2$) are in a bottle that contains 233 milliequivalents of magnesium citrate? Note: Magnesium has an atomic weight of 24 grams/mole and a +2 ionic charge; citrate has a molecular weight of 189 grams/mole and a -3 ionic charge.

10. How may millimoles of calcium are in a tablet of calcium citrate (Ca$_3$(C$_6$H$_5$O$_7$)$_2$) containing 3.3 mEq of elemental calcium and 250 international units of cholecalciferol? Note: Calcium has an atomic weight of 40 grams/mole and a +2 ionic charge.

SOLUTIONS *for* MILLIMOLARITY PROBLEMS

1. How many millimoles of sodium chloride are in a 500-mL infusion of one-half normal saline (½NS)? Note: Sodium has an atomic weight of 23 grams/mole and a +1 ionic charge; chlorine has an atomic weight of 35.5 grams/mole and a -1 ionic charge.

    STEP 1: Determine the number of milligrams of sodium chloride in a 500-mL infusion of ½NS.

    $$\frac{0.45 \text{ g of sodium chloride}}{100 \text{ mL of solution}} \times \frac{1{,}000 \text{ mg}}{\text{g}} \times 500 \text{ mL of solution} = 2{,}250 \text{ mg } of \text{ sodium chloride}$$

    NOTE: ½NS = 0.45% (w/v/) sodium chloride solution.

    STEP 2: Enter the values into the equation to convert milligrams to millimoles.

    $$\text{\# }of\text{ millimoles} = \frac{\text{\# }of\text{ milligrams}}{\text{molecular weight (grams/mole)}} = \frac{2{,}250 \text{ mg}}{(23 + 35.5) \text{ g/mole}} = 38.5 \text{ millimoles}$$

2. How many millimoles of calcium are in one 200-milligram dose of calcium chloride dihydrate ($CaCl_2 \bullet 2H_2O$)? Note: Calcium has an atomic weight of 40 grams/mole and a +2 ionic charge; chlorine has an atomic weight of 35.5 grams/mole and a -1 ionic charge.

    SOLUTION: Enter the values into the equation to convert milligrams to millimoles.

    $$\text{\# }of\text{ millimoles} = \frac{\text{\# }of\text{ milligrams}}{\text{molecular weight (grams/mole)}} = \frac{200 \text{ mg}}{(40 + (35.5 \times 2) + (18 \times 2)) \text{ g/mole}} = 1.36 \text{ millimoles}$$

    NOTE: Valence is irrelevant in this calculation.

3. How many millimoles of chlorine are contained in a 200-milligram dose of calcium chloride dihydrate?

    STEP 1: Enter the values into the equation to convert milligrams to millimoles.

    $$\text{\# }of\text{ millimoles} = \frac{\text{\# }of\text{ milligrams}}{\text{molecular weight (grams/mole)}} = \frac{200 \text{ mg}}{(40 + (35.5 \times 2) + (18 \times 2)) \text{ g/mole}} = 1.36 \text{ millimoles}$$

    NOTE: This is the number of millimoles of calcium chloride dihydrate in a 200-mg dose.

    STEP 2: Multiply by two for the number of millimoles of chlorine in a 200-mg dose.

    $$1.36 \text{ millimoles } of \text{ calcium chloride dihydrate} \times \frac{2 \text{ atoms } of \text{ chlorine}}{1 \text{ molecule } of \text{ calcium chloride dihydrate}} = 2.72 \text{ millimoles } of \text{ chlorine}$$

    NOTE: This step is necessary because each molecule of calcium chloride dihydrate ($CaCl_2 \bullet 2H_2O$) contains two atoms of chlorine.

4. Each milliliter of solution in a 10-milliliter vial of calcium gluconate contains 100 milligrams of calcium gluconate. What is the millimolar concentration of calcium gluconate? Note: Calcium has an atomic weight of 40 grams/mole and a +2 ionic charge; gluconate has a molecular weight of 195 grams/mole and a -1 ionic charge.

   STEP 1: Determine the number of millimoles of calcium gluconate in one milliliter of solution.

   $$\text{\# of millimoles} = \frac{\text{\# of milligrams}}{\text{molecular weight (grams/mole)}} = \frac{100 \text{ mg}}{(40 + (195 \times 2)) \text{ g/mole}} = 0.233 \text{ millimoles}$$

   NOTE: The concentration of the solution is 100 mg of calcium gluconate per milliliter.

   STEP 2: Convert concentration from mmol/mL to mmol/L.

   $$\frac{0.233 \text{ mmol of calcium gluconate}}{\text{mL of solution}} \times \frac{1{,}000 \text{ mL}}{\text{L}} = 233 \text{ mmol of calcium gluconate/L} = 233 \text{ mM calcium gluconate}$$

5. How many millimoles of calcium are present in a 1,000-milligram/10-milliliter vial of calcium gluconate ($Ca(C_6H_{11}O_7)_2$) solution? Note: Calcium has an atomic weight of 40 grams/mole and a +2 ionic charge; gluconate has a molecular weight of 195 grams/mole and a -1 ionic charge.

   STEP 1: Enter the values into the equation to convert milligrams to millimoles.

   $$\text{\# of millimoles} = \frac{\text{\# of milligrams}}{\text{molecular weight (grams/mole)}} = \frac{1{,}000 \text{ mg}}{((40 + (195 \times 2) \text{ g/mole})} = 2.33 \text{ mmol}$$

   NOTE: The number of millimoles of calcium is equivalent to the number of millimoles of calcium gluconate since each molecule of calcium gluconate contains only one atom of calcium.

6. How many millimoles of gluconate are present in a 1,000-milligram/10-milliliter vial of calcium gluconate ($Ca(C_6H_{11}O_7)_2$) solution? Note: Calcium has an atomic weight of 40 grams/mole and a +2 ionic charge; gluconate has a molecular weight of 195 grams/mole and a -1 ionic charge.

   STEP 1: Enter the values into the equation to convert milligrams to millimoles.

   $$\text{\# of millimoles} = \frac{\text{\# of milligrams}}{\text{molecular weight (grams/mole)}} = \frac{1{,}000 \text{ mg}}{((40 + (195 \times 2) \text{ g/mole})} \times \frac{2 \text{ molecules of gluconate}}{1 \text{ molecule of calcium gluconate}} = 4.65 \text{ mmol of gluconate}$$

   NOTE: Don't miss that there are two gluconate ions in each molecule of calcium gluconate.

7. What is the millimolar concentration of a 50-milliliter solution that contains 50 milliequivalents of sodium bicarbonate ($NaHCO_3$)?

   STEP 1: Enter the values into the equation to convert milliequivalents to millimoles.

   $$\text{\# of millimoles} = \frac{\text{\# of milliequivalents}}{\text{valence}} = \frac{50 \text{ mEq}}{1} = 50 \text{ mmol}$$

   NOTE: This is the amount present in 50 milliliters.

   STEP 2: Set up a proportion and solve for the unknown to determine the concentration in terms of millimoles per liter.

   $$\frac{50 \text{ mmol}}{50 \text{ mL}} = \frac{\text{UNKNOWN}}{1{,}000 \text{ mL}} \therefore \text{UNKNOWN} = \frac{50 \text{ mmol}}{50 \text{ mL}} \times 1{,}000 \text{ mL} = 1{,}000 \text{ mmol} \therefore 1{,}000 \text{ mM sodium bicarbonate}$$

   NOTE: 1,000 milliliters is equivalent to one liter.

8. How many millimoles of magnesium sulfate are in a 16.25-milliequivalent infusion? Note: Magnesium has an atomic weight of 24 grams/mole and a +2 ionic charge; sulfate has a molecular weight of 96 grams/mole and a -2 ionic charge.

   SOLUTION: Enter the values into the equation to convert milliequivalents to millimoles.

   $$\text{\# of millimoles} = \frac{\text{\# of milliequivalents}}{\text{valence}} = \frac{16.25 \text{ mEq}}{2} = 8.125 \text{ millimoles}$$

   NOTE: The valence is equal to the total charge of cations or anions in the compound. In this case, the valence is two.

9. How may millimoles of magnesium citrate ($Mg_3(C_6H_5O_7)_2$) are in a bottle that contains 233 milliequivalents of magnesium citrate? Note: Magnesium has an atomic weight of 24 grams/mole and a +2 ionic charge; citrate has a molecular weight of 189 grams/mole and a -3 ionic charge.

   SOLUTION: Enter the values into the equation to convert milliequivalents to millimoles.

   $$\text{\# of millimoles} = \frac{\text{\# of milliequivalents}}{\text{valence}} = \frac{233 \text{ mEq}}{6} = 38.8 \text{ millimoles}$$

   NOTE: The valence is equal to the total charge of cations or anions in the compound. In this case, the valence is six.

10. How may millimoles of calcium are in a tablet of calcium citrate ($Ca_3(C_6H_5O_7)_2$) containing 3.3 mEq of elemental calcium and 250 international units of cholecalciferol? Note: Calcium has an atomic weight of 40 grams/mole and a +2 ionic charge.

    SOLUTION: Enter the values into the equation to convert milliequivalents to millimoles.

    $$\text{\# of millimoles} = \frac{\text{\# of milliequivalents}}{\text{valence}} = \frac{3.3 \text{ mEq}}{2} = 1.65 \text{ millimoles}$$

    NOTE: The milliequivalent quantity of elemental calcium was given, and elemental calcium has a valence of two.

MILLIOSMOLARITY

CONVERT *from* MILLIGRAMS TO MILLIOSMOLES

$$\text{\# of milliosmoles (mOsmol)} = \frac{\text{\# of milligrams} \times n}{\text{molecular weight}}$$

CONVERT *from* MILLIEQUIVALENTS TO MILLIOSMOLES

$$\text{\# of milliosmoles (mOsmol)} = \frac{\text{\# of milliequivalents} \times n}{\text{valence}}$$

MILLIOSMOLAR CONCENTRATION*

$$\text{milliosmolarity (mOsmol/L)} = \frac{\text{\# of milligrams/liter} \times n}{\text{molecular weight}}$$

The variable "n" equals the number of particles (i.e., ions and/or molecules) in solution after the solute dissociates.

NOTE: Medication concentrations are typically small and measured in terms of milliosmoles (one milliosmole is 1/1,000th of an osmole).

> 600 mOsmol/L
central line required for intravenous infusions

> 900 mOsmol/L
central line required for total nutrient admixtures

NOTE: Administration via a peripheral line is generally acceptable at concentrations below these thresholds.

1. The solute in 10% (w/v) dextrose in water (D10W) is hydrous dextrose ($C_6H_{12}O_6 \cdot H_2O$), which has a molecular weight of 198.17 grams/mole. What is the milliosmolarity of D10W?

2. What is the concentration of mannitol 25% (w/v) injection solution in terms of mOsmol/mL? Note: Mannitol ($C_6H_{14}O_6$) has a molecular weight of 182 grams/mole.

3. How many milliosmoles of sodium bicarbonate are in a 50-mL syringe of 8.4% (w/v) sodium bicarbonate ($NaHCO_3$)? Note: Sodium has an atomic weight of 23 grams/mole and a +1 ionic charge; bicarbonate has a molecular weight of 61 grams/mole and a -1 ionic charge.

4. What is the milliosmolarity of normal saline solution? Note: Sodium has an atomic weight of 23 grams/mole and a +1 ionic charge; chlorine has an atomic weight of 35.5 grams/mole and a -1 ionic charge.

5. The solute in D5W (dextrose 5% (w/v) in water) is dextrose monohydrate ($C_6H_{12}O_6 \cdot H_2O$), which has a molecular weight of 198.17 grams/mole. What is the milliosmolarity of D5W?

6. Calcium chloride injection is commercially available in 10-milliliter vials as a 10% (w/v) solution. The solute is calcium chloride dihydrate ($CaCl_2 \cdot 2H_2O$). What is the milliosmolar concentration of this solution? Note: Calcium has an atomic weight of 40 grams/mole and a +2 ionic charge; chlorine has an atomic weight of 35.5 grams/mole and a -1 ionic charge; H_2O has a molecular weight of 18 grams/mole and is a nonelectrolyte.

7. What is the osmolarity of sodium chloride 3% infusion solution? Note: Sodium has an atomic weight of 23 grams/mole and a +1 ionic charge; chlorine has an atomic weight of 35.5 grams/mole and a -1 ionic charge.

8. One hundred milliliters of Lactated Ringer's solution contains 600 mg of sodium chloride, 310 mg of sodium lactate, 30 mg of potassium chloride, and 20 mg of calcium chloride dihydrate. What is the milliosmolarity of lactated Ringer's? Note: Sodium has an atomic weight of 23 grams/mole and a +1 ionic charge; chlorine has an atomic weight of 35.5 grams/mole and a -1 ionic charge; calcium has an atomic weight of 40 grams/mole and a +2 ionic charge; H_2O has a molecular weight of 18 grams/mole and is a nonelectrolyte; potassium has an atomic weight of 39 grams/mole and a +1 ionic charge; lactate has a molecular weight of 89 grams/mole and a -1 ionic charge.

9. The pharmacy stocks an infusion of sodium chloride 450 milligrams in 100 milliliters of water. What is the osmolarity of this solution? Note: Sodium has an atomic weight of 23 grams/mole; chlorine has an atomic weight of 35.5 grams/mole.

10. Sodium acetate has a molecular weight of 82 grams/mole. What is the osmolar concentration (mOsmol/mL) of a 2 mEq/mL solution of sodium acetate ($NaC_2H_3O_2$)?

11. What is the milliosmolarity of a one-liter solution that contains 300 milligrams of calcium ions as the solute? Note: Calcium has an atomic weight of 40 grams/mole and a +2 ionic charge.

12. How many milliosmoles are in 250 milliliters of a 10 mEq/mL solution of Mg^{2+} ions?

13. A 2,000-milliliter total parenteral nutrition infusion contains several ingredients, including 420 grams of hydrous dextrose. What is the milliosmolarity of the dextrose component? The molecular weight of hydrous dextrose is 198.17 grams/mole.

14. A total parenteral nutrition (TPN) formulation should be administered through a central line if the osmolarity exceeds 900 mOsmol/L; otherwise, it can be administered through a peripheral line. What is the osmolarity of the following TPN? Can it be administered through a peripheral line? Note: Hydrous dextrose has a molecular weight of 198.17 grams/mole and is a nonelectrolyte; sodium has an atomic weight of 23 grams/mole and a +1 ionic charge; chlorine has an atomic weight of 35.5 grams/mole and a -1 ionic charge; magnesium has an atomic weight of 24 grams/mole and a +2 ionic charge; sulfate has a molecular weight of 96 grams/mole and a -2 ionic charge; potassium has an atomic weight of 39 grams/mole and a +1 ionic charge; acetate has a molecular weight of 59 grams/mole and a -1 ionic charge; calcium has an atomic weight of 40 grams/mole and a +2 ionic charge; gluconate has a molecular weight of 195 grams/mole and a -1 ionic charge.

Hydrous dextrose	310 grams
Amino acids	105 grams
Multivitamin for infusion	10 milliliters
Sodium chloride	90 mEq
Magnesium sulfate	30 mEq
Potassium acetate	60 mEq
Calcium gluconate	12 mEq
SWFI qs	2,680 mL

NOTE: Assume the 10-milliliter multivitamin for infusion has an osmolar concentration of 40 mOsmol/10 mL. Also, assume 10 milliosmoles per gram of amino acids.

REFERENCES

1. Mannitol injection USP 25% [package insert]. Shirley, NY: American Regent, Inc; 2011.
2. Sodium bicarbonate injection solution [package insert]. Lake Forest, IL: Hospira, Inc; 2005.
3. Calcium chloride injection solution [package insert]. Lake Forest, IL: Hospira, Inc; 2018.
4. Alexander M, Corrigan A, Gorski L, Phillips L, eds. *Core Curriculum for Infusion Nursing*. 4th edition. Philadelphia, PA: Wolters Kluwer Health/Lippincott Williams & Wilkins; 2014:36-42.
5. Isaacs JW, Millikan WJ, Stackhouse J, Hersh T, Rudman D. Parenteral nutrition of adults with 900-milliosmolar solution via peripheral vein. *American Journal of Clinical Nutrition* 1977; 30:552–9.
6. Metheny N. *Fluid & Electrolyte Balance: Nursing Considerations*. 4th edition. Philadelphia, PA: Lippincott; 2000.

SOLUTIONS for MILLIOSMOLARITY PROBLEMS

1. The solute in 10% (w/v) dextrose in water (D10W) is hydrous dextrose ($C_6H_{12}O_6 \bullet H_2O$), which has a molecular weight of 198.17 grams/mole. What is the milliosmolarity of D10W?

   STEP 1: Convert units of concentration from percent (w/v) to milligrams per liter.

   $$\text{dextrose 10\% (w/v) solution} = \frac{10 \text{ g } of \text{ dextrose}}{100 \text{ mL } of \text{ solution}} \times \frac{1{,}000 \text{ mL}}{L} \times \frac{1{,}000 \text{ mg}}{g} = \frac{100{,}000 \text{ mg } of \text{ dextrose}}{L \: of \text{ solution}}$$

   STEP 2: Enter values into the equation to determine the milliosmolar concentration of the solution.

   $$\text{milliosmolarity (mOsmol/L)} = \frac{\# \: of \text{ milligrams/liter} \times n}{\text{molecular weight}} = \frac{100{,}000 \text{ mg/liter} \times 1}{198.17 \text{ g/mole}} = 505 \text{ mOsmol/L}$$

   NOTE: Dextrose monohydrate is a nonelectrolyte and, consequently, does not dissociate into multiple particles in solution ($\therefore n = 1$).

2. What is the concentration of mannitol 25% (w/v) injection solution in terms of mOsmol/mL? Note: Mannitol ($C_6H_{14}O_6$) has a molecular weight of 182 grams/mole.

   STEP 1: Convert units of concentration from percent (w/v) to milligrams per milliliter.

   $$\text{mannitol 25\% (w/v) solution} = \frac{25 \text{ g } of \text{ mannitol}}{100 \text{ mL } of \text{ solution}} \times \frac{1{,}000 \text{ mg}}{g} = \frac{250 \text{ mg } of \text{ mannitol}}{\text{mL } of \text{ solution}}$$

   NOTE: The question asks explicitly for milliosmoles per milliliter, so do **not** convert the volume from milliliters to liters for this one.

   STEP 2: Enter values into the equation to convert milligrams to milliosmoles.

   $$\# \: of \text{ milliosmoles (mOsmol)} = \frac{\# \: of \text{ milligrams} \times n}{\text{molecular weight}} = \frac{250 \text{ mg} \times 1}{182 \text{ g/mole}} = 1.37 \text{ mOsmol} \therefore 1.37 \text{ mOsmol/mL}$$

   NOTE: Each milliliter of solution contains 250 mg of mannitol, which is equivalent to 1.37 mOsmol. Mannitol is a nonelectrolyte and, consequently, does not dissociate into multiple particles in solution ($\therefore n = 1$).

3. How many milliosmoles of sodium bicarbonate are in a 50-mL syringe of 8.4% (w/v) sodium bicarbonate ($NaHCO_3$)? Note: Sodium has an atomic weight of 23 grams/mole and a +1 ionic charge; bicarbonate has a molecular weight of 61 grams/mole and a -1 ionic charge.

   STEP 1: Determine the mass of sodium bicarbonate in terms of milligrams in one syringe.

   $$\frac{8.4 \text{ g } of \text{ sodium bicarbonate}}{100 \text{ mL } of \text{ solution}} \times \frac{50 \text{ mL } of \text{ solution}}{\text{syringe}} \times \frac{1{,}000 \text{ mg}}{g} = \frac{4{,}200 \text{ mg } of \text{ sodium bicarbonate}}{\text{syringe}}$$

   STEP 2: Enter values into the equation to convert milligrams to milliosmoles.

   $$\# \: of \text{ milliosmoles (mOsmol)} = \frac{\# \: of \text{ milligrams} \times n}{\text{molecular weight}} = \frac{4{,}200 \text{ mg} \times 2}{(23 + 61) \text{ g/mole}} = 100 \text{ mOsmol}$$

   NOTE: $NaHCO_3$ is an electrolyte that dissociates into Na^+ and $HCO3^-$ in solution ($\therefore n = 2$).

4. What is the milliosmolarity of normal saline solution? Note: Sodium has an atomic weight of 23 grams/mole and a +1 ionic charge; chlorine has an atomic weight of 35.5 grams/mole and a -1 ionic charge.

   STEP 1: Express concentration in terms of milligrams per liter.

   $$\text{sodium chloride 0.9\% (w/v) solution} = \frac{0.9 \text{ g of NaCl}}{100 \text{ mL of solution}} \times \frac{1{,}000 \text{ mL}}{\text{L}} \times \frac{1{,}000 \text{ mg}}{\text{g}} = \frac{9{,}000 \text{ mg of NaCl}}{\text{L of solution}}$$

   STEP 2: Enter values into the equation to determine the milliosmolar concentration of the solution.

   $$\text{milliosmolarity (mOsmol/L)} = \frac{\text{\# of milligrams/liter} \times n}{\text{molecular weight}} = \frac{9{,}000 \text{ mg/L} \times 2}{(23 + 35.5) \text{ g/mole}} = 308 \text{ mOsmol/L}$$

   NOTE: NaCl is an electrolyte that dissociates into Na$^+$ and Cl$^-$ in solution ($\therefore$ n = 2).

5. The solute in D5W (dextrose 5% (w/v) in water) is dextrose monohydrate ($C_6H_{12}O_6 \bullet H_2O$), which has a molecular weight of 198.17 grams/mole. What is the milliosmolarity of D5W?

   STEP 1: Express concentration in terms of milligrams per liter.

   $$\text{dextrose 5\% (w/v) solution} = \frac{5 \text{ g of dextrose}}{100 \text{ mL of solution}} \times \frac{1{,}000 \text{ mL}}{\text{L}} \times \frac{1{,}000 \text{ mg}}{\text{g}} = \frac{50{,}000 \text{ mg of dextrose}}{\text{L of solution}}$$

   STEP 2: Enter values into the equation to determine the milliosmolar concentration of the solution.

   $$\text{milliosmolarity (mOsmol/L)} = \frac{\text{\# of milligrams/liter} \times n}{\text{molecular weight}} = \frac{50{,}000 \text{ mg/L} \times 1}{198.17 \text{ g/mole}} = 252 \text{ mOsmol/L}$$

   NOTE: Dextrose monohydrate is a nonelectrolyte and does not dissociate into multiple particles in solution ($\therefore$ n = 1).

6. Calcium chloride injection is commercially available in 10-milliliter vials as a 10% (w/v) solution. The solute is calcium chloride dihydrate ($CaCl_2 \bullet 2H_2O$). What is the milliosmolar concentration of this solution? Note: Calcium has an atomic weight of 40 grams/mole and a +2 ionic charge; chlorine has an atomic weight of 35.5 grams/mole and a -1 ionic charge; H_2O has a molecular weight of 18 grams/mole and is a nonelectrolyte.

   STEP 1: Express concentration in terms of milligrams per liter.

   $$\text{calcium chloride 10\% (w/v) solution} = \frac{10 \text{ g of calcium chloride}}{100 \text{ mL of solution}} \times \frac{1{,}000 \text{ mL}}{\text{L}} \times \frac{1{,}000 \text{ mg}}{\text{g}} = \frac{100{,}000 \text{ mg of calcium chloride}}{\text{L of solution}}$$

   STEP 2: Enter values into the equation to determine the milliosmolar concentration of the solution.

   $$\text{milliosmolarity (mOsmol/L)} = \frac{\text{\# of milligrams/liter} \times n}{\text{molecular weight}} = \frac{100{,}000 \text{ mg/L} \times 3}{(40 + (35.5 \times 2) + (18 \times 2)) \text{ g/mole}} = 2{,}041 \text{ mOsmol/L}$$

   NOTE: Calcium chloride is an electrolyte that dissociates into three particles in solution (Ca^{2+}, Cl^-, and Cl^- $\therefore$ n = 3). With a concentration of 2,041 mOsmol/L, this solution is very hypertonic. Unsurprisingly, the packaging displays a warning to "administer only by slow injection" (maximum administration rate: 1 mL/minute).

7. What is the osmolarity of sodium chloride 3% infusion solution? Note: Sodium has an atomic weight of 23 grams/mole and a +1 ionic charge; chlorine has an atomic weight of 35.5 grams/mole and a -1 ionic charge.

   STEP 1: Express concentration in terms of milligrams per liter.

   $$\text{sodium chloride 3\% (w/v) solution} = \frac{3 \text{ g of sodium chloride}}{100 \text{ mL of solution}} \times \frac{1{,}000 \text{ mL}}{\text{L}} \times \frac{1{,}000 \text{ mg}}{\text{g}} = \frac{30{,}000 \text{ mg of sodium chloride}}{\text{L of solution}}$$

   STEP 2: Enter values into the equation to determine the milliosmolar concentration of the solution.

   $$\text{milliosmolarity (mOsmol/L)} = \frac{\text{\# of milligrams/liter} \times n}{\text{molecular weight}} = \frac{30{,}000 \text{ mg/L} \times 2}{(23 + 35.5) \text{ g/mole}} = 1{,}026 \text{ mOsmol/L}$$

   NOTE: Sodium chloride is an electrolyte that dissociates into two particles in solution (Na^+ and Cl^- $\therefore$ n = 2). A central line is typically recommended for infusions with an osmolarity ≥ 600 mOsmol/L (or >900 mOsmol/L for parenteral nutrition).

8. One hundred milliliters of Lactated Ringer's solution contains 600 mg of sodium chloride, 310 mg of sodium lactate, 30 mg of potassium chloride, and 20 mg of calcium chloride dihydrate. What is the milliosmolarity of lactated Ringer's? Note: Sodium has an atomic weight of 23 grams/mole and a +1 ionic charge; chlorine has an atomic weight of 35.5 grams/mole and a -1 ionic charge; calcium has an atomic weight of 40 grams/mole and a +2 ionic charge; H_2O has a molecular weight of 18 grams/mole and is a nonelectrolyte; potassium has an atomic weight of 39 grams/mole and a +1 ionic charge; lactate has a molecular weight of 89 grams/mole and a -1 ionic charge.

   STEP 1: Determine the number of milliosmoles of each ingredient using the equation to convert milligrams to milliosmoles.

   SODIUM CHLORIDE:

   $$\text{\# of milliosmoles (mOsmol)} = \frac{\text{\# of milligrams} \times n}{\text{molecular weight}} = \frac{600 \text{ mg} \times 2}{(23 + 35.5) \text{ g/mole}} = 20.5 \text{ mOsmol}$$

   SODIUM LACTATE:

   $$\text{\# of milliosmoles (mOsmol)} = \frac{\text{\# of milligrams} \times n}{\text{molecular weight}} = \frac{310 \text{ mg} \times 2}{(23 + 89) \text{ g/mole}} = 5.5 \text{ mOsmol}$$

   POTASSIUM CHLORIDE:

   $$\text{\# of milliosmoles (mOsmol)} = \frac{\text{\# of milligrams} \times n}{\text{molecular weight}} = \frac{30 \text{ mg} \times 2}{(39 + 35.5) \text{ g/mole}} = 0.8 \text{ mOsmol}$$

   CALCIUM CHLORIDE DIHYDRATE:

   $$\text{\# of milliosmoles (mOsmol)} = \frac{\text{\# of milligrams} \times n}{\text{molecular weight}} = \frac{20 \text{ mg} \times 3}{(40 + (35.5 \times 2) + (18 \times 2)) \text{ g/mole}} = 0.4 \text{ mOsmol}$$

   STEP 2: Add the milliosmoles of each component to determine the total milliosmoles.

   $$20.5 \text{ mOsmol} + 5.5 \text{ mOsmol} + 0.8 \text{ mOsmol} + 0.4 \text{ mOsmol} = 27.2 \text{ mOsmol}$$

   NOTE: This is the amounts present in 100 mL; however, the units of milliosmolarity are mOsmol/L.

   STEP 3: Convert concentration from milliosmoles per 100 mL to milliosmoles per liter to determine the milliosmolarity.

   $$\frac{27.2 \text{ mOsmol}}{100 \text{ mL}} \times \frac{1{,}000 \text{ mL}}{\text{L}} = 272 \text{ mOsmol/L}$$

9. The pharmacy stocks an infusion of sodium chloride 450 milligrams in 100 milliliters of water. What is the osmolarity of this solution? Note: Sodium has an atomic weight of 23 grams/mole; chlorine has an atomic weight of 35.5 grams/mole.

   STEP 1: Express concentration in terms of milligrams per liter.

   $$\frac{450 \text{ mg of sodium chloride}}{100 \text{ mL of solution}} \times \frac{1,000 \text{ mL}}{\text{L}} = \frac{4,500 \text{ mg of sodium chloride}}{\text{L of solution}}$$

   STEP 2: Enter values into the equation to determine the milliosmolar concentration of the solution.

   $$\text{milliosmolarity (mOsmol/L)} = \frac{\text{\# of milligrams/liter} \times n}{\text{molecular weight}} = \frac{4,500 \text{ mg/L} \times 2}{(23 + 35.5) \text{ g/mole}} = 154 \text{ mOsmol/L}$$

10. Sodium acetate ($NaC_2H_3O_2$) has a molecular weight of 82 grams/mole. What is the osmolar concentration (mOsmol/mL) of a 2 mEq/mL solution of sodium acetate?

    SOLUTION: Determine the number of milliosmoles using the equation to convert milliequivalents to milliosmoles.

    $$\text{\# of milliosmoles (mOsmol)} = \frac{\text{\# of milliequivalents} \times n}{\text{valence}} = \frac{2 \times 2}{1} = 4 \text{ mOsmol} \therefore \text{osmolar concentration} = 4 \text{ mOsmol/mL}$$

11. What is the milliosmolarity of a one-liter solution that contains 300 milligrams of calcium ions as the solute? Note: Calcium has an atomic weight of 40 grams/mole and a +2 ionic charge.

    SOLUTION: Enter values into the equation to determine the milliosmolar concentration of the solution.

    $$\text{milliosmolarity (mOsmol/L)} = \frac{\text{\# of milligrams/liter} \times n}{\text{molecular weight}} = \frac{300 \text{ mg/L} \times 1}{40 \text{ g/mole}} = 7.5 \text{ mOsmol/L}$$

    NOTE: Free calcium ions (Ca^{2+}) do not dissociate into multiple particles in solution ($\therefore n = 1$).

12. How many milliosmoles are in 250 milliliters of a 10 mEq/mL solution of Mg^{2+} ions?

    STEP 1: Determine the total mass of magnesium in solution.

    $$\frac{10 \text{ mEq}}{\text{mL}} \times 250 \text{ mL} = 2,500 \text{ mEq}$$

    STEP 2: Enter values into the equation to convert milliequivalents to milliosmoles.

    $$\text{\# of milliosmoles (mOsmol)} = \frac{\text{\# of milliequivalents} \times n}{\text{valence}} = \frac{2,500 \text{ mEq} \times 1}{2} = 1,250 \text{ mOsmol}$$

    NOTE: Free calcium ions (Mg^{2+}) do not dissociate into multiple particles in solution ($\therefore n = 1$).

13. A 2,000-milliliter total parenteral nutrition infusion contains several ingredients, including 420 grams of hydrous dextrose. What is the milliosmolarity of the dextrose component? The molecular weight of hydrous dextrose is 198.17 grams/mole.

    STEP 1: Express the concentration of dextrose in terms of milligrams per liter.

    $$\frac{420 \text{ g}}{2 \text{ L}} \times \frac{1,000 \text{ mg}}{\text{g}} = 210,000 \text{ mg/L}$$

    STEP 2: Enter values into the equation to determine the milliosmolar concentration of the solution.

    $$\text{milliosmolarity (mOsmol/L)} = \frac{\text{\# of milligrams/liter} \times n}{\text{molecular weight}} = \frac{210,000 \text{ mg/L} \times 1}{198.17 \text{ g/mol}} = 1,060 \text{ mOsmol/L}$$

    NOTE: Hydrous dextrose (or "dextrose monohydrate") is a nonelectrolyte and therefore does not dissociate in solution.

15. A total parenteral nutrition (TPN) formulation should be administered through a central line if the osmolarity exceeds 900 mOsmol/L; otherwise, it can be administered through a peripheral line. What is the osmolarity of the following TPN? Can it be administered through a peripheral line? Note: Hydrous dextrose has a molecular weight of 198.17 grams/mole and is a nonelectrolyte; sodium has an atomic weight of 23 grams/mole and a +1 ionic charge; chlorine has an atomic weight of 35.5 grams/mole and a -1 ionic charge; magnesium has an atomic weight of 24 grams/mole and a +2 ionic charge; sulfate has a molecular weight of 96 grams/mole and a -2 ionic charge; potassium has an atomic weight of 39 grams/mole and a +1 ionic charge; acetate has a molecular weight of 59 grams/mole and a -1 ionic charge; calcium has an atomic weight of 40 grams/mole and a +2 ionic charge; gluconate has a molecular weight of 195 grams/mole and a -1 ionic charge.

Hydrous dextrose	310 grams
Amino acids	105 grams
Multivitamin for infusion	10 milliliters
Sodium chloride	90 mEq
Magnesium sulfate	30 mEq
Potassium acetate	60 mEq
Calcium gluconate	12 mEq
SWFI qs	2,680 mL

NOTE: Assume the 10 milliliters of multivitamin for infusion has an osmolar concentration of 40 mOsmol/10 mL. Also, assume 10 milliosmoles per gram of amino acids.

STEP 1: Determine the number of milliosmoles of each ingredient and add them together for a total.

HYDROUS DEXTROSE

$$\text{\# of milliosmoles (mOsmol)} = \frac{\text{\# of milligrams} \times n}{\text{molecular weight}} = \frac{310 \text{ g} \times 1}{198.17 \text{ g/mole}} \times \frac{1{,}000 \text{ mg}}{\text{g}} = 1{,}564 \text{ mOsmol}$$

AMINO ACIDS

$$105 \text{ grams} \times \frac{10 \text{ mOsmol}}{\text{gram}} = 1{,}050 \text{ mOsmol}$$

MULTIVITAMINS

$$10 \text{ mL} \times \frac{40 \text{ mOsmol}}{10 \text{ mL}} = 40 \text{ mOsmol}$$

SODIUM CHLORIDE

$$\text{\# of milliosmoles (mOsmol)} = \frac{\text{\# of milliequivalents} \times n}{\text{valence}} = \frac{90 \text{ mEq} \times 2}{1} = 180 \text{ mOsmol}$$

MAGNESIUM SULFATE

$$\text{\# of milliosmoles (mOsmol)} = \frac{\text{\# of milliequivalents} \times n}{\text{valence}} = \frac{30 \text{ mEq} \times 2}{2} = 30 \text{ mOsmol}$$

POTASSIUM ACETATE

$$\text{\# of milliosmoles (mOsmol)} = \frac{\text{\# of milliequivalents} \times n}{\text{valence}} = \frac{60 \text{ mEq} \times 2}{1} = 120 \text{ mOsmol}$$

CALCIUM GLUCONATE

$$\text{\# of milliosmoles (mOsmol)} = \frac{\text{\# of milliequivalents} \times n}{\text{valence}} = \frac{12 \text{ mEq} \times 3}{2} = 18 \text{ mOsmol}$$

Total # of milliosmoles = (1,564 + 1,050 + 40 + 180 + 30 + 120 + 18) mOsmol = 3,002 mOsmol

NOTE: According to the question, the overall volume of the TPN is 2,680 mL (per instructions to qs with SWFI to 2,680 mL).

STEP 2: Express the concentration in terms of milliosmoles per liter.

$$\frac{3{,}002 \text{ mOsmol}}{2{,}680 \text{ mL}} \times \frac{1{,}000 \text{ mL}}{\text{L}} = 1{,}120 \text{ mOsmol/L}$$

∴ No, do not administer through a peripheral line since the osmolarity exceeds 900 mOsmol/L.

SIMPLE DILUTION

DILUTION EQUATION

$$V_1 \times C_1 = V_2 \times C_2$$

Simple dilution problems can be solved quickly using this old equation from high school chemistry class. The mass of the solute remains constant; therefore, changes in concentration are proportional to changes in volume. V_1 and C_1 represent the volume and concentration of the solution before dilution; meanwhile, V_2 and C_2 represent the volume and concentration of the solution after dilution.

1. If 250 milliliters of water is added to 250 milliliters of ethyl alcohol 4% (v/v) solution, what is the resultant percent concentration (v/v) of ethyl alcohol?

2. How many milliliters of epinephrine 1:10,000 solution can be created by diluting 500 milliliters of epinephrine 1:2,500 solution?

3. If one 10-unit vial of 10-unit/mL Pitocin® (oxytocin) is diluted to a volume of 1,000 mL with Ringer's lactate, then what is the final concentration of oxytocin in terms of units per milliliter?

4. If we dilute 453 grams of zinc oxide 40% (w/w) ointment to a mass of 1,510 grams, what is the resultant percent concentration (w/w) of zinc oxide?

5. What is the percent concentration (w/v) of sodium hypochlorite after adding 1,419 milliliters of sterile water to 473 milliliters of sodium hypochlorite 1:200 (w/v) solution?

6. How many milliliters of sterile water for injection (SWFI) must be added to 1,000 milliliters of sodium chloride 3% (w/v) solution to create normal saline solution (NSS)?

7. How many liters of dextrose 5% (w/v) solution can be created from a 2,000-milliliter bag of dextrose 70% (w/v) solution?

8. How many milliliters of a 1:20,000 solution of a medication can be prepared from 375 milliliters of a 0.025% stock solution?

9. Acyclovir 500 mg lyophilized powder must be reconstituted with 10 milliliters of sterile water for injection (SWFI) to produce a solution of 50 mg/mL acyclovir. According to the package insert, the highest recommended concentration for the infusion of acyclovir is 7 mg/mL. How many milliliters of diluent must be admixed with a reconstituted 500-milligram vial of acyclovir to create a 7 mg/mL solution?

10. Azithromycin 500 mg lyophilized powder must be reconstituted with 4.8 milliliters of SWFI to produce a 100 mg/mL solution. What is the total volume of a 2 mg/mL infusion solution that contains 500 milligrams of azithromycin?

SOLUTIONS for SIMPLE DILUTION PROBLEMS

1. If 250 milliliters of water is added to 250 milliliters of ethyl alcohol 4% (v/v) solution, what is the resultant percent concentration (v/v) of ethyl alcohol?

   STEP 1: Enter the values into the equation $V_1 \times C_1 = V_2 \times C_2$.

   $$250 \text{ mL} \times 4\% = 500 \text{ mL} \times C_2$$

   STEP 2: Solve for the unknown (C_2).

   $$C_2 = \frac{250 \text{ mL} \times 4\%}{500 \text{ mL}} = 2\% \therefore 2\% \text{ ethyl alcohol}$$

2. How many milliliters of epinephrine 1:10,000 solution can be created by diluting 500 milliliters of epinephrine 1:2,500 solution?

   STEP 1: Enter the values into the equation $V_1 \times C_1 = V_2 \times C_2$.

   $$V_1 \times 1/10{,}000 = 500 \text{ mL} \times 1/2{,}500$$

   STEP 2: Solve for the unknown (V_1).

   $$V_1 = \frac{500 \text{ mL} \times 1/2{,}500}{1/10{,}000} = 2{,}000 \text{ mL} \therefore 2{,}000 \text{ mL } of \text{ solution}$$

3. If one 10-unit vial of 10-unit/mL Pitocin® (oxytocin) is diluted to a volume of 1,000 mL with Ringer's lactate, then what is the final concentration of oxytocin in terms of units per milliliter?

   STEP 1: Enter the values into the equation $V_1 \times C_1 = V_2 \times C_2$.

   $$1 \text{ mL} \times 10 \text{ units/mL of oxytocin} = 1{,}000 \text{ mL} \times C_2$$

   STEP 2: Solve for the unknown (C_2).

   $$C_2 = \frac{1 \text{ mL} \times 10 \text{ units/mL}}{1{,}000 \text{ mL}} = 0.01 \text{ units/mL} \therefore 0.01 \text{ units } of \text{ oxytocin/mL}$$

4. If we dilute 453 grams of zinc oxide 40% (w/w) ointment to a mass of 1,510 grams, what is the resultant percent concentration (w/w) of zinc oxide?

   STEP 1: Enter the values into the equation $V_1 \times C_1 = V_2 \times C_2$.

   $$453 \text{ g} \times 40\% = 1{,}510 \text{ g} \times C_2$$

   NOTE: The variables V_1 and V_2 may represent volume or mass, depending on the problem at hand.

   STEP 2: Solve for the unknown (C_2).

   $$C_2 = \frac{453 \text{ g} \times 40\%}{1{,}510 \text{ g}} = 12\% \therefore \text{ zinc oxide } 12\% \text{ (w/w) ointment}$$

5. What is the percent concentration (w/v) of sodium hypochlorite after adding 1,419 milliliters of sterile water to 473 milliliters of sodium hypochlorite 1:200 (w/v) solution?

   STEP 1: Enter the values into the equation $V_1 \times C_1 = V_2 \times C_2$.

   $$473 \text{ mL} \times 1/200 = 1,892 \text{ mL} \times C_2$$

   NOTE: V_2 is equal to the sum of the volume of the original solution (473 mL) and the volume of the diluent (1,419 mL).

   STEP 2: Solve for the unknown (C_2).

   $$C_2 = \frac{473 \text{ mL} \times 1/200}{1,892 \text{ mL}} = 0.00125 \therefore \text{ sodium hypochlorite 0.125\% (w/v) solution}$$

   NOTE: Sodium hypochlorite 0.125% (w/v) solution is quarter-strength Dakin's® solution.

6. How many milliliters of sterile water for injection (SWFI) must be added to 1,000 milliliters of sodium chloride 3% (w/v) solution to create normal saline solution (NSS)?

   STEP 1: Enter the values into the equation $V_1 \times C_1 = V_2 \times C_2$.

   $$1,000 \text{ mL} \times 3\% = V_2 \times 0.9\%$$

   NOTE: NSS = sodium chloride 0.9% (w/v) solution

   STEP 2: Solve for the unknown (V_2).

   $$V_2 = \frac{1,000 \text{ mL} \times 3\%}{0.9\%} = 3,333 \text{ mL}$$

   STEP 3: Revisit the question. How many milliliters of SWFI must be **added** to create NSS?

   1,000 mL *of* sodium chloride 3% (w/v) solution + UNKNOWN mL *of* SWFI = 3,333 mL *of* sodium chloride 0.9% (w/v) solution

   $\therefore$ UNKNOWN mL *of* SWFI = 3,333 mL *of* sodium chloride 0.9% (w/v) solution − 1,000 mL *of* sodium chloride 3% (w/v) solution

   = 2,333 mL *of* SWFI

ALERT!
Read questions carefully! Always double-check to see if they are asking for the **volume** or the **change in volume**.

---

7. How many liters of dextrose 5% (w/v) solution can be created from a 2,000-milliliter bag of dextrose 70% (w/v) solution?

   STEP 1: Enter the values into the equation $V_1 \times C_1 = V_2 \times C_2$.

   $$V_1 \times 5\% = 2,000 \text{ mL} \times 70\%$$

   STEP 2: Solve for the unknown (V_1).

   $$V_1 = \frac{2,000 \text{ mL} \times 70\%}{5\%} = 28,000 \text{ mL} \therefore 28,000 \text{ mL } of \text{ dextrose 5\% (w/v) solution}$$

   STEP 3: Convert volume from milliliters to liters to answer the question correctly.

   $$28,000 \text{ mL } of \text{ dextrose 5\% (w/v) solution} \times \frac{\text{liter}}{1,000 \text{ mL } of \text{ solution}} = 28 \text{ L } of \text{ dextrose 5\% (w/v) solution}$$

8. How many milliliters of a 1:20,000 solution of a medication can be prepared from 375 milliliters of a 0.025% stock solution?

    STEP 1: Convert the ratio strength to percent concentration.

    $$\frac{1 \text{ g of medication}}{20,000 \text{ mL of solution}} = \frac{\text{UNKNOWN}}{100 \text{ mL of solution}} \therefore \text{UNKNOWN} = \frac{1 \text{ g of medication}}{20,000 \text{ mL of solution}} \times 100 \text{ mL of solution} = 0.005 \text{ g of medication}$$

    $$\frac{0.005 \text{ g of medication}}{100 \text{ mL of solution}} = 0.005\% \text{ solution of medication}$$

    STEP 2: Enter the values into the equation $V_1 \times C_1 = V_2 \times C_2$.

    $$375 \text{ mL} \times 0.025\% = V_2 \times 0.005\%$$

    STEP 3: Solve for the unknown (V_2).

    $$V_2 = \frac{375 \text{ mL} \times 0.025\%}{0.005\%} = 1,875 \text{ mL} \therefore 1,875 \text{ mL of 1:20,000 solution of medication}$$

9. Acyclovir 500 mg lyophilized powder must be reconstituted with 10 milliliters of sterile water for injection (SWFI) to produce a solution of 50 mg/mL acyclovir. According to the package insert, the highest recommended concentration for the infusion of acyclovir is 7 mg/mL. How many milliliters of diluent must be admixed with a reconstituted 500-milligram vial of acyclovir to create a 7 mg/mL solution?

    STEP 1: Enter the values into the equation $V_1 \times C_1 = V_2 \times C_2$.

    $$10 \text{ mL} \times 50 \text{ mg/mL} = V_2 \times 7 \text{ mg/mL}$$

    STEP 2: Solve for the unknown (V_2).

    $$V_2 = \frac{10 \text{ mL} \times 50 \text{ mg/mL}}{7 \text{ mg/mL}} = 71.4 \text{ mL}$$

    STEP 3: Revisit the question. How many mLs of diluent must be **added** to a 10-mL vial of 500-mg acyclovir to yield a 7 mg/mL solution?

    $$10 \text{ mL of acyclovir 50 mg/mL solution} + \text{UNKNOWN mL of diluent} = 71.4 \text{ mL of acyclovir 7 mg/mL solution}$$

    $$\therefore \text{UNKNOWN mL of diluent} = 71.4 \text{ mL of acyclovir 7 mg/mL solution} - 10 \text{ mL of acyclovir 50 mg/mL solution} = 61.4 \text{ mL of diluent}$$

10. Azithromycin 500 mg lyophilized powder must be reconstituted with 4.8 milliliters of SWFI to produce a 100 mg/mL solution. What is the total volume of a 2 mg/mL infusion solution that contains 500 milligrams of azithromycin?

    STEP 1: Enter the values into the equation $V_1 \times C_1 = V_2 \times C_2$.

    $$5 \text{ mL} \times 100 \text{ mg/mL} = V_2 \times 2 \text{ mg/mL}$$

    NOTE: Only 4.8 mL of SWFI was added to the vial, but the reconstituted volume was 5 mL due to the displacement value of the powder. In this case, the reconstituted powder occupied 0.2 mL of space. All powders have a displacement value, but it is not always significant. The previous example of acyclovir is a case in which the displacement value was negligible.

    STEP 2: Solve for the unknown (V_2).

    $$V_2 = \frac{5 \text{ mL} \times 100 \text{ mg/mL}}{2 \text{ mg/mL}} = 250 \text{ mL} \therefore 250 \text{ mL of azithromycin infusion solution}$$

REFERENCES
1. Acyclovir [package insert]. Eatontown, NJ: West-Ward Pharmaceuticals; 2016.
2. Zithromax [package insert]. New York, NY: Pfizer Inc; 2018.

ALLIGATION MEDIAL

Alligation medial is a method of calculating the concentration of a formulation that was prepared by combining two or more components of differing concentrations.

1. What is the percent concentration (w/w) of hydrocortisone in a mixture that contains 15 grams of hydrocortisone 1% (w/w) ointment and 30 grams of hydrocortisone 2.5% (w/w) ointment?

2. What is the percent concentration (v/v) of alcohol in a mixture that contains 50 milliliters of 50% (v/v) alcohol, 90 milliliters of 70% (v/v) alcohol, and 135 milliliters of 91% (v/v) alcohol?

3. What is the percent concentration (w/v) of sodium chloride in a mixture that contains 240 milliliters of 0.225% (w/v) sodium chloride solution, 480 milliliters of 0.45% (w/v) sodium chloride solution, and 180 milliliters of 3% (w/v) sodium chloride solution?

4. What is the concentration (% w/w) of triamcinolone in a mixture that contains 23.0 grams of 0.025% triamcinolone cream, 23.0 grams of 0.1% triamcinolone cream, and 34.5 grams of 0.5% triamcinolone cream?

5. What is the ratio strength of epinephrine in a mixture that contains 70 milliliters of epinephrine 1:10,000 solution, 25 milliliters of epinephrine 1:5,000 solution, and 5 milliliters of epinephrine 1:1,000 solution?

6. What is the percent concentration (w/v) of timolol in a mixture of 10 milliliters of timolol 0.5% (w/v) ophthalmic solution and 5 milliliters of timolol 0.25% (w/v) ophthalmic solution?

7. What concentration (% w/w) results from mixing 290 grams of urea 47% (w/w) cream with 80 grams of urea 10% (w/w) cream?

8. If 60 milliliters of bupivacaine 0.125% (w/v) solution, 5 milliliters of bupivacaine 0.75% (w/v) solution, and 25 milliliters of fentanyl 2 mcg/mL solution are combined, then what is the ratio strength of bupivacaine?

9. What is the percent concentration (w/v) of a mixture that contains 65 milliliters of lidocaine 2% (w/v) injection solution, 227.5 milliliters of lidocaine 4% (w/v) topical solution, and 65 milliliters of lidocaine 0.5% (w/v) injection solution?

10. What is the percent concentration of a mixture of 30 grams of zinc oxide 15%–lanolin 14.5% ointment, 58 grams of a zinc oxide 20% ointment, 454 grams of a zinc oxide 40% (w/w) diaper rash ointment, and 125 grams of a Calmoseptine® ointment, which contains lanolin 15.7%, menthol 0.44%, petrolatum 24%, and zinc oxide 20.6% (w/w)?

SOLUTIONS for ALLIGATION MEDIAL PROBLEMS

1. What is the percent concentration (w/w) of hydrocortisone in a mixture that contains 15 grams of hydrocortisone 1% (w/w) ointment and 30 grams of hydrocortisone 2.5% (w/w) ointment?

   SOLUTION: Divide the mass of hydrocortisone by the total mass of the mixture to determine the concentration.

1 g *of* hydrocortisone/100 g *of* ointment	x	15 g *of* ointment =	0.15 g *of* hydrocortisone
2.5 g *of* hydrocortisone/100 g *of* ointment	x	30 g *of* ointment =	0.75 g *of* hydrocortisone
Total Amount:		45 g *of* ointment	0.90 g *of* hydrocortisone

   $$\text{Final Concentration} = \frac{\text{Total Amount of Active Ingredient}}{\text{Total Amount of Ointment}} = \frac{0.90 \text{ grams}}{45 \text{ grams}} = 0.02 \therefore \text{ hydrocortisone 2\% (w/w) ointment}$$

2. What is the percent concentration (v/v) of alcohol in a mixture that contains 50 milliliters of 50% (v/v) alcohol, 90 milliliters of 70% (v/v) alcohol, and 135 milliliters of 91% (v/v) alcohol?

   SOLUTION: Divide the volume of alcohol by the total volume of the mixture to determine the concentration.

50 mL *of* alcohol/100 mL of solution	x	50 mL *of* solution =	25 mL *of* alcohol
70 mL *of* alcohol/100 mL of solution	x	90 mL *of* solution =	63 mL *of* alcohol
91 mL *of* alcohol/100 mL of solution	x	135 mL *of* solution =	122.85 mL *of* alcohol
Total Amount:		275 mL *of* solution	210.85 mL *of* alcohol

   $$\text{Final Concentration} = \frac{\text{Total Amount of Active Ingredient}}{\text{Total Amount of Solution}} = \frac{210.85 \text{ mL}}{275 \text{ mL}} = 0.767 \therefore \text{ alcohol 77\% (v/v) solution}$$

3. What is the percent concentration (w/v) of sodium chloride in a mixture that contains 240 milliliters of 0.225% (w/v) sodium chloride solution, 480 milliliters of 0.45% (w/v) sodium chloride solution, and 180 milliliters of 3% (w/v) sodium chloride solution?

   SOLUTION: Divide the mass of sodium chloride by the total volume of the mixture to determine the concentration.

0.225 g *of* sodium chloride/100 mL *of* solution	x	240 mL *of* solution =	0.54 g *of* sodium chloride
0.45 g *of* sodium chloride/100 mL *of* solution	x	480 mL *of* solution =	2.16 g *of* sodium chloride
3 g *of* sodium chloride/100 mL *of* solution	x	180 mL *of* solution =	5.40 g *of* sodium chloride
Total Amount:		900 mL *of* solution	8.10 g *of* sodium chloride

   $$\text{Final Concentration} = \frac{\text{Total Amount of Active Ingredient}}{\text{Total Amount of Solution}} = \frac{8.10 \text{ g}}{900 \text{ mL}} = 0.009 \therefore \text{ sodium chloride 0.9\% (w/v) solution}$$

4. What is the concentration (% w/w) of triamcinolone in a mixture that contains 23.0 grams of 0.025% triamcinolone cream, 23.0 grams of 0.1% triamcinolone cream, and 34.5 grams of 0.5% triamcinolone cream?

   SOLUTION: Divide the mass of triamcinolone by the total mass of the mixture to determine the concentration.

0.025 g *of* triamcinolone/100 g *of* cream	x	23.0 g *of* cream =	0.00575 g *of* triamcinolone
0.1 g *of* triamcinolone/100 g *of* cream	x	23.0 g *of* cream =	0.023 g *of* triamcinolone
0.5 g *of* triamcinolone/100 g *of* cream	x	34.5 g *of* cream =	0.1725 g *of* triamcinolone
Total Amount:		80.5 g *of* cream	0.20125 g *of* triamcinolone

   $$\text{Final Concentration} = \frac{\text{Total Amount of Active Ingredient}}{\text{Total Amount of Cream}} = \frac{0.20125 \text{ g}}{80.5 \text{ g}} = 0.0025 \therefore \text{ triamcinolone 0.25\% (w/w) cream}$$

5. What is the ratio strength of epinephrine in a mixture that contains 70 milliliters of epinephrine 1:10,000 solution, 25 milliliters of epinephrine 1:5,000 solution, and 5 milliliters of epinephrine 1:1,000 solution?

   STEP 1: Divide the mass of epinephrine by the total volume of the mixture to determine the concentration.

   1 g *of* epinephrine/10,000 mL *of* solution   x   70 mL *of* solution   =   0.007 g *of* epinephrine
   1 g *of* epinephrine/5,000 mL *of* solution   x   25 mL *of* solution   =   0.005 g *of* epinephrine
   1 g *of* epinephrine/1,000 mL *of* solution   x   5 mL *of* solution   =   0.005 g *of* epinephrine
   Total Amount: 100 mL *of* solution   0.017 g *of* epinephrine

   $$\text{Final Concentration} = \frac{\text{Total Amount } of \text{ Active Ingredient}}{\text{Total Amount } of \text{ Solution}} = \frac{0.017 \text{ g}}{100 \text{ mL}} = 0.00017 \therefore \text{epinephrine 0.017\% (w/v) solution}$$

   STEP 2: Determine the ratio strength by setting up a proportion and solving for the unknown.

   $$\frac{0.017 \text{ g } of \text{ epinephrine}}{100 \text{ mL } of \text{ solution}} = \frac{1 \text{ g } of \text{ epinephrine}}{\text{UNKNOWN}} \therefore \text{UNKNOWN} = \frac{100 \text{ mL } of \text{ solution}}{0.017 \text{ g } of \text{ epinephrine}} \times 1 \text{ g } of \text{ epinephrine} = 5,882 \text{ mL } of \text{ solution}$$

   $$\therefore \frac{1 \text{ g } of \text{ epinephrine}}{5,882 \text{ mL } of \text{ solution}} = \text{epinephrine 1:5,882 solution}$$

6. What is the percent concentration (w/v) of timolol in a mixture of 10 milliliters of timolol 0.5% (w/v) ophthalmic solution and 5 milliliters of timolol 0.25% (w/v) ophthalmic solution?

   SOLUTION: Divide the mass of timolol by the total volume of the mixture to determine the concentration.

   0.5 g *of* timolol/100 mL *of* solution   x   10 mL *of* solution   =   0.05 g *of* timolol
   0.25 g *of* timolol/100 mL *of* solution   x   5 mL *of* solution   =   0.0125 g *of* timolol
   Total Amount: 15 mL *of* solution   0.0625 g *of* timolol

   $$\text{Final Concentration} = \frac{\text{Total Amount } of \text{ Active Ingredient}}{\text{Total Amount } of \text{ Solution}} = \frac{0.0625 \text{ g}}{15 \text{ mL}} = 0.004167 \therefore \text{timolol 0.42\% (w/v) ophthalmic solution}$$

7. What concentration (% w/w) results from mixing 290 grams of urea 47% (w/w) cream with 80 grams of urea 10% (w/w) cream?

   SOLUTION: Divide the mass of urea by the total mass of the mixture to determine the concentration.

   47 g *of* urea/100 g *of* cream   x   290 g *of* cream   =   136.3 g *of* urea
   10 g *of* urea/100 g *of* cream   x   80 g *of* cream   =   8 g *of* urea
   Total Amount: 370 g *of* cream   144.3 g *of* urea

   $$\text{Final Concentration} = \frac{\text{Total Amount } of \text{ Active Ingredient}}{\text{Total Amount } of \text{ Cream}} = \frac{144.3 \text{ g}}{370 \text{ g}} = 0.39 \therefore \text{urea 39\% (w/w) cream}$$

8. If 60 milliliters of bupivacaine 0.125% (w/v) solution, 5 milliliters of bupivacaine 0.75% (w/v) solution, and 25 milliliters of fentanyl 2 mcg/mL solution are combined, then what is the ratio strength of bupivacaine?

   SOLUTION: Divide the mass of bupivacaine by the total volume of the mixture to determine the concentration.

   0.125 g *of* bupivacaine/100 mL *of* solution   x   60 mL *of* solution   =   0.075 g *of* bupivacaine
   0.75 g *of* bupivacaine/100 mL *of* solution   x   5 mL *of* solution   =   0.0375 g *of* bupivacaine
   0.00 g *of* bupivacaine/100 mL *of* solution   x   25 mL *of* solution   =   0.000 g *of* bupivacaine
   Total Amount: 90 mL *of* solution   0.1125 g *of* bupivacaine

   NOTE: Because fentanyl 2 mcg/mL solution contains no bupivacaine, it is equivalent to bupivacaine 0% solution.

   $$\text{Final Concentration} = \frac{\text{Total Amount } of \text{ Active Ingredient}}{\text{Total Amount } of \text{ Solution}} = \frac{0.1125 \text{ g}}{90 \text{ mL}} = 0.00125 \therefore \text{bupivacaine 0.125\% (w/v) solution}$$

9. What is the percent concentration (w/v) of a mixture that contains 65 milliliters of lidocaine 2% (w/v) injection solution, 227.5 milliliters of lidocaine 4% (w/v) topical solution, and 65 milliliters of lidocaine 0.5% (w/v) injection solution?

   SOLUTION: Divide the mass of lidocaine by the total volume of the mixture to determine the concentration.

2 g *of* lidocaine/100 mL *of* solution	x	65 mL *of* solution	=	1.3 g *of* lidocaine
4 g *of* lidocaine/100 mL *of* solution	x	227.5 mL *of* solution	=	9.1 g *of* lidocaine
0.5 g *of* lidocaine/100 mL *of* solution	x	65 mL *of* solution	=	0.325 g *of* lidocaine
Total Amount:		357.5 mL *of* solution		10.725 g *of* lidocaine

   $$\text{Final Concentration} = \frac{\text{Total Amount of Active Ingredient}}{\text{Total Amount of Solution}} = \frac{10.725 \text{ g}}{357.5 \text{ mL}} = 0.03 \therefore \text{ lidocaine 3\% (w/v) solution}$$

10. What is the percent concentration of zinc oxide in the following mixture: 30 grams of zinc oxide 15%–lanolin 14.5% ointment, 58 grams of zinc oxide 20% ointment, 454 grams of zinc oxide 40% (w/w) diaper rash ointment, and 125 grams of a Calmoseptine® ointment, which contains lanolin 15.7%, menthol 0.44%, petrolatum 24%, and zinc oxide 20.6% (w/w)?

    SOLUTION: Divide the mass of zinc oxide by the total mass of the mixture to determine the concentration.

15 g *of* zinc oxide/100 g *of* ointment	x	30 g *of* ointment	=	4.5 g *of* zinc oxide
20 g *of* zinc oxide/100 g *of* ointment	x	58 g *of* ointment	=	11.6 g *of* zinc oxide
40 g *of* zinc oxide/100 g *of* ointment	x	454 g *of* ointment	=	181.6 g *of* zinc oxide
20.6 g *of* zinc oxide/100 g *of* ointment	x	125 g *of* ointment	=	25.75 g *of* zinc oxide
Total Amount:		667 g *of* ointment		223.45 g *of* zinc oxide

    $$\text{Final Concentration} = \frac{\text{Total Amount of Active Ingredient}}{\text{Total Amount of Solution}} = \frac{223.45 \text{ g}}{667 \text{ g}} = 0.335 \therefore \text{ zinc oxide 33.5\% (w/w) ointment}$$

ALLIGATION ALTERNATE

ALLIGATION ALTERNATE METHOD

The alligation alternate method is employed when the desired concentration of a product is unavailable but can be created by combing two other products with differing concentrations (one higher and one lower than the desired concentration).

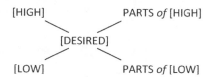

[HIGH] = product concentration higher than desired, [LOW] = product concentration lower than desired, [DESIRED] = concentration desired

[HIGH], [LOW], and [DESIRED] are given in the problem. The "parts of [HIGH]" and "parts of [LOW]" needed to create [DESIRED] are equivalent to the absolute value of the difference between [LOW] – [DESIRED] and [HIGH] – [DESIRED], respectively.

1. How much triamcinolone 0.025% (w/w) ointment and triamcinolone 0.1% (w/w) ointment must be combined to create 30 grams of triamcinolone 0.075% (w/w) ointment?

2. How many grams of petroleum jelly and hydrocortisone 2.5% (w/w) ointment must be mixed to prepare a 454-gram jar of hydrocortisone 1% (w/w) ointment?

3. How many milliliters of 90% alcohol solution and sterile water must be combined to create 1,000 milliliters of 70% alcohol solution?

4. How many milliliters of sodium chloride 5% (w/v) solution and normal saline solution must be mixed to create 300 milliliters of sodium chloride 3% (w/v) solution?

5. How many grams of pure fluconazole powder must be combined with 82 grams of polyethylene glycol ointment and 64 grams of Dermabase™ to create a fluconazole 12% (w/w) ointment?

6. How many milliliters of 5% dextrose in water (D5W) must be added to 20 milliliters of a 50 mg/mL vancomycin solution to create a 2.5 mg/mL vancomycin infusion solution?

7. How many milliliters of 3% KCl solution and water must be combined to create 50 milliliters of 1% KCl solution?

8. How many milliliters of magnesium sulfate (MgSO$_4$) 1 g/2 mL solution and MgSO$_4$ 10 mg/mL solution must be admixed to create 500 milliliters of MgSO$_4$ 40 mg/mL solution?

9. How many milliliters of sodium bicarbonate 4.2% (w/v) solution must be mixed with 50 milliliters of sodium bicarbonate 8.4% (w/v) solution to create sodium bicarbonate 7.5% (w/v) solution?

10. How many milliliters of gentamicin 40 mg/mL solution must be added to a 100-milliliter infusion solution that already contains 80 milligrams of gentamicin to create a gentamicin 1 mg/mL solution?

SOLUTIONS *for* ALLIGATION ALTERNATE PROBLEMS

1. How much triamcinolone 0.025% (w/w) ointment and triamcinolone 0.1% (w/w) ointment must be combined to create 30 grams of triamcinolone 0.075% (w/w) ointment?

   STEP 1: Write the given [HIGH] at the top left, the given [LOW] at the bottom left, and the [DESIRED] in the center. Follow each diagonal line to calculate the difference between the value on the left and the value in the center. Write the result in the alternate diagonal space to the right.

   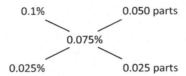

   0.050 part *of* triamcinolone 0.1% ointment + 0.025 part *of* triamcinolone 0.025% ointment = 0.075 total parts

   STEP 2: Set up a proportion and solve for the unknown to determine the mass of triamcinolone 0.1% ointment needed.

   $$\frac{0.050 \text{ parts } of \text{ triamcinolone 0.1\% ointment}}{0.075 \text{ parts total}} = \frac{\text{UNKNOWN}}{30 \text{ g total}}$$

   $$\therefore \text{UNKNOWN} = \frac{0.050 \text{ parts } of \text{ triamcinolone 0.1\% ointment}}{0.075 \text{ parts total}} \times 30 \text{ grams total} = 20 \text{ grams } of \text{ 0.1\% triamcinolone ointment}$$

   STEP 3: Set up a proportion and solve for the unknown to determine the mass of triamcinolone 0.025% ointment needed.

   $$\frac{0.025 \text{ parts } of \text{ triamcinolone 0.025\% ointment}}{0.075 \text{ parts total}} = \frac{\text{UNKNOWN}}{30 \text{ g total}}$$

   $$\therefore \text{UNKNOWN} = \frac{0.025 \text{ parts } of \text{ triamcinolone 0.025\% ointment}}{0.075 \text{ parts total}} \times 30 \text{ grams total} = 10 \text{ grams } of \text{ 0.025\% triamcinolone ointment}$$

2. How many grams of petroleum jelly and hydrocortisone 2.5% (w/w) ointment must be mixed to prepare a 454-gram jar of hydrocortisone 1% (w/w) ointment?

   STEP 1: Write the given value for [HIGH] at the top left, the given value for [LOW] at the bottom left, and the [DESIRED] in the center. Follow each line and write the difference between the respective values in the alternate space to the right.

   NOTE: Because petroleum jelly does not contain any active ingredient, it is treated mathematically as hydrocortisone 0% (w/w) ointment.

   1 part *of* hydrocortisone 2.5% ointment + 1.5 parts *of* petroleum jelly = 2.5 total parts

   STEP 2: Set up a proportion and solve for the unknown to determine the mass of hydrocortisone 2.5% ointment needed.

   $$\frac{1 \text{ part } of \text{ hydrocortisone 2.5\% ointment}}{2.5 \text{ parts total}} = \frac{\text{UNKNOWN}}{454 \text{ g total}}$$

   $$\therefore \text{UNKNOWN} = \frac{1 \text{ part } of \text{ hydrocortisone 2.5\% ointment}}{2.5 \text{ parts total}} \times 454 \text{ grams total} = 181.6 \text{ grams } of \text{ hydrocortisone 2.5\% ointment}$$

   STEP 3: Set up a proportion and solve for the unknown to determine the mass of petroleum jelly needed.

   $$\frac{1.5 \text{ parts } of \text{ petroleum jelly}}{2.5 \text{ parts total}} = \frac{\text{UNKNOWN}}{454 \text{ g total}}$$

   $$\therefore \text{UNKNOWN} = \frac{1.5 \text{ parts } of \text{ petroleum jelly}}{2.5 \text{ parts total}} \times 454 \text{ grams total} = 272.4 \text{ grams } of \text{ petroleum jelly}$$

3. How many milliliters of 90% alcohol solution and sterile water must be combined to create 1,000 milliliters of 70% alcohol solution?

   STEP 1: Write the given value for [HIGH] at the top left, the given value for [LOW] at the bottom left, and the [DESIRED] in the center. Follow each line and write the difference between the respective values in the alternate space to the right.

   NOTE: Because sterile water does not contain any active ingredient, it is treated mathematically as a 0% alcohol solution.

   70 parts *of* 90% alcohol solution + 20 parts *of* sterile water = 90 total parts

   STEP 2: Set up a proportion and solve for the unknown to determine the volume of 90% alcohol solution needed.

   $$\frac{70 \text{ parts } of \text{ 90\% alcohol solution}}{90 \text{ parts total}} = \frac{\text{UNKNOWN}}{1{,}000 \text{ mL total}}$$

   $$\therefore \text{UNKNOWN} = \frac{70 \text{ parts } of \text{ 90\% alcohol solution}}{90 \text{ parts total}} \times 1{,}000 \text{ mL total} = 778 \text{ mL } of \text{ 90\% alcohol solution}$$

   STEP 3: Set up a proportion and solve for the unknown to determine the volume of sterile water needed.

   $$\frac{20 \text{ parts } of \text{ sterile water}}{90 \text{ parts total}} = \frac{\text{UNKNOWN}}{1{,}000 \text{ mL total}} \quad \therefore \text{UNKNOWN} = \frac{20 \text{ parts } of \text{ sterile water}}{90 \text{ parts total}} \times 1{,}000 \text{ mL total} = 222 \text{ mL } of \text{ sterile water}$$

4. How many milliliters of sodium chloride 5% (w/v) solution and normal saline solution must be mixed to create 300 milliliters of sodium chloride 3% (w/v) solution?

   STEP 1: Write the given value for [HIGH] at the top left, the given value for [LOW] at the bottom left, and the [DESIRED] in the center. Follow each line and write the difference between the respective values in the alternate space to the right.

   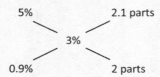

   NOTE: Normal saline solution is sodium chloride 0.9% solution.

   2.1 parts *of* sodium chloride 5% solution + 2 parts *of* normal saline solution = 4.1 total parts

   STEP 2: Set up a proportion and solve for the unknown to determine the volume of sodium chloride 5% solution needed.

   $$\frac{2.1 \text{ parts } of \text{ sodium chloride 5\% solution}}{4.1 \text{ parts total}} = \frac{\text{UNKNOWN}}{300 \text{ mL total}}$$

   $$\therefore \text{UNKNOWN} = \frac{2.1 \text{ parts } of \text{ sodium chloride 5\% solution}}{4.1 \text{ parts total}} \times 300 \text{ mL total} = 154 \text{ mL } of \text{ sodium chloride 5\% (w/v) solution}$$

   STEP 3: Set up a proportion and solve for the unknown to determine the volume of normal saline needed.

   $$\frac{2 \text{ parts } of \text{ normal saline solution}}{4.1 \text{ parts total}} = \frac{\text{UNKNOWN}}{300 \text{ mL total}}$$

   $$\therefore \text{UNKNOWN} = \frac{2 \text{ parts } of \text{ normal saline solution}}{4.1 \text{ parts total}} \times 300 \text{ mL total} = 146 \text{ mL } of \text{ normal saline solution}$$

5. How many grams of pure fluconazole powder must be combined with 82 grams of polyethylene glycol ointment and 64 grams of Dermabase™ to create a fluconazole 12% (w/w) ointment?

   STEP 1: Write the given value for [HIGH] at the top left, the given value for [LOW] at the bottom left, and the [DESIRED] in the center. Follow each line and write the difference between the respective values in the alternate space to the right.

   NOTE: The question is asking, how many grams of fluconazole 100% powder must be combined with 146 grams of fluconazole 0% ointment to create fluconazole 12% ointment? Since polyethylene glycol ointment and Dermabase™ do not contain any active ingredient, we regard these two ingredients ("ointment bases") mathematically as fluconazole 0% ointment.

   STEP 2: Set up a proportion and solve for the unknown to determine the mass of fluconazole powder needed.

   $$\frac{12 \text{ parts } of \text{ fluconazole 100\% powder}}{88 \text{ parts } of \text{ ointment bases}} = \frac{\text{UNKNOWN}}{146 \text{ grams } of \text{ ointment bases}}$$

   $$\therefore \text{UNKNOWN} = \frac{12 \text{ parts } of \text{ fluconazole 100\% powder}}{88 \text{ parts } of \text{ ointment bases}} \times 146 \text{ grams } of \text{ ointment bases} = 19.9 \text{ g } of \text{ fluconazole 100\% powder}$$

6. How many milliliters of 5% dextrose in water (D5W) must be added to 20 milliliters of a 50 mg/mL vancomycin solution to create a 2.5 mg/mL vancomycin infusion solution?

   STEP 1: Write the given value for [HIGH] at the top left, the given value for [LOW] at the bottom left, and the [DESIRED] in the center. Follow each line and write the difference between the respective values in the alternate space to the right.

   NOTE: Because D5W does not contain any active ingredient, it is regarded mathematically as vancomycin 0 mg/mL solution.

   STEP 2: Set up a proportion and solve for the unknown to determine the volume of D5W needed.

   $$\frac{2.5 \text{ parts } of \text{ vancomycin 50 mg/mL solution}}{47.5 \text{ parts } of \text{ D5W}} = \frac{20 \text{ mL } of \text{ vancomycin 50 mg/mL solution}}{\text{UNKNOWN}}$$

   $$\therefore \text{UNKNOWN} = \frac{47.5 \text{ parts } of \text{ D5W}}{2.5 \text{ parts } of \text{ vancomycin 50 mg/mL solution}} \times 20 \text{ mL } of \text{ vancomycin 50 mg/mL solution} = 380 \text{ mL } of \text{ D5W}$$

7. How many milliliters of 3% KCl solution and water must be combined to create 50 milliliters of 1% KCl solution?

   STEP 1: Write the given value for [HIGH] at the top left, the given value for [LOW] at the bottom left, and the [DESIRED] in the center. Follow each line and write the difference between the respective values in the alternate space to the right.

   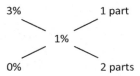

   NOTE: Because water does not contain any active ingredient, it is regarded mathematically as a 0% KCl solution.

   1 part *of* 3% KCl solution + 2 parts *of* water = 3 total parts

   STEP 2: Set up a proportion and solve for the unknown to determine the volume of 3% KCl solution needed.

   $$\frac{1 \text{ part } of \text{ 3% KCl solution}}{3 \text{ parts total}} = \frac{\text{UNKNOWN}}{50 \text{ mL total}}$$

   $$\therefore \text{UNKNOWN} = \frac{1 \text{ part } of \text{ 3% KCl solution}}{3 \text{ parts total}} \times 50 \text{ mL total} = 16.7 \text{ mL } of \text{ 3% KCl solution}$$

   STEP 3: Set up a proportion and solve for the unknown to determine the volume of water needed.

   $$\frac{2 \text{ parts } of \text{ water}}{3 \text{ parts total}} = \frac{\text{UNKNOWN}}{50 \text{ mL total}}$$

   $$\therefore \text{UNKNOWN} = \frac{2 \text{ parts } of \text{ water}}{3 \text{ parts total}} \times 50 \text{ mL total} = 33.3 \text{ mL } of \text{ water}$$

8. How many milliliters of magnesium sulfate ($MgSO_4$) 1 g/2 mL solution and $MgSO_4$ 10 mg/mL solution must be admixed to create 500 milliliters of $MgSO_4$ 40 mg/mL solution?

   STEP 1: Standardize the $MgSO_4$ units of concentration to mg/mL.

   $$\frac{1 \text{ g}}{2 \text{ mL}} \times \frac{1{,}000 \text{ mg}}{\text{g}} = 500 \text{ mg/mL}$$

   NOTE: The choice of units is inconsequential; they just need to be the same. We chose mg/mL because it is the easiest option, as two of the three concentrations provided are already expressed in these terms.

   STEP 2: Write the given value for [HIGH] at the top left, the given value for [LOW] at the bottom left, and the [DESIRED] in the center. Follow each line and write the difference between the respective values in the alternate space to the right.

   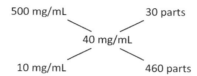

   30 parts *of* $MgSO_4$ 500 mg/mL solution + 460 parts *of* $MgSO_4$ 10 mg/mL solution = 490 total parts

   STEP 3: Set up a proportion and solve for the unknown to determine the volume of $MgSO_4$ 1 g/2 mL solution needed.

   $$\frac{30 \text{ parts } of \text{ } MgSO_4 \text{ 500 mg/mL solution}}{490 \text{ parts total}} = \frac{\text{UNKNOWN}}{500 \text{ mL total}}$$

   $$\therefore \text{UNKNOWN} = \frac{30 \text{ parts } of \text{ } MgSO_4 \text{ 500 mg/mL sol.}}{490 \text{ parts total}} \times 500 \text{ mL total} = 30.6 \text{ mL } of \text{ } MgSO_4 \text{ 500 mg/mL sol.} \therefore 30.6 \text{ mL } of \text{ } MgSO_4 \text{ 1 g/2 mL solution}$$

   STEP 4: Set up a proportion and solve for the unknown to determine the volume of $MgSO_4$ 10 mg/mL solution needed.

   $$\frac{460 \text{ parts } of \text{ } MgSO_4 \text{ 10 mg/mL solution}}{490 \text{ parts total}} = \frac{\text{UNKNOWN}}{500 \text{ mL total}}$$

   $$\therefore \text{UNKNOWN} = \frac{460 \text{ parts } of \text{ } MgSO_4 \text{ 10 mg/mL solution}}{490 \text{ parts total}} \times 500 \text{ mL total} = 469.4 \text{ mL } of \text{ } MgSO_4 \text{ 10 mg/mL solution}$$

9. How many milliliters of sodium bicarbonate 4.2% (w/v) solution must be mixed with 50 milliliters of sodium bicarbonate 8.4% (w/v) solution to create sodium bicarbonate 7.5% (w/v) solution?

   STEP 1: Write the given value for [HIGH] at the top left, the given value for [LOW] at the bottom left, and the [DESIRED] in the center. Follow each line and write the difference between the respective values in the alternate space to the right.

   NOTE: Because water does not contain any active ingredient, it is regarded mathematically as a 0% sodium bicarbonate solution.

   STEP 2: Set up a proportion and solve for the unknown to determine the volume of 4.2% sodium bicarbonate needed.

   $$\frac{0.9 \text{ parts } of \text{ 4.2\% sodium bicarbonate}}{3.3 \text{ parts } of \text{ 8.4\% sodium bicarbonate}} = \frac{\text{UNKNOWN}}{50 \text{ mL } of \text{ 8.4\% sodium bicarbonate}}$$

   $$\therefore \text{UNKNOWN} = \frac{0.9 \text{ parts } of \text{ 4.2\% sodium bicarbonate}}{3.3 \text{ parts } of \text{ 8.4\% sodium bicarbonate}} \times 50 \text{ mL } of \text{ 8.4\% sodium bicarbonate} = 13.6 \text{ mL } of \text{ 4.2\% sodium bicarbonate}$$

10. How many milliliters of gentamicin 40 mg/mL solution must be added to a 100-milliliter infusion solution that already contains 80 milligrams of gentamicin to create a gentamicin 1 mg/mL solution?

   STEP 1: Express the concentration of the existing infusion solution in terms of mg/mL.

   $$\frac{\text{gentamicin 80 mg}}{\text{100 mL solution}} = \text{gentamicin 0.8 mg/mL solution}$$

   STEP 2: Write the given value for [HIGH] at the top left, the given value for [LOW] at the bottom left, and the [DESIRED] in the center. Follow each line and write the difference between the respective values in the alternate space to the right.

   STEP 2: Set up a proportion and solve for the unknown to determine the volume of gentamicin 40 mg/mL needed.

   $$\frac{0.2 \text{ parts } of \text{ gentamicin 40 mg/mL}}{39 \text{ parts } of \text{ gentamicin 0.8 mg/mL}} = \frac{\text{UNKNOWN}}{100 \text{ mL } of \text{ gentamicin 0.8 mg/mL}}$$

   $$\therefore \text{UNKNOWN} = \frac{0.2 \text{ parts } of \text{ gentamicin 40 mg/mL}}{39 \text{ parts } of \text{ gentamicin 0.8 mg/mL}} \times 100 \text{ mL } of \text{ gentamicin 0.8 mg/mL} = 0.51 \text{ mL } of \text{ gentamicin 40 mg/mL solution}$$

PRESCRIPTION BALANCES

PERCENT ERROR EQUATION

$$\text{Percent Error} = \frac{|\text{Measured Quantity} - \text{True Quantity}|}{\text{True Quantity}} \times 100\%$$

PERCENT ERROR EQUATION for BALANCES & SCALES

$$\text{Percent Error} = \frac{\text{Sensitivity Requirement}}{\text{Measured Weight}} \times 100\%$$

NOTE: Apparent quantity (or apparent weight) is the amount according to the reading on the measurement device.

SENSITIVITY REQUIREMENT
The sensitivity requirement is the weight required to move the indicator on the balance one division.

MINIMUM WEIGHABLE QUANTITY (MWQ)
Also known as the "least weighable quantity," this is the smallest weight that can be measured with a given balance or scale within a chosen percent error. As the acceptable percent error decreases, the MWQ increases. In pharmacy, 5% is commonly considered to be the maximum acceptable percent error.

SENSITIVITY REQUIREMENT	PERCENT ERROR	MINIMUM WEIGHABLE QUANTITY
6 mg	5%	120 mg
6 mg	4%	150 mg
6 mg	2%	300 mg

1. If a technician measures 120 milliliters of a substance, but the actual volume is later determined to be 127 milliliters, what was the percent error in the original measurement?

2. Suppose a pharmacist measures 50 milliliters of a substance, but the actual volume of the substance obtained by the measurement is later determined to be 48 milliliters. What was the percent error in the original measurement?

3. If a torsion balance with a sensitivity requirement of 6 milligrams measures a mass of 960 milligrams, what is the expected percent error in the measurement?

4. If a torsion balance with a sensitivity requirement of 6 milligrams measures a mass of 240 milligrams, what is the expected percent error in the measurement?

5. If a torsion balance with a sensitivity requirement of 6 milligrams measures a mass of 120 milligrams, what is the expected percent error in the measurement?

6. If a torsion balance with a sensitivity requirement of 6 milligrams measures a mass of 60 milligrams, what is the expected percent error in the measurement?

7. What is the percent error in a 60-milligram measurement on a scale with a three-milligram sensitivity requirement?

8. What is the percent error in a 60-milligram measurement on a scale with a one and one-half-milligram sensitivity requirement?

9. What is the smallest mass measurable on a scale with a sensitivity requirement of one milligram if 5% error is acceptable?

10. What is the smallest mass measurable on a scale with a sensitivity requirement of 20 milligrams if only a 2% error is acceptable?

11. What is the sensitivity requirement of a double pan torsion balance capable of measuring 120 milligrams with a 5% error?

12. What is the sensitivity requirement of a scale capable of measuring two milligrams with a 5% error?

SOLUTIONS for PRESCRIPTION BALANCE PROBLEMS

1. If a technician measures 120 milliliters of a substance, but the actual volume is later determined to be 127 milliliters, what was the percent error in the original measurement?

   SOLUTION: Enter the values into the equation for percent error.

   $$\text{Percent Error} = \frac{|\text{Measured Quantity} - \text{True Quantity}|}{\text{True Quantity}} \times 100\% = \frac{|120 \text{ mL} - 127 \text{ mL}|}{127 \text{ mL}} \times 100\% = \frac{|-7 \text{ mL}|}{127 \text{ mL}} \times 100\% = 5.51\%$$

2. Suppose a pharmacist measures 50 milliliters of a substance, but the actual volume of the substance obtained by the measurement is later determined to be 48 milliliters. What was the percent error in the original measurement?

   SOLUTION: Enter the values into the equation for percent error.

   $$\text{Percent Error} = \frac{|\text{Measured Quantity} - \text{True Quantity}|}{\text{True Quantity}} \times 100\% = \frac{|48 \text{ mL} - 50 \text{ mL}|}{48 \text{ mL}} \times 100\% = \frac{|-2 \text{ mL}|}{48 \text{ mL}} \times 100\% = 4.17\%$$

3. If a torsion balance with a sensitivity requirement of 6 milligrams measures a mass of 960 milligrams, what is the expected percent error in the measurement?

   SOLUTION: Enter the values for sensitivity requirement and measured weigh into the percent error equation for balances and scales.

   $$\text{Percent Error} = \frac{\text{Sensitivity Requirement}}{\text{Measured Weight}} \times 100\% = \frac{6 \text{ mg}}{960 \text{ mg}} \times 100\% = 0.625\%$$

4. If a torsion balance with a sensitivity requirement of 6 milligrams measures a mass of 240 milligrams, what is the expected percent error in the measurement?

   SOLUTION: Enter the values for sensitivity requirement and measured weigh into the percent error equation for balances and scales.

   $$\text{Percent Error} = \frac{\text{Sensitivity Requirement}}{\text{Measured Weight}} \times 100\% = \frac{6 \text{ mg}}{240 \text{ mg}} \times 100\% = 2.5\%$$

5. If a torsion balance with a sensitivity requirement of 6 milligrams measures a mass of 120 milligrams, what is the expected percent error in the measurement?

   SOLUTION: Enter the values for sensitivity requirement and measured weigh into the percent error equation for balances and scales.

   $$\text{Percent Error} = \frac{\text{Sensitivity Requirement}}{\text{Measured Weight}} \times 100\% = \frac{6 \text{ mg}}{120 \text{ mg}} \times 100\% = 5\%$$

6. If a torsion balance with a sensitivity requirement of 6 milligrams measures a mass of 60 milligrams, what is the expected percent error in the measurement?

   SOLUTION: Enter the values for sensitivity requirement and measured weigh into the percent error equation for balances and scales.

   $$\text{Percent Error} = \frac{\text{Sensitivity Requirement}}{\text{Measured Weight}} \times 100\% = \frac{6 \text{ mg}}{60 \text{ mg}} \times 100\% = 10\%$$

7. What is the percent error in a 60-milligram measurement on a scale with a three-milligram sensitivity requirement?

   SOLUTION: Enter the values for sensitivity requirement and measured weigh into the percent error equation for balances and scales.

$$\text{Percent Error} = \frac{\text{Sensitivity Requirement}}{\text{Measured Weight}} \times 100\% = \frac{3 \text{ mg}}{60 \text{ mg}} \times 100\% = 5\%$$

8. What is the percent error in a 60-milligram measurement on a scale with a one and one-half-milligram sensitivity requirement?

   SOLUTION: Enter the values for sensitivity requirement and measured weigh into the percent error equation for balances and scales.

$$\text{Percent Error} = \frac{\text{Sensitivity Requirement}}{\text{Measured Weight}} \times 100\% = \frac{1.5 \text{ mg}}{60 \text{ mg}} \times 100\% = 2.5\%$$

9. What is the smallest mass measurable on a scale with a sensitivity requirement of one milligram if 5% error is acceptable?

   SOLUTION: Rearrange the percent error equation for balances and scales to solve for measured weight.

$$\text{Percent Error} = \frac{\text{Sensitivity Requirement}}{\text{Measured Weight}} \times 100\% \therefore \text{Measured Weight} = \frac{\text{Sensitivity Requirement}}{\text{Percent Error}} \times 100\% = \frac{1 \text{ mg}}{5\%} \times 100\% = 20 \text{ mg}$$

   NOTE: The "minimum weighable quantity" (or least weighable quantity) is used as the "measured weight" variable in the percent error equation for balances and scales. With this device, given its sensitivity requirement, measuring masses > 20 mg would produce measurements with a percent error < 5%; meanwhile, measuring masses < 20 mg would produce measurements with a percent error > 5%.

10. What is the smallest mass measurable on a scale with a sensitivity requirement of 20 milligrams if only a 2% error is acceptable?

    SOLUTION: Rearrange the percent error equation for balances and scales to solve for measured weight.

$$\text{Percent Error} = \frac{\text{Sensitivity Requirement}}{\text{Measured Weight}} \times 100\% \therefore \text{Measured Weight} = \frac{\text{Sensitivity Requirement}}{\text{Percent Error}} \times 100\% = \frac{20 \text{ mg}}{2\%} \times 100\% = 1{,}000 \text{ mg}$$

    NOTE: Once again, measuring masses > 1,000 mg using this scale would produce a percent error < 2%, and measuring masses < 1,000 mg would produce a percent error > 2%.

11. What is the sensitivity requirement of a double pan torsion balance capable of measuring 120 milligrams with a 5% error?

    SOLUTION: Rearrange the percent error equation for balances and scales to solve for sensitivity requirement.

$$\text{Percent Error} = \frac{\text{Sensitivity Requirement}}{\text{Measured Weight}} \times 100\% \therefore \text{Sensitivity Requirement} = \frac{\text{Percent Error}}{100\%} \times \text{Measured Weight} = \frac{5\%}{100\%} \times 120 \text{ mg} = 6 \text{ mg}$$

    NOTE: The standard Class A (or Class III) prescription balance is a double pan torsion balance with a sensitivity requirement of 6 milligrams.

12. What is the sensitivity requirement of a scale capable of measuring two milligrams with a 5% error?

    SOLUTION: Rearrange the percent error equation for balances and scales to solve for sensitivity requirement.

$$\text{Percent Error} = \frac{\text{Sensitivity Requirement}}{\text{Measured Weight}} \times 100\% \therefore \text{Sensitivity Requirement} = \frac{\text{Percent Error}}{100\%} \times \text{Measured Weight} = \frac{5\%}{100\%} \times 2 \text{ mg} = 0.1 \text{ mg}$$

HENDERSON-HASSELBALCH

THE HENDERSON-HASSELBALCH EQUATION

WEAK ACIDS

$$pH = pK_a + \log \frac{[A^-]}{[HA]}$$

WEAK BASES

$$pH = pK_a + \log \frac{[B]}{[BH^+]}$$

CONVERTING from $pK_a \rightarrow pK_b$

If you're working a problem with a weak base, and the dissociation constant is given as K_b, then pK_a can be calculated using this equation:

$$pK_a + pK_b = 14 \therefore pK_a = 14 - pK_b$$

NOTE: The letter "p" stands for "– log." Meanwhile, K_a is the dissociation constant for weak acids, and K_b is the dissociation constant for weak bases. Typically, for drugs, dissociation constants are written as "K_a" for weak acids and weak bases, so there is a low likelihood that you will have to use this equation.

pH – pKa	ACIDIC SUBSTANCES [A⁻]/[HA]	BASIC SUBSTANCES [B]/[BH⁺]
6	1,000,000/1	1,000,000/1
5	100,000/1	100,000/1
4	10,000/1	10,000/1
3	1,000/1	1,000/1
2	100/1	100/1
1	10/1	10/1
0	1/1	1/1
–1	1/10	1/10
–2	1/100	1/100
–3	1/1,000	1/1,000
–4	1/10,000	1/10,000
–5	1/100,000	1/100,000
–6	1/1,000,000	1/1,000,000

log (1) = 0
log (10) = 1
log (100) = 2
log (1,000) = 3
log (10,000) = 4
log (100,000) = 5
log (1,000,000) = 6
log (10,000,000) = 7

WEAK ACIDS
As the alkalinity of the environment increases, a greater proportion of an acidic drug donates its proton and becomes ionized.

WEAK BASES
As the acidity of the environment increases, a greater proportion of a basic drug accepts a proton and becomes ionized.

THE EFFECT of IONIZATION ON SOLUBILITY & ABSORPTION
Ionized drugs are more water-soluble than unionized drugs; however, unionized drugs are more lipid-soluble and consequently better absorbed.

HENDERSON-HASSELBALCH

1. Ibuprofen is a weak acid with a pKa of 4.43. The stomach's pH is 2.43. What is the expected ratio of ionized to unionized ibuprofen in the stomach?

2. Aspirin (acetylsalicylic acid) is a weak acid with a pKa of 3.5. The pH in the lumen of the duodenum is 6. What is the expected ratio of unionized to ionized aspirin inside the duodenum?

3. Codeine is a weak base with a pKa of 7.9. The pH in the lumen of the jejunum is 7.9. What percentage of codeine do we expect to exist ionized inside the jejunum?

4. Amphetamine is a weak base with a pKa of 9.9, and the stomach has a pH of 2.9. What percentage of an oral dose of amphetamine do we expect to exist unionized in the stomach?

5. If amphetamine (a weak base with a pKa of 9.9) distributes to the duodenum, where the pH is 5.9, what percentage of the drug would we expect to exist unionized?

6. Lidocaine is a weak base with a pKa of 7.86, and the pH of blood is 7.4. What percentage of lidocaine would likely exist unionized immediately after injection into the bloodstream?

7. Oxycodone, a weak base with a pKa of 8.9, is dissolved in an oral solution with a pH of 4.0. What percentage of oxycodone would likely exist unionized within the solution?

8. Acetaminophen is a weak acid with a pKa of 9.4. The pH of the rectum is 8.4. After administering an acetaminophen rectal suppository, what percentage of acetaminophen would likely exist unionized?

9. Morphine, a weak base with a pKa of 7.9, is dissolved in a sterile injection solution with a pH of 3.25. What is the expected ratio of unionized to ionized morphine?

10. Furosemide is a weak acid with a pKa of 3.9. What percentage of furosemide will exist in the ionized form when placed in an environment with a pH of 3?

11. Phenytoin, a weak acid with a pK_a of 8.3, is dissolved in an alkaline injection solution (pH 12). What percentage of phenytoin would we expect to exist unionized in the injection solution?

12. A nurse injects phenytoin (a weak acid with a pKa of 8.3) into a muscle with a pH of 6.8. What percentage of phenytoin could we expect to be present unionized within the muscle?

13. If the dissociation constant (K_a) for benzoic acid is 6.25×10^{-5}, what is the pH of a buffer solution that contains 0.4 M benzoic acid and 0.06 M sodium benzoate?

14. The dissociation constant (K_a) for formic acid is 1.8×10^{-4}. What is the pH of a buffer solution comprised of 0.7 M formic acid and 0.7 M sodium formate?

15. The dissociation constant (K_a) for lactic acid is 1.4×10^{-4}. What is the pH of a buffer solution made up of 0.24 M lactic acid and 0.16 M sodium lactate?

16. If the dissociation constant (K_b) for ammonia is 1.8×10^{-5}, what is the pH of a buffer solution that contains 0.9 M ammonia and 0.1 M ammonium chloride?

SOLUTIONS *for* HENDERSON-HASSELBALCH PROBLEMS

1. Ibuprofen is a weak acid with a pKa of 4.43. The stomach's pH is 2.43. What is the expected ratio of ionized to unionized ibuprofen in the stomach?

    STEP 1: Rearrange the Henderson-Hasselbalch equation (for weak acids) to solve for [A⁻]/[HA].

    $$pH = pK_a + \log\frac{[A^-]}{[HA]} \therefore \log\frac{[A^-]}{[HA]} = pH - pK_a = 2.43 - 4.43 = -2$$

    $$\therefore \frac{[A^-]}{[HA]} = 10^{-2} = 0.01 = \frac{1}{100}$$

    STEP 2: Determine the ratio of ionized to unionized ibuprofen based on the information from STEP 1.

    From STEP 1, we know that the proportion of [A⁻] = 1 and [HA] = 100.

    [ionized ibuprofen]:[unionized ibuprofen] = [A⁻]:[HA] = 1:100

    NOTE: This answer should make sense considering that acidic drugs are expected to retain their proton when the pH of the environment < pKa of the drug.

2. Aspirin (acetylsalicylic acid) is a weak acid with a pKa of 3.5. The pH in the lumen of the duodenum is 6. What is the expected ratio of unionized to ionized aspirin inside the duodenum?

    STEP 1: Rearrange the Henderson-Hasselbalch equation (for weak acids) to solve for [A⁻]/[HA].

    $$pH = pK_a + \log\frac{[A^-]}{[HA]} \therefore \log\frac{[A^-]}{[HA]} = pH - pK_a = 6 - 3.5 = 2.5$$

    $$\therefore \frac{[A^-]}{[HA]} = 10^{2.5} = 316 = \frac{316}{1}$$

    STEP 2: Determine the ratio of unionized to ionized aspirin based on the information from STEP 1.

    From STEP 1, we know that the proportion of [A⁻] = 316 and [HA] = 1.

    [unionized aspirin]:[ionized aspirin] = [HA]:[A⁻] = 1: 316

    NOTE: This answer should make sense considering that acidic drugs are expected to ionize when the pH of the environment > the pKa of the drug.

3. Codeine is a weak base with a pKa of 7.9. The pH in the lumen of the jejunum is 7.9. What percentage of codeine do we expect to exist ionized inside the jejunum?

    STEP 1: Rearrange the Henderson-Hasselbalch equation (for weak bases) to solve for [B]/[BH⁺].

    $$pH = pK_a + \log\frac{[B]}{[BH^+]} \therefore \log\frac{[B]}{[BH^+]} = pH - pK_a = 7.9 - 7.9 = 0 \therefore \frac{[B]}{[BH^+]} = 10^0 = 1 = \frac{1}{1}$$

    STEP 2: Determine the percentage of codeine that is ionized based on the information from STEP 1.

    From STEP 1, we know that the proportion of [B] = 1 and [BH⁺] = 1.

    $$\text{percentage } of \text{ ionized codeine} = \frac{[\text{ionized codeine}]}{[\text{ionized codeine}] + [\text{unionized codeine}]} = \frac{[BH^+]}{[BH^+] + [B]} = \frac{1}{1+1} = \frac{1}{2} = 50\%$$

    NOTE: This answer should make sense, as we expect equal portions of ionized and unionized drug when the pH of the environment = the pKa of the drug.

4. Amphetamine is a weak base with a pKa of 9.9, and the stomach has a pH of 2.9. What percentage of an oral dose of amphetamine do we expect to exist unionized in the stomach?

   STEP 1: Rearrange the Henderson-Hasselbalch equation (for weak bases) to solve for [B]/[BH⁺].

   $$pH = pK_a + \log\frac{[B]}{[BH^+]} \therefore \log\frac{[B]}{[BH^+]} = pH - pK_a = 2.9 - 9.9 = -7 \therefore \frac{[B]}{[BH^+]} = 10^{-7} = 0.0000001 = \frac{1}{10,000,000}$$

   STEP 2: Determine the percentage of amphetamine that is unionized based on the information from STEP 1.

   From STEP 1, we know that the proportion of [B] = 1 and [BH⁺] = 10,000,000.

   $$\text{percentage } of \text{ unionized amphetamine} = \frac{[\text{unionized amphetamine}]}{[\text{ionized amphetamine}] + [\text{unionized amphetamine}]} = \frac{[B]}{[BH^+] + [B]} = \frac{1}{10,000,000 + 1}$$

   $$= \frac{1}{10,000,001} = 0.0000001 \therefore 0.00001\%$$

5. If amphetamine (a weak base with a pKa of 9.9) distributes to the duodenum, where the pH is 5.9, what percentage of the drug would we expect to exist unionized?

   STEP 1: Rearrange the Henderson-Hasselbalch equation (for weak bases) to solve for [B]/[BH⁺].

   $$pH = pK_a + \log\frac{[B]}{[BH^+]} \therefore \log\frac{[B]}{[BH^+]} = pH - pK_a = 5.9 - 9.9 = -4 \therefore \frac{[B]}{[BH^+]} = 10^{-4} = 0.0001 = \frac{1}{10,000}$$

   STEP 2: Determine the percentage of amphetamine that is unionized based on the information from STEP 1.

   From STEP 1, we know that the proportion of [B] = 1 and [BH⁺] = 10,000.

   $$\text{percentage } of \text{ unionized amphetamine} = \frac{[\text{unionized amphetamine}]}{[\text{ionized amphetamine}] + [\text{unionized amphetamine}]} = \frac{[B]}{[BH^+] + [B]} = \frac{1}{10,000 + 1}$$

   $$= \frac{1}{10,001} = 0.0001 \therefore 0.01\%$$

6. Lidocaine is a weak base with a pKa of 7.86, and the pH of blood is 7.4. What percentage of lidocaine would likely exist unionized immediately after injection into the bloodstream?

   STEP 1: Rearrange the Henderson-Hasselbalch equation (for weak bases) to solve for [B]/[BH⁺].

   $$pH = pK_a + \log\frac{[B]}{[BH^+]} \therefore \log\frac{[B]}{[BH^+]} = pH - pK_a = 7.4 - 7.86 = -0.46$$

   $$\therefore \frac{[B]}{[BH^+]} = 10^{-0.46} = 0.347 = \frac{1}{2.88}$$

   STEP 2: Determine the percentage of amphetamine that is unionized based on the information from STEP 1.

   From STEP 1, we know that the proportion of [B] = 1 and [BH⁺] = 2.88.

   $$\text{percentage } of \text{ unionized lidocaine} = \frac{[\text{unionized lidocaine}]}{[\text{ionized lidocaine}] + [\text{unionized lidocaine}]} = \frac{[B]}{[BH^+] + [B]} = \frac{1}{2.88 + 1}$$

   $$= \frac{1}{3.88} = 0.258 \therefore 25.8\%$$

7. Oxycodone, a weak base with a pKa of 8.9, is dissolved in an oral solution with a pH of 4.0. What percentage of oxycodone would likely exist unionized within the solution?

   STEP 1: Rearrange the Henderson-Hasselbalch equation (for weak bases) to solve for [B]/[BH$^+$].

   $$pH = pK_a + \log\frac{[B]}{[BH^+]} \therefore \log\frac{[B]}{[BH^+]} = pH - pK_a = 4.0 - 8.9 = -4.9$$

   $$\therefore \frac{[B]}{[BH^+]} = 10^{-4.9} = 0.0000126 = \frac{1}{79,400}$$

   STEP 2: Determine the percentage of amphetamine that is unionized based on the information from STEP 1.

   From STEP 1, we know that the proportion of [B] = 1 and [BH$^+$] = 2.88.

   $$\text{percentage } of \text{ unionized amphetamine} = \frac{[\text{unionized amphetamine}]}{[\text{ionized amphetamine}] + [\text{unionized amphetamine}]} = \frac{[B]}{[BH^+] + [B]} = \frac{1}{79,400 + 1}$$

   $$= \frac{1}{79,401} = 0.0000126 \therefore 0.00126\%$$

8. Acetaminophen is a weak acid with a pKa of 9.4. The pH of the rectum is 8.4. After administering an acetaminophen rectal suppository, what percentage of acetaminophen would likely exist unionized?

   STEP 1: Rearrange the Henderson-Hasselbalch equation (for weak acids) to solve for [A$^-$]/[HA].

   $$pH = pK_a + \log\frac{[A^-]}{[HA]} \therefore \log\frac{[A^-]}{[HA]} = pH - pK_a = 8.4 - 9.4 = -1$$

   $$\therefore \frac{[A^-]}{[HA]} = 10^{-1} = 0.1 = \frac{1}{10}$$

   STEP 2: Determine the percentage of acetaminophen that is unionized based on the information from STEP 1.

   From STEP 1, we know that the proportion of [A$^-$] = 1 and [HA] = 10.

   $$\text{percentage } of \text{ unionized amphetamine} = \frac{[\text{unionized acetaminophen}]}{[\text{ionized acetaminophen}] + [\text{unionized acetaminophen}]} = \frac{[HA]}{[A^-] + [HA]} = \frac{10}{1 + 10}$$

   $$= \frac{10}{11} = 0.909 \therefore 90.9\%$$

9. Morphine, a weak base with a pKa of 7.9, is dissolved in a sterile injection solution with a pH of 3.25. What is the expected ratio of unionized to ionized morphine?

   STEP 1: Rearrange the Henderson-Hasselbalch equation (for weak bases) to solve for [B]/[BH$^+$].

   $$pH = pK_a + \log\frac{[B]}{[BH^+]} \therefore \log\frac{[B]}{[BH^+]} = pH - pK_a = 3.25 - 7.9 = -4.65$$

   $$\therefore \frac{[B]}{[BH^+]} = 10^{-4.65} = 0.00002239 = \frac{1}{44,700}$$

   STEP 2: Determine the ratio of unionized to ionized morphine based on the information from STEP 1.

   From STEP 1, we know that the proportion of [B] = 1 and [BH$^+$] = 44,700.

   [unionized morphine]:[ionized morphine] = [B]: [BH$^+$] = 1: 44,700

10. Furosemide is a weak acid with a pKa of 3.9. What percentage of furosemide will exist in the ionized form when placed in an environment with a pH of 3?

   STEP 1: Rearrange the Henderson-Hasselbalch equation (for weak acids) to solve for [A⁻]/[HA].

   $$pH = pK_a + \log\frac{[A^-]}{[HA]} \therefore \log\frac{[A^-]}{[HA]} = pH - pK_a = 3 - 3.0 = -0.9 \therefore \frac{[A^-]}{[HA]} = 10^{-0.9} = 0.126 = \frac{1}{7.94}$$

   STEP 2: Determine the percentage of furosemide that is ionized based on the information from STEP 1.

   From STEP 1, we know that the proportion of [A⁻] = 1 and [HA] = 7.94.

   $$\text{percentage } of \text{ unionized furosemide} = \frac{[\text{unionized furosemide}]}{[\text{ionized furosemide}] + [\text{unionized furosemide}]} = \frac{[A^-]}{[A^-]+[HA]} = \frac{1}{1+7.94}$$

   $$= \frac{1}{8.94} = 0.112 \therefore 11.2\%$$

11. Phenytoin, a weak acid with a pK$_a$ of 8.3, is dissolved in an alkaline injection solution (pH 12). What percentage of phenytoin would we expect to exist unionized in the injection solution?

   STEP 1: Rearrange the Henderson-Hasselbalch equation (for weak acids) to solve for [A⁻]/[HA].

   $$pH = pK_a + \log\frac{[A^-]}{[HA]} \therefore \log\frac{[A^-]}{[HA]} = pH - pK_a = 12 - 8.3 = 3.7 \therefore \frac{[A^-]}{[HA]} = 10^{3.7} = 5{,}012 = \frac{5{,}012}{1}$$

   STEP 2: Determine the percentage of phenytoin that is unionized based on the information from STEP 1.

   From STEP 1, we know that the proportion of [A⁻] = 5,012 and [HA] = 1.

   $$\text{percentage } of \text{ unionized phenytoin} = \frac{[\text{unionized phenytoin}]}{[\text{ionized phenytoin}] + [\text{unionized phenytoin}]} = \frac{[HA]}{[A^-]+[HA]} = \frac{1}{5{,}012+1} = \frac{1}{5{,}013} = 0.0002 \therefore 0.02\%$$

   NOTE: The injection solution has a pH of 12, ensuring that phenytoin is ionized, so it will remain in solution. Unionized phenytoin is relatively insoluble and highly prone to precipitation.

12. A nurse injects phenytoin (a weak acid with a pKa of 8.3) into a muscle with a pH of 6.8. What percentage of phenytoin could we expect to be present unionized within the muscle?

   STEP 1: Rearrange the Henderson-Hasselbalch equation (for weak acids) to solve for [A⁻]/[HA].

   $$pH = pK_a + \log\frac{[A^-]}{[HA]} \therefore \log\frac{[A^-]}{[HA]} = pH - pK_a = 6.8 - 8.3 = -1.5 \therefore \frac{[A^-]}{[HA]} = 10^{-1.5} = 0.0316 = \frac{1}{31.6}$$

   STEP 2: Determine the percentage of phenytoin that is unionized based on the information from STEP 1.

   From STEP 1, we know that the proportion of [A⁻] = 1 and [HA] = 31.6.

   $$\text{percentage } of \text{ unionized phenytoin} = \frac{[\text{unionized phenytoin}]}{[\text{ionized phenytoin}] + [\text{unionized phenytoin}]} = \frac{[HA]}{[A^-]+[HA]} = \frac{31.6}{1+31.6}$$

   $$= \frac{31.6}{32.6} = 0.969 \therefore 96.9\%$$

NOTE: Because phenytoin is almost entirely unionized in the muscle, it precipitates and then slowly dissolves over time. To account for this, according to the package insert, the dose of intramuscular phenytoin should be 50% greater than an equivalent oral dose.

13. If the dissociation constant (K_a) for benzoic acid is 6.25 x 10^{-5}, what is the pH of a buffer solution that contains 0.4 M benzoic acid and 0.06 M sodium benzoate?

    STEP 1: Calculate the pK_a of benzoic acid.

    $$pK_a = -\log(K_a) = -\log(6.25 \times 10^{-5}) = 4.20$$

    STEP 2: Apply the Henderson-Hasselbalch equation (for weak acids) to determine the pH of the buffer solution.

    $$pH = pK_a + \log\frac{[A^-]}{[HA]} = 4.20 + \log\frac{[0.06]}{[0.4]} = 4.20 + (-0.8) = 3.4$$

14. The dissociation constant (K_a) for formic acid is 1.8 x 10^{-4}. What is the pH of a buffer solution comprised of 0.7 M formic acid and 0.7 M sodium formate?

    STEP 1: Calculate the pK_a of formic acid.

    $$pK_a = -\log(K_a) = -\log(1.8 \times 10^{-4}) = 3.74$$

    STEP 2: Apply the Henderson-Hasselbalch equation (for weak acids) to determine the pH of the buffer solution.

    $$pH = pK_a + \log\frac{[A^-]}{[HA]} = 3.74 + \log\frac{[0.7]}{[0.7]} = 3.74 + 0 = 3.74$$

15. The dissociation constant (K_a) for lactic acid is 1.4 x 10^{-4}. What is the pH of a buffer solution made up of 0.24 M lactic acid and 0.16 M sodium lactate?

    STEP 1: Calculate the pK_a of lactic acid.

    $$pK_a = -\log(K_a) = -\log(1.4 \times 10^{-4}) = 3.85$$

    STEP 2: Apply the Henderson-Hasselbalch equation (for weak acids) to determine the pH of the buffer solution.

    $$pH = pK_a + \log\frac{[A^-]}{[HA]} = 3.85 + \log\frac{[0.16]}{[0.24]} = 3.85 + (-0.176) = 3.7$$

16. If the dissociation constant (K_b) for ammonia is 1.8 x 10^{-5}, what is the pH of a buffer solution that contains 0.9 M ammonia and 0.1 M ammonium chloride?

    STEP 1: Calculate the pK_b of ammonia.

    $$pK_b = -\log(K_b) = -\log(1.8 \times 10^{-5}) = 4.74$$

    STEP 2: Apply the equation to convert pK_b to pK_a.

    $$pK_a + pK_b = 14 \therefore pK_a = 14 - pK_b = 14 - 4.74 = 9.26$$

    STEP 3: Apply the Henderson-Hasselbalch equation (for weak bases) to determine the pH of the buffer solution.

    $$pH = pK_a + \log\frac{[B]}{[BH^+]} = 9.26 + \log\frac{[0.9]}{[0.1]} = 9.26 + 0.95 = 10.2$$

PARENTERAL NUTRITION

ENTERAL MACRONUTRIENT	KILOCALORIES/GRAM	PARENTERAL EQUIVALENT	KILOCALORIES/GRAM
Carbohydrate	4 kilocalories/gram	Dextrose Solution	3.4 kilocalories/gram
Protein	4 kilocalories/gram	Amino Acid Solution	4 kilocalories/gram
Fat	9 kilocalories/gram	Lipid Emulsion	10 - 11 kilocalories/gram

NOTE: The monohydrate in dextrose monohydrate injection solution dilutes the caloric density from 4 kcal/g to 3.4 kcal/g. Meanwhile, the emulsifiers in intravenous fat emulsions add one extra kcal/g (total 10 kcal/g) for 20–30% fat emulsions and two extra kcal/g (total 11 kcal/g) for 10% fat emulsions.

ROUGH ESTIMATE of BASAL METABOLIC RATE (BMR) for ADULTS

STRESS	DAILY CALORIE REQUIREMENT
None	25 kcal/kg
Mild	30 kcal/kg
Moderate	35 kcal/kg
Severe	40 kcal/kg

NOTE: BMR may also be referred to as resting metabolic rate (RMR), basal energy expenditure (BEE), resting energy expenditure (REE), and resting metabolic energy (RME). The Harris-Benedict equations can be used to estimate BMR; however, the equations are rather complex, and the estimates they produce are still only accurate to within ±20% (95% confidence interval).

ADJUSTED BODY WEIGHT for OBESE PATIENTS

Calorie requirement calculations for obese patients should be based on adjusted body weight (ABW):

$$ABW = IBW + [0.25 \times (\text{Actual Weight} - IBW)]$$

REFERENCE: Krenitsky J. Adjusted body weight, pro: evidence to support the use of adjusted body weight in calculating calorie requirements. Nutr Clin Pract. 2005;20(4):468-73.

ROUGH ESTIMATE of PROTEIN REQUIREMENT

STRESS	DAILY PROTEIN REQUIREMENT
None	0.8 g/kg
Mild	1 g/kg
Moderate	1.5 g/kg
Severe	2 g/kg

NOTE: Some clinicians do not count calories from protein toward the total daily calorie requirement.

EQUATION for NITROGEN BALANCE (NB)

NB = Nitrogen Intake − Nitrogen Loss = [Protein Intake (grams)/6.25] − [24-hour Urinary Urea Nitrogen (grams) + 4 grams]

NOTE: Nitrogen accounts for 16% of the average weight of an amino acid. Dividing by a factor of 6.25 is equivalent to multiplying by 0.16. Four grams are added to the 24-hour urinary urea nitrogen because approximately 4 additional grams of nitrogen are lost daily via routes other than urine urea (e.g., hair, skin, stool, sweat).

THE HOLLIDAY-SEGAR METHOD for ESTIMATING FLUID REQUIREMENT

BODY WEIGHT	DAILY FLUID REQUIREMENT
< 10 kilograms	100 mL/kg
10–20 kilograms	1,000 mL + 50 mL/kg for each kg over 10 kg
> 20 kilograms	1,500 mL + 20 mL/kg for each kg over 20 kg

AVERAGE DAILY FLUID REQUIREMENT for ADULTS: APPROXIMATELY 30 ML/KG

PARENTERAL NUTRITION

1. How many milliliters of dextrose 70% (w/v) injection solution will provide 1,428 kilocalories from carbohydrates?

2. How many milliliters of dextrose 50% (w/v) injection solution will provide 1,292 kilocalories from carbohydrates?

3. How many milliliters of ProSol™ (amino acid 20% injection solution) will provide 624 kilocalories from protein?

4. How many milliliters of Aminosyn® (amino acid 10% injection solution) will provide 396 kilocalories from protein?

5. How many milliliters of Clinisol® (amino acid 15% injection solution) will provide 840 Calories from protein?

6. How many milliliters of Intralipid® 20% (intravenous fat emulsion) will provide 820 kilocalories from fat?

7. How many milliliters of Intralipid® 10% (intravenous fat emulsion) will provide 429 kilocalories from fat?

8. How many milliliters of Intralipid® 30% (intravenous fat emulsion) will provide 195 Calories from fat?

9. If a patient receives parenteral nutrition with 88 grams of amino acids, how many kilocalories from protein is the patient receiving?

10. A 135-pound non-obese patient requires 25 non-protein kilocalories per kilogram with 70% of calories from carbohydrates and 30% of calories from fat. How many kilocalories from carbohydrates and fat are needed?

11. How many kilocalories will a patient receive from a total nutrient admixture (3-in-1) that contains 455 grams of dextrose from D70W, 62 grams of lipids from a 20% intravenous fat emulsion, and 95 grams of amino acids from a 10% amino acid solution?

12. How many kilocalories will a patient receive from a total nutrient admixture (3-in-1) that contains 72 milliliters of Intralipid® 30% (fat 30% intravenous emulsion), 433 milliliters of Travasol® 10% (amino acid 10% injection solution), and 721 milliliters of dextrose 70% (w/v) solution?

13. A patient weighs 121 pounds and must receive a total nutrient admixture (3-in-1) that supplies 30 kilocalories per kilogram of body weight per day with 72% of non-protein calories from carbohydrates and 28% of non-protein calories from fat plus another 1.5 grams of protein per kilogram of body weight. Assuming the clinician counts calories from protein toward the daily calorie requirement, how many kilocalories per day will the patient receive from each macronutrient?

14. A patient weighs 143 pounds and must receive a total nutrient admixture (3-in-1) that supplies 25 non-protein kilocalories per kilogram of body weight per day with 80% of non-protein calories from carbohydrates and 20% of non-protein calories from fat plus another 0.8 grams of protein per kilogram. How many milliliters of D50W, Intralipid® 20%, and Travasol® 10% should the patient receive each day?

15. If a patient weighs 90 kilograms and must receive a total nutrient admixture (3-in-1) that supplies a total of 35 kilocalories per kilogram of body weight per day with 68% of calories from carbohydrates, 24% of calories from fat, and 8% of calories from protein, then how many milliliters of D70W, Intralipid® 30%, and Travasol® 10% should the patient receive each day?

16. CW is a 55-year-old female who is 64 inches tall and weighs 129 pounds. She is under severe metabolic stress and unable to take anything orally. Her physician orders a total nutrient admixture (3-in-1) to supply 40 non-protein kilocalories per kilogram of ideal body weight plus an additional 2 grams of protein per kilogram of ideal body weight. The physician wants 75% of non-protein calories from carbohydrates and 25% from fat. How many grams of dextrose, lipids, and amino acids should CW receive daily from this formulation? Assume fat source will be a 20% intravenous fat emulsion.

17. What is the protein requirement for an obese 297-pound male trauma patient who measures 5' 11" in height and is under moderate metabolic stress? Assume the protein requirement is 1.5 grams per kilogram per day since the patient is under moderate stress and base the calculation on adjusted body weight with an adjustment factor of 0.25 for excess body weight since the patient is obese.

18. What is the daily calorie requirement for an obese female patient that is 5 ft 1 in tall, weighs 199 pounds, and is under no metabolic stress? Assume the daily calorie requirement is 25 kcal/kg per day for no stress and base the calculation on adjusted body weight with an adjustment factor of 0.25 for excess body weight since the patient is obese.

19. What is the daily calorie requirement based on ideal body weight (IBW) for a male patient that is 6 ft 2 in tall, weighs 206 pounds, and is under mild metabolic stress? Assume the daily calorie requirement is 30 kcal/kg per day for mild stress.

20. What is the daily calorie requirement based on actual body weight for a female patient that is 1.78 meters tall, weighs 61.4 kilograms, and is under moderate metabolic stress? Assume the daily calorie requirement is 35 kcal/kg per day for moderate stress.

21. What is the daily calorie requirement for a male patient that is 5 ft 8 in tall, weighs 187 pounds, and is under severe metabolic stress? Assume the daily calorie requirement is 40 kcal/kg per day for severe stress and base the calculation on ideal body weight if the patient is not obese or adjusted body weight with an adjustment factor of 0.25 for excess body weight if the patient is obese.

22. What is the daily calorie requirement for a female patient that is 5 ft 8 in tall, weighs 187 pounds, and is under moderate metabolic stress? Assume the daily calorie requirement is 35 kcal/kg per day for moderate stress and base the calculation on ideal body weight if the patient is not obese or adjusted body weight with an adjustment factor of 0.25 for excess body weight if the patient is obese.

23. How many grams of protein should be administered in one day to a female patient that is 5 ft tall and under severe metabolic stress? Assume the daily protein requirement is 2 g/kg per day for severe stress and base the calculation on ideal body weight (IBW).

24. How many grams of protein should be administered in one day to a male patient that is 6 ft tall and under mild metabolic stress? Assume the daily protein requirement is 1 g/kg per day for mild stress and base the calculation on ideal body weight (IBW).

25. If a 67-kilogram patient must receive 1.2 grams of protein per day, how many grams of nitrogen will the patient receive each day?

26. If a 76-kilogram female patient is 5 ft 7 in tall and has a 24-hour UUN of 12.1 grams, what is the patient's estimated daily nitrogen loss?

27. Suppose a male patient has a 24-hour urine urea nitrogen (UUN) of 15.2 grams. What is his estimated nitrogen balance (NB) if he receives 920 milliliters of Travasol® 10% (amino acid 10% solution) daily as his only protein intake source?

28. If a patient receives 122.4 grams of protein intravenously per day, how many grams of nitrogen is the patient receiving each day?

29. If a 164-kilogram patient has a 24-hour UUN of 16.3 grams, what is the patient's estimated daily nitrogen loss?

30. If a patient's 24-hour urine urea nitrogen (UUN) level is 11.9 grams, what is their nitrogen balance (NB), assuming they receive 100 grams of protein daily?

31. What is the estimated daily fluid requirement for a child that weighs 16 kilograms?

32. What is the estimated daily fluid requirement for an infant that weighs 18.7 pounds?

33. What is the estimated daily fluid requirement for a 70-year-old male that weighs 165 pounds?

34. What is the estimated daily fluid requirement for a 4-month-old female that weighs 6.5 kilograms?

35. What is the estimated daily fluid requirement for a male patient that weighs 42.9 pounds with a creatinine clearance of 100 mL/min?

36. What is the estimated daily fluid requirement for a 20-year-old female that weighs 105.6 pounds?

37. What is the estimated daily fluid requirement for a 34-year-old male that weighs 78 kilograms?

38. What is the estimated daily fluid requirement for a 48-year-old male that weighs 209 pounds?

SOLUTIONS *for* PARENTERAL NUTRITION PROBLEMS

1. How many milliliters of dextrose 70% (w/v) injection solution will provide 1,428 kilocalories from carbohydrates?

    SOLUTION: Perform dimensional analysis.

    $$1{,}428 \text{ kilocalories} \times \frac{\text{gram of dextrose}}{3.4 \text{ kilocalories}} \times \frac{100 \text{ mL of solution}}{70 \text{ grams of dextrose}} = 600 \text{ mL of solution}$$

    NOTE: Dextrose injection solution contains dextrose monohydrate ($C_6H_{12}O_6 \bullet H_2O$), which provides 3.4 kcal/gram rather than 4 kcal/gram due to the presence of H_2O. Anhydrous dextrose (i.e., the dry powder form of dextrose) contains 4 kcal/gram since H_2O is absent.

2. How many milliliters of dextrose 50% (w/v) injection solution will provide 1,292 kilocalories from carbohydrates?

    SOLUTION: Perform dimensional analysis.

    $$1{,}292 \text{ kilocalories} \times \frac{\text{gram of dextrose}}{3.4 \text{ kilocalories}} \times \frac{100 \text{ mL of solution}}{50 \text{ grams of dextrose}} = 760 \text{ mL of solution}$$

3. How many milliliters of ProSol™ (amino acid 20% injection solution) will provide 624 kilocalories from protein?

    SOLUTION: Perform dimensional analysis.

    $$624 \text{ kilocalories} \times \frac{\text{gram of protein}}{4 \text{ kilocalories}} \times \frac{100 \text{ mL of solution}}{20 \text{ grams of protein}} = 780 \text{ mL of solution}$$

    NOTE: The terms "protein" and "amino acids" can be considered interchangeable in the context of parenteral nutrition.

4. How many milliliters of Aminosyn® (amino acid 10% injection solution) will provide 396 kilocalories from protein?

    SOLUTION: Perform dimensional analysis.

    $$396 \text{ kilocalories} \times \frac{\text{gram of protein}}{4 \text{ kilocalories}} \times \frac{100 \text{ mL of solution}}{10 \text{ grams of protein}} = 990 \text{ mL of solution}$$

5. How many milliliters of Clinisol® (amino acid 15% injection solution) will provide 840 Calories from protein?

    SOLUTION: Perform dimensional analysis.

    $$840 \text{ kilocalories} \times \frac{\text{gram of protein}}{4 \text{ kilocalories}} \times \frac{100 \text{ mL of solution}}{15 \text{ grams of protein}} = 1{,}400 \text{ mL of solution}$$

    NOTE: 1 Calorie = 1 kilocalorie.

6. How many milliliters of Intralipid® 20% (intravenous fat emulsion) will provide 820 kilocalories from fat?

    SOLUTION: Perform dimensional analysis.

    $$820 \text{ kilocalories} \times \frac{\text{gram of fat}}{10 \text{ kilocalories}} \times \frac{100 \text{ mL of emulsion}}{20 \text{ grams of fat}} = 410 \text{ mL of emulsion}$$

7. How many milliliters of Intralipid® 10% (intravenous fat emulsion) will provide 429 kilocalories from fat?

   SOLUTION: Perform dimensional analysis.

   $$429 \text{ kilocalories} \times \frac{\text{gram of fat}}{11 \text{ kilocalories}} \times \frac{100 \text{ mL of emulsion}}{10 \text{ grams of fat}} = 390 \text{ mL of emulsion}$$

   NOTE: Lipid 10% emulsions provide 11 kilocalories/gram; whereas, lipid 20% and 30% emulsions provide 10 kilocalories/gram.

8. How many milliliters of Intralipid® 30% (intravenous fat emulsion) will provide 195 Calories from fat?

   SOLUTION: Perform dimensional analysis.

   $$195 \text{ kilocalories} \times \frac{\text{gram of fat}}{10 \text{ kilocalories}} \times \frac{100 \text{ mL of emulsion}}{30 \text{ grams of fat}} = 65 \text{ mL of emulsion}$$

   NOTE: 1 Calorie = 1 kilocalorie.

9. If a patient receives parenteral nutrition with 88 grams of amino acids, how many kilocalories from protein is the patient receiving?

   SOLUTION: Perform dimensional analysis.

   $$88 \text{ grams of protein} \times \frac{4 \text{ kilocalories}}{\text{gram of protein}} = 352 \text{ kilocalories}$$

10. A 135-pound non-obese patient requires 25 non-protein kilocalories per kilogram with 70% of calories from carbohydrates and 30% of calories from fat. How many kilocalories from carbohydrates and fat are needed?

    STEP 1: Convert the weight from units of pounds to kilograms and use dimensional analysis to calculate the daily calorie requirement.

    $$135 \text{ pounds} \times \frac{\text{kg}}{2.2 \text{ pounds}} \times \frac{25 \text{ kilocalories}}{\text{kg}} = 1{,}534 \text{ kilocalories}$$

    STEP 2: Multiply the total daily calories by the decimal fraction of each component (carbohydrates and fat).

    $$1{,}534 \text{ kilocalories} \times 0.70 \text{ carbohydrates} = 1{,}074 \text{ kilocalories from carbohydrates}$$

    $$1{,}534 \text{ kilocalories} \times 0.30 \text{ fat} = 460 \text{ kilocalories from fat}$$

11. How many kilocalories will a patient receive from a total nutrient admixture (3-in-1) that contains 455 grams of dextrose from D70W, 62 grams of lipids from a 20% intravenous fat emulsion, and 95 grams of amino acids from a 10% amino acid solution?

    SOLUTION: Use dimensional analysis to calculate the number of kilocalories from each source and add them together for a total.

    $$\left[455 \text{ g of dextrose} \times \frac{3.4 \text{ kcal}}{\text{g}}\right] + \left[62 \text{ g of lipids} \times \frac{10 \text{ kcal}}{\text{g}}\right] + \left[95 \text{ g of amino acids} \times \frac{4 \text{ kcal}}{\text{g}}\right] = 2{,}547 \text{ kcal}$$

    NOTE: A 20% fat emulsion supplies 10 kilocalories of energy per gram of lipids.

12. How many kilocalories will a patient receive from a total nutrient admixture (3-in-1) that contains 72 milliliters of Intralipid® 30% (fat 30% intravenous emulsion), 433 milliliters of Travasol® 10% (amino acid 10% injection solution), and 721 milliliters of dextrose 70% (w/v) solution?

    SOLUTION: Use dimensional analysis to calculate the number of kilocalories from each source and add them together for a total.

    $$72 \text{ mL of Intralipid}^{\circledR} 30\% \times \frac{30 \text{ grams of lipids}}{100 \text{ mL of Intralipid}^{\circledR} 30\%} \times \frac{10 \text{ kcal}}{\text{gram of lipids}} = 216 \text{ kcal}$$

    $$433 \text{ mL of Travasol}^{\circledR} 10\% \times \frac{10 \text{ grams of amino acids}}{100 \text{ mL of Travasol}^{\circledR} 10\%} \times \frac{4 \text{ kcal}}{\text{gram of amino acids}} = 173 \text{ kcal}$$

    $$721 \text{ mL of D70W} \times \frac{70 \text{ grams of dextrose}}{100 \text{ mL of D70W}} \times \frac{3.4 \text{ kcal}}{\text{gram of dextrose}} = 1{,}716 \text{ kcal}$$

    Total kilocalories = 216 kcal + 173 kcal + 1,716 kcal = 2,105 kcal

13. A patient weighs 121 pounds and must receive a total nutrient admixture (3-in-1) that supplies 30 kilocalories per kilogram of body weight per day with 72% of non-protein calories from carbohydrates and 28% of non-protein calories from fat plus another 1.5 grams of protein per kilogram of body weight. Assuming the clinician counts calories from protein toward the daily calorie requirement, how many kilocalories per day will the patient receive from each macronutrient?

    STEP 1: Convert the weight from units of pounds to kilograms.

    $$121 \text{ pounds} \times \frac{\text{kg}}{2.2 \text{ pounds}} = 55 \text{ kg}$$

    STEP 2: Use dimensional analysis to determine the total kilocalories the patient must receive each day.

    $$55 \text{ kg} \times \frac{30 \text{ kcal}}{\text{kg}} = 1{,}650 \text{ kcal}$$

    STEP 3: Use dimensional analysis to determine the kilocalories from protein the patient must receive each day.

    $$55 \text{ kg} \times \frac{1.5 \text{ grams of protein}}{\text{kg}} \times \frac{4 \text{ kcal}}{\text{gram of protein}} = 330 \text{ kcal of protein}$$

    STEP 4: Subtract the protein kilocalories (STEP 3) from total kilocalories (STEP 2) to determine daily non-protein kilocalories.

    $$1{,}650 \text{ kcal} - 330 \text{ kcal} = 1{,}320 \text{ kcal}$$

    STEP 5: Multiply the decimal fraction of carbohydrate and fat by the non-protein kilocalories.

    $$0.72 \text{ of carbohydrates} \times 1{,}320 \text{ kcal} = 950 \text{ kcal of carbohydrates}$$

    $$0.28 \text{ of fat} \times 1{,}320 \text{ kcal} = 370 \text{ kcal of fat}$$

    FINAL ANSWER: 330 kcal *of* protein, 950 kcal *of* carbohydrates, and 370 kcal *of* fat.

14. A patient weighs 143 pounds and must receive a total nutrient admixture (3-in-1) that supplies 25 non-protein kilocalories per kilogram of body weight per day with 80% of non-protein calories from carbohydrates and 20% of non-protein calories from fat plus another 0.8 grams of protein per kilogram. How many milliliters of D50W, Intralipid® 20%, and Travasol® 10% should the patient receive each day?

    STEP 1: Convert the weight from units of pounds to kilograms.

    $$143 \text{ pounds} \times \frac{\text{kg}}{2.2 \text{ pounds}} = 65 \text{ kg}$$

    STEP 2: Use dimensional analysis to determine the total kilocalories the patient must receive each day from carbohydrates and fat.

    $$65 \text{ kg} \times \frac{25 \text{ kcal}}{\text{kg}} = 1,625 \text{ kcal}$$

    STEP 3: Multiply the decimal fraction of carbohydrates and fat, respectively, by the non-protein kilocalories calculated in STEP 2.

    $$0.80 \text{ of carbohydrates} \times 1,625 \text{ kcal} = 1,300 \text{ kcal of carbohydrates}$$

    $$0.20 \text{ of fat} \times 1,625 \text{ kcal} = 325 \text{ kcal of fat}$$

    STEP 4: Use dimensional analysis to determine the volume of D50W, Intralipid 20%, and Travasol® 10% the patient must get each day.

    $$1,300 \text{ kcal of carbohydrates} \times \frac{\text{gram of dextrose}}{3.4 \text{ kcal of carbohydrates}} \times \frac{100 \text{ mL of D50W}}{50 \text{ grams of dextrose}} = 764.7 \text{ mL of D50W}$$

    $$325 \text{ kcal of fat} \times \frac{\text{gram of lipids}}{10 \text{ kcal of fat}} \times \frac{100 \text{ mL of Intralipid® 20\%}}{20 \text{ grams of lipids}} = 162.5 \text{ mL of Intralipid® 20\%}$$

    $$65 \text{ kg} \times \frac{0.8 \text{ grams of protein}}{\text{kg}} \times \frac{100 \text{ mL of Travasol® 10\%}}{10 \text{ gram of protein}} = 520 \text{ mL of Travasol® 10\%}$$

15. If a patient weighs 90 kilograms and must receive a total nutrient admixture (3-in-1) that supplies a total of 35 kilocalories per kilogram of body weight per day with 68% of calories from carbohydrates, 24% of calories from fat, and 8% of calories from protein, then how many milliliters of D70W, Intralipid® 30%, and Travasol® 10% should the patient receive each day?

    STEP 1: Use dimensional analysis to determine the total kilocalories the patient must receive each day.

    $$90 \text{ kg} \times \frac{35 \text{ kcal}}{\text{kg}} = 3,150 \text{ kcal}$$

    STEP 2: Multiply the decimal fraction of carbohydrates, fat, and protein by the total daily kilocalories.

    $$0.68 \text{ of carbohydrates} \times 3,150 \text{ kcal} = 2,142 \text{ kcal of carbohydrates}$$

    $$0.24 \text{ of fat} \times 3,150 \text{ kcal} = 756 \text{ kcal of fat}$$

    $$0.08 \text{ of protein} \times 3,150 \text{ kcal} = 252 \text{ kcal of protein}$$

    STEP 3: Use dimensional analysis to determine the volume of D70W Intralipid 30%, and Travasol® 10% needed.

    $$2,142 \text{ kcal of carbohydrates} \times \frac{\text{gram of dextrose}}{3.4 \text{ kcal of carbohydrates}} \times \frac{100 \text{ mL of D70W}}{70 \text{ grams of dextrose}} = 900 \text{ mL of D70W}$$

    $$756 \text{ kcal of fat} \times \frac{\text{gram of lipids}}{10 \text{ kcal of fat}} \times \frac{100 \text{ mL of Intralipid® 30\%}}{30 \text{ grams of lipids}} = 252 \text{ mL of Intralipid® 30\%}$$

    $$252 \text{ kcal of protein} \times \frac{\text{gram of amino acids}}{4 \text{ kcal of protein}} \times \frac{100 \text{ mL of Travasol® 10\%}}{10 \text{ grams of amino acids}} = 630 \text{ mL of Travasol® 10\%}$$

16. CW is a 55-year-old female who is 64 inches tall and weighs 129 pounds. She is under severe metabolic stress and unable to take anything orally. Her physician orders a total nutrient admixture (3-in-1) to supply 40 non-protein kilocalories per kilogram of ideal body weight plus an additional 2 grams of protein per kilogram of ideal body weight. The physician wants 75% of non-protein calories from carbohydrates and 25% from fat. How many grams of dextrose, lipids, and amino acids should CW receive daily from this formulation? Assume fat source will be a 20% intravenous fat emulsion.

   STEP 1: Calculate ideal body weight.

   $$\text{IBW (female)} = 45.5 \text{ kg} + (2.3 \text{ kg for each inch of height over 5 feet}) = 45.5 \text{ kg} + (2.3 \text{ kg} \times 4) = 54.7 \text{ kg}$$

   NOTE: 5 feet = 60 inches.

   STEP 2: Use dimensional analysis to determine the non-protein kilocalories the patient must receive each day.

   $$54.7 \text{ kg} \times \frac{40 \text{ kcal}}{\text{kg}} = 2{,}188 \text{ kcal}$$

   STEP 3: Multiply decimal fraction of carbohydrate and fat by the total daily non-protein kilocalories.

   $$0.75 \text{ of carbohydrates} \times 2{,}188 \text{ kcal} = 1{,}641 \text{ kcal of carbohydrates}$$

   $$0.25 \text{ of fat} \times 2{,}188 \text{ kcal} = 547 \text{ kcal of fat}$$

   STEP 4: Use dimensional analysis to determine the mass of dextrose and lipids needed.

   $$1{,}641 \text{ kcal of carbohydrates} \times \frac{\text{gram of dextrose}}{3.4 \text{ kcal of carbohydrates}} = 482.6 \text{ grams of dextrose}$$

   $$547 \text{ kcal of fat} \times \frac{\text{gram of lipids}}{10 \text{ kcal of fat}} = 54.7 \text{ g of lipids}$$

   $$54.7 \text{ kg} \times \frac{2 \text{ grams of protein}}{\text{kg}} = 109.4 \text{ g of amino acids}$$

   NOTE: The caloric density of fat from a 20% intravenous fat emulsion is 10 kcal/gram.

17. What is the protein requirement for an obese 297-pound male trauma patient who measures 5' 11" in height and is under moderate metabolic stress? Assume the protein requirement is 1.5 grams per kilogram per day since the patient is under moderate stress and base the calculation on adjusted body weight with an adjustment factor of 0.25 for excess body weight since the patient is obese.

    STEP 1: Convert the weight from units of pounds to kilograms.

    $$297 \text{ pounds} \times \frac{\text{kg}}{2.2 \text{ pounds}} = 135 \text{ kg}$$

    STEP 2: Calculate ideal body weight.

    $$\text{IBW (male)} = 50 \text{ kg} + (2.3 \text{ kg for each inch of height over 5 feet}) = 50 \text{ kg} + (2.3 \times 11) = 75.3 \text{ kg}$$

    STEP 3: Calculate adjusted body weight with an adjustment factor of 0.25 for excess body weight.

    $$\text{ABW} = \text{IBW} + [0.25 \times (\text{Actual Weight} - \text{IBW})] = 75.3 \text{ kg} + [0.25 \times (135 \text{ kg} - 75.3 \text{ kg})] = 90.2 \text{ kg}$$

    STEP 4: Multiply adjusted body weight by daily protein requirement to determine the final answer.

    $$90.2 \text{ kg} \times \frac{1.5 \text{ grams of protein}}{\text{kg}} = 135 \text{ grams of protein}$$

18. What is the daily calorie requirement for an obese female patient that is 5 ft 1 in tall, weighs 199 pounds, and is under no metabolic stress? Assume the daily calorie requirement is 25 kcal/kg per day for no stress and base the calculation on adjusted body weight with an adjustment factor of 0.25 for excess body weight since the patient is obese.

    STEP 1: Convert the weight from units of pounds to kilograms.

    $$199 \text{ pounds} \times \frac{\text{kg}}{2.2 \text{ pounds}} = 90.5 \text{ kg}$$

    STEP 2: Calculate ideal body weight.

    $$\text{IBW (female)} = 45.5 \text{ kg} + (2.3 \text{ kg for each inch of height over 5 feet}) = 45.5 \text{ kg} + (2.3 \text{ kg} \times 1) = 47.8 \text{ kg}$$

    STEP 3: Calculate adjusted body weight with an adjustment factor of 0.25 for excess body weight.

    $$\text{ABW} = \text{IBW} + [0.25 \times (\text{Actual Weight} - \text{IBW})] = 47.8 \text{ kg} + [0.25 \times (90.5 \text{ kg} - 47.8 \text{ kg})] = 58.5 \text{ kg}$$

    STEP 4: Multiply adjusted body weight by daily protein requirement to determine the final answer.

    $$58.5 \text{ kg} \times \frac{25 \text{ kilocalories}}{\text{kg}} = 1{,}460 \text{ kilocalories}$$

19. What is the daily calorie requirement based on ideal body weight (IBW) for a male patient that is 6 ft 2 in tall, weighs 206 pounds, and is under mild metabolic stress? Assume the daily calorie requirement is 30 kcal/kg per day for mild stress.

    STEP 1: Calculate ideal body weight.

    $$\text{IBW (male)} = 50 \text{ kg} + (2.3 \text{ kg for each inch of height over 5 feet}) = 50 \text{ kg} + (2.3 \text{ kg} \times 14) = 82.2 \text{ kg}$$

    STEP 2: Multiply IBW by daily calorie requirement to determine the final answer.

    $$82.2 \text{ kg} \times \frac{30 \text{ kilocalories}}{\text{kg}} = 2{,}466 \text{ kilocalories}$$

20. What is the daily calorie requirement based on actual body weight for a female patient that is 1.78 meters tall, weighs 61.4 kilograms, and is under moderate metabolic stress? Assume the daily calorie requirement is 35 kcal/kg per day for moderate stress.

    SOLUTION: Multiply actual body weight by daily calorie requirement to determine the answer.

    $$61.4 \text{ kg} \times \frac{35 \text{ kilocalories}}{\text{kg}} = 2{,}149 \text{ kilocalories}$$

21. What is the daily calorie requirement for a male patient that is 5 ft 8 in tall, weighs 187 pounds, and is under severe metabolic stress? Assume the daily calorie requirement is 40 kcal/kg per day for severe stress and base the calculation on ideal body weight if the patient is not obese or adjusted body weight with an adjustment factor of 0.25 for excess body weight if the patient is obese.

    STEP 1: Convert the weight from units of pounds to kilograms.

    $$187 \text{ pounds} \times \frac{\text{kg}}{2.2 \text{ pounds}} = 85 \text{ kg}$$

    STEP 2: Calculate ideal body weight.

    IBW (male) = 50 kg + (2.3 kg for each inch of height over 5 feet) = 50 kg + (2.3 kg x 8) = 68.4 kg

    STEP 3: Determine whether actual weight is > 30% above IBW.

    $$\frac{\text{Actual Weight} - \text{IBW}}{\text{IBW}} = \frac{85 \text{ kg} - 68.4 \text{ kg}}{68.4 \text{ kg}} = 0.243 = 24.3\%$$

    NOTE: Excess body weight does not exceed 30% of IBW; therefore, the patient is not obese.

    STEP 4: Multiply the IBW by the daily calorie requirement.

    $$68.4 \text{ kg} \times \frac{40 \text{ kilocalories}}{\text{kg}} = 2{,}736 \text{ kilocalories}$$

22. What is the daily calorie requirement for a female patient that is 5 ft 8 in tall, weighs 187 pounds, and is under moderate metabolic stress? Assume the daily calorie requirement is 35 kcal/kg per day for moderate stress and base the calculation on ideal body weight if the patient is not obese or adjusted body weight with an adjustment factor of 0.25 for excess body weight if the patient is obese.

    STEP 1: Convert the weight from units of pounds to kilograms.

    $$187 \text{ pounds} \times \frac{\text{kg}}{2.2 \text{ pounds}} = 85 \text{ kg}$$

    STEP 2: Calculate ideal body weight.

    IBW (female) = 45.5 kg + (2.3 kg for each inch of height over 5 feet) = 45.5 kg + (2.3 kg x 8) = 63.9 kg

    STEP 3: Determine whether actual weight is > 30% above IBW.

    $$\frac{\text{Actual Weight} - \text{IBW}}{\text{IBW}} = \frac{85 \text{ kg} - 63.9 \text{ kg}}{63.9 \text{ kg}} = 0.33 = 33\%$$

    NOTE: Excess body weight exceeds 30% of IBW; therefore, the patient is obese.

    STEP 4: Calculate the adjusted body weight with an adjustment factor of 0.25 for excess body weight.

    ABW = IBW + [0.25 x (Actual Weight − IBW)] = 63.9 kg + [0.25 x (85 kg − 63.9 kg)] = 69.2 kg

    STEP 5: Multiply IBW by daily protein requirement to determine the final answer.

    $$69.2 \text{ kg} \times \frac{35 \text{ kilocalories}}{\text{kg}} = 2{,}420 \text{ kilocalories}$$

23. How many grams of protein should be administered in one day to a female patient that is 5 ft tall and under severe metabolic stress? Assume the daily protein requirement is 2 g/kg per day for severe stress and base the calculation on ideal body weight (IBW).

    STEP 1: Calculate IBW.

    $$\text{IBW (female)} = 45.5 \text{ kg} + (2.3 \text{ kg for each inch of height over 5 feet}) = 45.5 \text{ kg} + (2.3 \text{ kg} \times 0) = 45.5 \text{ kg}$$

    STEP 2: Multiply the IBW by the daily protein requirement.

    $$45.5 \text{ kg} \times \frac{2 \text{ grams } of \text{ protein}}{\text{kg}} = 91 \text{ grams } of \text{ protein}$$

24. How many grams of protein should be administered in one day to a male patient that is 6 ft tall and under mild metabolic stress? Assume the daily protein requirement is 1 g/kg per day for mild stress and base the calculation on ideal body weight (IBW).

    STEP 1: Calculate IBW.

    $$\text{IBW (male)} = 50 \text{ kg} + (2.3 \text{ kg for each inch of height over 5 feet}) = 50 \text{ kg} + (2.3 \text{ kg} \times 12) = 77.6 \text{ kg}$$

    STEP 2: Multiply the IBW by the daily protein requirement.

    $$77.6 \text{ kg} \times \frac{1 \text{ grams } of \text{ protein}}{\text{kg}} = 77.6 \text{ grams } of \text{ protein}$$

25. If a 67-kilogram patient must receive 1.2 grams of protein per day, how many grams of nitrogen will the patient receive each day?

    STEP 1: Use dimensional analysis to determine the daily protein intake.

    $$67 \text{ kg} \times \frac{1.2 \text{ grams}}{\text{kg}} = 80.4 \text{ grams}$$

    STEP 2: Estimated daily nitrogen intake can be derived from the equation for nitrogen balance (NB).

    $$\text{NB} = \text{Nitrogen Intake} - \text{Nitrogen Loss} = [\text{Protein Intake (grams)}/6.25] - [\text{24-hour Urinary Urea Nitrogen (grams)} + 4 \text{ grams}]$$

    $$\therefore \text{Nitrogen Intake} = \text{Protein Intake (grams)}/6.25 = 80.4 \text{ grams}/6.25 = 12.9 \text{ grams } of \text{ nitrogen}$$

26. If a 76-kilogram female patient is 5 ft 7 in tall and has a 24-hour UUN of 12.1 grams, what is the patient's estimated daily nitrogen loss?

    SOLUTION: Derive an equation for estimated daily nitrogen loss from the equation for nitrogen balance (NB).

    $$\text{NB} = \text{Nitrogen Intake} - \text{Nitrogen Loss} = [\text{Protein Intake (grams)}/6.25] - [\text{24-hour Urinary Urea Nitrogen (grams)} + 4 \text{ grams}]$$

    $$\therefore \text{Nitrogen Loss} = \text{24-hour Urinary Urea Nitrogen (grams)} + 4 \text{ grams} = 12.1 \text{ grams} + 4 \text{ grams} = 16.1 \text{ grams } of \text{ nitrogen}$$

27. Suppose a male patient has a 24-hour urine urea nitrogen (UUN) of 15.2 grams. What is his estimated nitrogen balance (NB) if he receives 920 milliliters of Travasol® 10% (amino acid 10% solution) daily as his only protein intake source?

    STEP 1: Determine the amount of protein that is contained in his daily dose of Travasol® 10%.

    $$920 \text{ mL } of \text{ Travasol® 10% solution} \times \frac{10 \text{ grams } of \text{ protein}}{100 \text{ mL } of \text{ Travasol® 10% solution}} = 92 \text{ grams } of \text{ protein}$$

    STEP 2: Enter the values for protein intake and UUN into the equation to determine NB.

    $$\text{NB} = [\text{Protein Intake (grams)}/6.25] - [\text{24-hour UUN (grams)} + 4 \text{ grams}] = [92 \text{ grams}/6.25] - [15.2 \text{ grams} + 4 \text{ grams}]$$

    $$= -4.5 \text{ grams}$$

28. If a patient receives 122.4 grams of protein intravenously per day, how many grams of nitrogen is the patient receiving each day?

    SOLUTION: Estimated daily nitrogen intake can be derived from the equation for nitrogen balance (NB).

    NB = Nitrogen Intake − Nitrogen Loss = [Protein Intake (grams)/6.25] − [24-hour Urinary Urea Nitrogen (grams) + 4 grams]

    ∴ Nitrogen Intake = Protein Intake (grams)/6.25 = 122.4 grams/6.25 = 19.6 grams *of* nitrogen

29. If a 164-kilogram patient has a 24-hour UUN of 16.3 grams, what is the patient's estimated daily nitrogen loss?

    SOLUTION: Derive an equation for estimated daily nitrogen loss from the equation for nitrogen balance (NB).

    NB = Nitrogen Intake − Nitrogen Loss = [Protein Intake (grams)/6.25] − [24-hour Urinary Urea Nitrogen (grams) + 4 grams]

    ∴ Nitrogen Loss = 24-hour Urinary Urea Nitrogen (grams) + 4 grams = 16.3 grams + 4 grams = 20.3 grams

30. If a patient's 24-hour urine urea nitrogen (UUN) level is 11.9 grams, what is their nitrogen balance (NB), assuming they receive 100 grams of protein daily?

    SOLUTION: Enter the values for protein intake and UUN into the equation to determine NB.

    NB = [Protein Intake (grams)/6.25] − [24-hour UUN (grams) + 4 grams]

    = [100 grams/6.25] − [11.9 grams + 4 grams]

    = 0.1 grams *of* nitrogen

31. What is the estimated daily fluid requirement for a child that weighs 16 kilograms?

    SOLUTION: Estimate the fluid requirement according to the equation for patients with a bodyweight between 10–20 kg.

    Estimated daily fluid requirement = 1,000 mL + 50 mL/kg for each kg over 10 kg

    $1,000 \text{ mL} + \left[\frac{50 \text{ mL}}{\text{kg}} \times (16 \text{ kg} - 10 \text{ kg})\right] = 1,000 \text{ mL} + 300 \text{ mL} = 1,300 \text{ mL}$

32. What is the estimated daily fluid requirement for an infant that weighs 18.7 pounds?

    STEP 1: Convert the weight from units of pounds to kilograms.

    $18.7 \text{ pounds} \times \frac{\text{kg}}{2.2 \text{ pounds}} = 8.5 \text{ kg}$

    STEP 2: Estimate the fluid requirement according to the equation for patients with a bodyweight below 10 kg.

    Estimated daily fluid requirement = 100 mL/kg

    $\frac{100 \text{ mL}}{\text{kg}} \times 8.5 \text{ kg} = 850 \text{ mL}$

33. What is the estimated daily fluid requirement for a 70-year-old male that weighs 165 pounds?

    STEP 1: Convert the weight from pounds to kilograms.

    $$165 \text{ pounds} \times \frac{\text{kg}}{2.2 \text{ pounds}} = 75 \text{ kg}$$

    STEP 2: Estimate the fluid requirement according to the equation for patients with a bodyweight above 20 kg.

    $$1{,}500 \text{ mL} + 20 \text{ mL/kg for each kg over } 20 \text{ kg}$$

    $$1{,}500 \text{ mL} + \left[\frac{20 \text{ mL}}{\text{kg}} \times (75 \text{ kg} - 20 \text{ kg})\right] = 1{,}500 \text{ mL} + 1{,}100 \text{ mL} = 2{,}600 \text{ mL}$$

34. What is the estimated daily fluid requirement for a 4-month-old female that weighs 6.5 kilograms?

    SOLUTION: Estimate the fluid requirement according to the equation for patients with a bodyweight below 10 kg.

    $$\text{Estimated daily fluid requirement} = 100 \text{ mL/kg}$$

    $$\frac{100 \text{ mL}}{\text{kg}} \times 6.5 \text{ kg} = 650 \text{ mL}$$

35. What is the estimated daily fluid requirement for a male patient that weighs 42.9 pounds with a creatinine clearance of 100 mL/min?

    STEP 1: Convert the weight from pounds to kilograms.

    $$42.9 \text{ pounds} \times \frac{\text{kg}}{2.2 \text{ pounds}} = 19.5 \text{ kg}$$

    STEP 2: Estimate the fluid requirement according to the equation for patients with a bodyweight between 10–20 kg.

    $$\text{Estimated daily fluid requirement} = 1{,}000 \text{ mL} + 50 \text{ mL/kg for each kg over } 10 \text{ kg}$$

    $$1{,}000 \text{ mL} + \left[\frac{50 \text{ mL}}{\text{kg}} \times (19.5 \text{ kg} - 10 \text{ kg})\right] = 1{,}000 \text{ mL} + 475 \text{ mL} = 1{,}475 \text{ mL}$$

    NOTE: A creatinine clearance of 100 mL/min is normal. If the patient had renal failure (i.e., CrCl < 15 mL/min) or was on dialysis, then we would reduce his fluid intake. Conditions that increase the fluid requirement include diarrhea and fever; meanwhile, conditions that decrease the fluid requirement include renal failure and heart failure.

36. What is the estimated daily fluid requirement for a 20-year-old female that weighs 105.6 pounds?

    STEP 1: Convert the weight from pounds to kilograms.

    $$105.6 \text{ pounds} \times \frac{\text{kg}}{2.2 \text{ pounds}} = 48 \text{ kg}$$

    STEP 2: Estimate the fluid requirement according to the equation for patients with a bodyweight above 20 kg.

    $$1{,}500 \text{ mL} + 20 \text{ mL/kg for each kg over } 20 \text{ kg}$$

    $$1{,}500 \text{ mL} + \left[\frac{20 \text{ mL}}{\text{kg}} \times (48 \text{ kg} - 20 \text{ kg})\right] = 1{,}500 \text{ mL} + 560 \text{ mL} = 2{,}060 \text{ mL}$$

37. What is the estimated daily fluid requirement for a 34-year-old male that weighs 78 kilograms?

    SOLUTION: Estimate the fluid requirement according to the equation for patients with a bodyweight above 20 kg.

    $$1,500 \text{ mL} + 20 \text{ mL/kg for each kg over 20 kg}$$

    $$1,500 \text{ mL} + \left[\frac{20 \text{ mL}}{\text{kg}} \times (78 \text{ kg} - 20 \text{ kg})\right] = 1,500 \text{ mL} + 1,160 \text{ mL} = 2,660 \text{ mL}$$

38. What is the estimated daily fluid requirement for a 48-year-old male that weighs 209 pounds?

    STEP 1: Convert the weight from pounds to kilograms.

    $$209 \text{ pounds} \times \frac{\text{kg}}{2.2 \text{ pounds}} = 95 \text{ kg}$$

    STEP 2: Estimate the fluid requirement according to the equation for patients with a bodyweight that exceeds 20 kg.

    $$1,500 \text{ mL} + 20 \text{ mL/kg for each kg over 20 kg}$$

    $$1,500 \text{ mL} + \left[\frac{20 \text{ mL}}{\text{kg}} \times (95 \text{ kg} - 20 \text{ kg})\right] = 1,500 \text{ mL} + 1,500 \text{ mL} = 3,000 \text{ mL}$$

REFERENCES
1. Holliday MG, Segar WE. The maintenance need for water in parenteral fluid therapy. Pediatrics. 1957; 19:823–832.

INFUSION FLOW RATE/DRIP RATE

STANDARD UNITS *for* FLOW RATE
mL/min (or mL/hr)

STANDARD UNITS *for* DRIP RATE
drops/min

Rather than using an equation, we can solve these problems via dimensional analysis.

NOTE: Flow rate and drip rate are proportional, as both values quantify the rate of infusion.

1. If a 500-milliliter infusion solution contains two grams of the active ingredient, what should the flow rate be in milliliters per minute for the patient to receive 200 mg of the active ingredient per hour?

2. If the infusion rate is 0.83 milliliters per minute and the infusion administration set delivers 60 drops per milliliter, what is the drip rate?

3. An infusion bag that contains 250 milliliters of heparin 100 unit/milliliter solution is delivered to a patient's bedside with instructions to administer 15,000 units per hour. If the infusion administration set delivers 20 drops per milliliter, then what is the correct drip rate?

4. A 250-milliliter infusion contains 25 units of vasopressin. If the patient must receive 30 milliunits of vasopressin per minute and the administration set delivers 20 drops per milliliter, what is the correct drip rate?

5. Milrinone is dosed at 0.33 mcg/kg/min for a particular 222.2-pound patient. Meanwhile, the infusion bag contains milrinone 40 milligrams in 200 milliliters of dextrose 5% in water, and the bag is attached to a microdrip infusion administration set (delivers 60 drops per milliliter). What is the correct drip rate for this patient?

6. If a 250-milliliter bag that contains one gram of vancomycin in normal saline solution must be infused over one hour using a microdrip infusion administration set (delivers 60 drops per milliliter), then what is the correct drip rate?

7. An infusion administration set that delivers 30 drops per milliliter is used to infuse a 160-milliliter bag of magnesium sulfate solution over 120 minutes. What was the correct drip rate?

8. A 176-pound patient must receive 10 mcg/kg/hr of a medication supplied as a premixed 100-microgram per milliliter infusion. What is the correct drip rate if the solution is administered with a microdrip infusion administration set?

9. JH must receive a one-liter infusion over 24 hours. If the administration set delivers 19 drops/mL, then what is the correct drip rate?

10. Four milliliters of a 1:10,000 stock solution of medication is diluted to a final volume of 300 milliliters, and the patient must receive 4 micrograms of the medication per minute. What is the correct flow rate?

11. One vial of Keppra® (levetiracetam) 500 milligram/5 milliliters is added to 100 milliliters of diluent and infused over 15 minutes. What is the flow rate?

12. A medication is flowing through an infusion administration set at the rate of 15 drops per minute, and the administration set delivers 10 drops per milliliter. What is the flow rate in milliliters per hour?

13. An infusion solution is flowing through an administration set at the rate of 150 milliliters per hour, and 50 drops enter the administration set every 60 seconds. How many drops per milliliter is the administration set producing?

14. If a 200-milliliter infusion solution contains 5,000 micrograms of the active ingredient, what flow rate ensures the patient will receive 20 micrograms of medication per minute?

SOLUTIONS for FLOW RATE/DRIP RATE PROBLEMS

1. If a 500-milliliter infusion solution contains two grams of the active ingredient, what should the flow rate be in milliliters per minute for the patient to receive 200 mg of the active ingredient per hour?

    STEP 1: Determine the concentration of the active ingredient in terms of milligrams per milliliter.

    $$\frac{2 \text{ grams}}{500 \text{ mL}} \times \frac{1{,}000 \text{ mg}}{\text{gram}} = 4 \text{ mg/mL}$$

    STEP 2: Use the answer from STEP 1 to convert the administration rate from milligrams per hour to milliliters per minute.

    $$\frac{200 \text{ mg}}{\text{hr}} \times \frac{\text{mL}}{4 \text{ mg}} \times \frac{\text{hr}}{60 \text{ min}} = 0.83 \text{ mL/min}$$

2. If the infusion rate is 0.83 milliliters per minute and the infusion administration set delivers 60 drops per milliliter, what is the drip rate?

    SOLUTION: Determine the drip rate using dimensional analysis.

    $$\frac{0.83 \text{ mL}}{\text{min}} \times \frac{60 \text{ drops}}{\text{mL}} = 50 \text{ drops/min}$$

    NOTE: Infusion administration sets are typically calibrated to deliver 10-60 drops per milliliter. The most commonly employed administration sets deliver 10 gtts/mL, 15 gtts/mL, or 60 gtts/mL.

3. An infusion bag that contains 250 milliliters of heparin 100 unit/milliliter solution is delivered to a patient's bedside with instructions to administer 15,000 units per hour. If the infusion administration set delivers 20 drops per milliliter, then what is the correct drip rate?

    SOLUTION: Determine the drip rate using dimensional analysis.

    $$\frac{15{,}000 \text{ units}}{\text{hr}} \times \frac{\text{mL}}{100 \text{ units}} \times \frac{20 \text{ drops}}{\text{mL}} \times \frac{\text{hr}}{60 \text{ min}} = 50 \text{ drops/min}$$

4. A 250-milliliter infusion contains 25 units of vasopressin. If the patient must receive 30 milliunits of vasopressin per minute and the administration set delivers 20 drops per milliliter, what is the correct drip rate?

    SOLUTION: Determine the drip rate using dimensional analysis.

    $$\frac{30 \text{ milliunits}}{\text{min}} \times \frac{\text{unit}}{1{,}000 \text{ milliunits}} \times \frac{250 \text{ mL}}{25 \text{ units}} \times \frac{20 \text{ drops}}{\text{mL}} = 6 \text{ drops/min}$$

5. Milrinone is dosed at 0.33 mcg/kg/min for a particular 222.2-pound patient. Meanwhile, the infusion bag contains milrinone 40 milligrams in 200 milliliters of dextrose 5% in water, and the bag is attached to a microdrip infusion administration set (delivers 60 drops per milliliter). What is the correct drip rate for this patient?

    STEP 1: Convert the patient's weight from pounds to kilograms.

    $$222.2 \text{ pounds} \times \frac{\text{kg}}{2.2 \text{ pounds}} = 101 \text{ kg}$$

    STEP 2: Determine the drip rate using dimensional analysis.

    $$101 \text{ kg} \times \frac{0.33 \text{ mcg}}{\text{kg} \times \text{min}} \times \frac{1 \text{ mg}}{1{,}000 \text{ mcg}} \times \frac{200 \text{ mL}}{40 \text{ mg}} \times \frac{60 \text{ drops}}{\text{mL}} = 9.999 \text{ drops/min} \therefore 10 \text{ drops/min}$$

6. If a 250-milliliter bag that contains one gram of vancomycin in normal saline solution must be infused over one hour using a microdrip infusion administration set (delivers 60 drops per milliliter), then what is the correct drip rate?

    SOLUTION: Determine the drip rate using dimensional analysis.

    $$\frac{250 \text{ mL}}{\text{hr}} \times \frac{60 \text{ drops}}{\text{mL}} \times \frac{\text{hr}}{60 \text{ min}} = 250 \text{ drops/min}$$

7. An infusion administration set that delivers 30 drops per milliliter is used to infuse a 160-milliliter bag of magnesium sulfate solution over 120 minutes. What was the correct drip rate?

    SOLUTION: Determine the drip rate using dimensional analysis.

    $$\frac{30 \text{ drops}}{\text{mL}} \times \frac{160 \text{ mL}}{120 \text{ min}} = 40 \text{ drops/min}$$

    NOTE: The rate of administration was given in the question (160 mL infused over 120 minutes).

8. A 176-pound patient must receive 10 mcg/kg/hr of a medication supplied as a premixed 100-microgram per milliliter infusion. What is the correct drip rate if the solution is administered with a microdrip infusion administration set?

    STEP 1: Convert the patient's weight from pounds to kilograms.

    $$176 \text{ pounds} \times \frac{\text{kg}}{2.2 \text{ pounds}} = 80 \text{ kg}$$

    STEP 2: Determine the drip rate using dimensional analysis.

    $$80 \text{ kg} \times \frac{10 \text{ mcg}}{\text{kg} \times \text{hr}} \times \frac{\text{mL}}{100 \text{ mcg}} \times \frac{60 \text{ drops}}{\text{mL}} \times \frac{\text{hr}}{60 \text{ min}} = 8 \text{ drops/min}$$

    REMEMBER: Microdrip infusion administration sets deliver 60 drops per milliliter.

9. JH must receive a one-liter infusion over 24 hours. If the administration set delivers 19 drops/mL, then what is the correct drip rate?

    SOLUTION: Determine the drip rate using dimensional analysis.

    $$\frac{1 \text{ liter}}{24 \text{ hr}} \times \frac{1{,}000 \text{ mL}}{\text{liter}} \times \frac{\text{hr}}{60 \text{ min}} \times \frac{19 \text{ drops}}{\text{mL}} = 13.2 \text{ drops/min} \therefore 13 \text{ drops/min}$$

10. Four milliliters of a 1:10,000 stock solution of medication is diluted to a final volume of 300 milliliters, and the patient must receive 4 micrograms of the medication per minute. What is the correct flow rate?

    STEP 1: Determine the mass of medication using dimensional analysis.

    $$\frac{1 \text{ g } of \text{ medication}}{10{,}000 \text{ mL } of \text{ stock solution}} \times \frac{1{,}000{,}000 \text{ mcg}}{\text{g}} \times 4 \text{ mL } of \text{ stock solution} = 400 \text{ mcg } of \text{ medication}$$

    STEP 2: Determine the flow rate using dimensional analysis.

    $$\frac{4 \text{ mcg } of \text{ medication}}{\text{min}} \times \frac{300 \text{ mL } of \text{ infusion solution}}{400 \text{ mcg } of \text{ medication}} = 3 \text{ mL/min}$$

11. One vial of Keppra® (levetiracetam) 500 milligram/5 milliliters is added to 100 milliliters of diluent and infused over 15 minutes. What is the flow rate?

    SOLUTION: Divide the total volume of the infusion by the administration time to determine the flow rate.

    $$\frac{105 \text{ mL}}{15 \text{ min}} = 7 \text{ mL/min}$$

NOTE: Read the question carefully. Unlike the previous problem where the final volume was 300 milliliters, this question states that we are adding 5 milliliters of the active ingredient to 100 milliliters of diluent, which would yield a final volume of 105 milliliters.

12. A medication is flowing through an infusion administration set at the rate of 15 drops per minute, and the administration set delivers 10 drops per milliliter. What is the flow rate in milliliters per hour?

    SOLUTION: Determine the flow rate in terms of milliliters per hour using dimensional analysis.

    $$\frac{15 \text{ drops}}{\text{min}} \times \frac{\text{mL}}{10 \text{ drops}} \times \frac{60 \text{ min}}{\text{hr}} = 90 \text{ mL/hr}$$

13. An infusion solution is flowing through an administration set at the rate of 150 milliliters per hour, and 50 drops enter the administration set every 60 seconds. How many drops per milliliter is the administration set producing?

    SOLUTION: Determine the number of drops per milliliter delivered by the administration set using dimensional analysis.

    $$\frac{50 \text{ drops}}{60 \text{ seconds}} \times \frac{3{,}600 \text{ seconds}}{\text{hr}} \times \frac{\text{hr}}{150 \text{ mL}} = 20 \text{ drops/mL}$$

14. If a 200-milliliter infusion solution contains 5,000 micrograms of the active ingredient, what flow rate ensures the patient will receive 20 micrograms of medication per minute?

    SOLUTION: Determine the flow rate using dimensional analysis.

    $$\frac{20 \text{ mcg}}{\text{min}} \times \frac{200 \text{ mL}}{5{,}000 \text{ mcg}} = 0.8 \text{ mL/min}$$

DISSOCIATION FACTOR (*i*)

DISSOCIATION FACTOR (*i*)

The dissociation factor is the decimal fraction of the number of particles after dissociation versus the number of particles before dissociation.

$$i = \frac{\text{\# of particles after dissociation}}{\text{\# of particles before dissociation}}$$

NOTE: The term "particle" in this context includes ions and molecules.

ESTIMATE *of* DISSOCIATION FACTOR (*i*)

Nonelectrolyte	1.0
Two ions	1.8
Three ions	2.6
Four ions	3.4
Five ions	4.2

NOTE: All of the above dissociation factor estimates assume 80% dissociation for electrolytes. It is safe to assume 80% dissociation unless the problem specifies otherwise.

---

1. What is the dissociation factor (*i*) of sodium bicarbonate ($NaHCO_3$) if 80% of the compound dissociates in solution?

2. What is the dissociation factor (*i*) of sodium carbonate ($Na_2(CO_3^{2-})$) if 80% of the compound dissociates in solution?

3. What is the dissociation factor (*i*) of sodium citrate dihydrate ($Na_3(C_6H_5O_7) \bullet 2H_2O$) if 80% of the compound dissociates in solution?

4. What is the dissociation factor (*i*) of dextrose ($C_6H_{12}O_6$) if none of the compound dissociates in solution?

5. What is the dissociation factor (*i*) of a mystery compound composed of five ions if 30% of the compound dissociates in solution?

SOLUTIONS for DISSOCIATION FACTOR PROBLEMS

1. What is the dissociation factor (*i*) of sodium bicarbonate ($NaHCO_3$) if 80% of the compound dissociates in solution?

    STEP 1: Account for all of the particles present after 80% dissociation of 100 molecules of solute.

    $$80 \text{ Na+ ions} + 80 \text{ HCO}_3^- \text{ ions} + 20 \text{ NaHCO}_3 \text{ molecules} = 180 \text{ particles}$$

    STEP 2: Enter values into the equation to determine the dissociation factor.

    $$i = \frac{\text{\# of particles after dissociation}}{\text{\# of particles before dissociation}} = \frac{180 \text{ particles}}{100 \text{ particles}} = 1.8$$

2. What is the dissociation factor (*i*) of sodium carbonate ($Na_2(CO_3^{2-})$) if 80% of the compound dissociates in solution?

    STEP 1: Account for all of the particles present after 80% dissociation of 100 molecules of solute.

    $$80 \text{ Na}^+ \text{ ions} + 80 \text{ Na}^+ \text{ ions} + 80 \text{ CO}_3^{2-} \text{ ions} + 20 \text{ Na}_2\text{CO}_3 \text{ molecules} = 260 \text{ particles}$$

    STEP 2: Enter the values into the equation to determine the dissociation factor.

    $$i = \frac{\text{\# of particles after dissociation}}{\text{\# of particles before dissociation}} = \frac{260 \text{ particles}}{100 \text{ particles}} = 2.6$$

3. What is the dissociation factor (*i*) of sodium citrate dihydrate ($Na_3(C_6H_5O_7) \cdot 2H_2O$) if 80% of the compound dissociates in solution?

    STEP 1: Account for all of the particles present after 80% dissociation of 100 molecules of solute.

    $$80 \text{ Na}^+ \text{ ions} + 80 \text{ Na}^+ \text{ ions} + 80 \text{ Na}^+ \text{ ions} + 80 \text{ C}_6\text{H}_5\text{O}_7^{3-} \text{ ions} + 20 \text{ Na}_3(\text{C}_6\text{H}_5\text{O}_7) \text{ molecules} = 340 \text{ particles}$$

    STEP 2: Enter values into the equation to determine the dissociation factor.

    $$i = \frac{\text{\# of particles after dissociation}}{\text{\# of particles before dissociation}} = \frac{340 \text{ particles}}{100 \text{ particles}} = 3.4$$

4. What is the dissociation factor (*i*) of dextrose ($C_6H_{12}O_6$) if none of the compound dissociates in solution?

    STEP 1: Account for all of the particles present after 80% dissociation of 100 molecules of solute.

    $$100 \text{ C}_6\text{H}_{12}\text{O}_6 \text{ molecules} = 100 \text{ particles}$$

    STEP 2: Enter values into the equation to determine the dissociation factor.

    $$i = \frac{\text{\# of particles after dissociation}}{\text{\# of particles before dissociation}} = \frac{100 \text{ particles}}{100 \text{ particles}} = 1.0$$

5. What is the dissociation factor (*i*) of a mystery compound composed of five ions if 30% of the compound dissociates in solution?

    STEP 1: Account for all of the particles present after 80% dissociation of 100 molecules of solute.

    $$30 \text{ ion \#1} + 30 \text{ ion \#2} + 30 \text{ ion \#3} + 30 \text{ ion \#4} + 30 \text{ ion \#5} + 70 \text{ undissociated molecules} = 220 \text{ particles}$$

    STEP 2: Enter the values into the equation to determine the dissociation factor.

    $$i = \frac{\text{\# of particles after dissociation}}{\text{\# of particles before dissociation}} = \frac{220 \text{ particles}}{100 \text{ particles}} = 2.2$$

SODIUM CHLORIDE EQUIVALENTS (E VALUES)

EQUATION for the SODIUM CHLORIDE EQUIVALENT MASS of A SUBSTANCE

equivalent mass *of* NaCl = mass *of* substance x E value *of* substance

EQUATION for the E VALUE of A SUBSTANCE

$$\text{E value of substance} = \frac{(58.5) \times (i \text{ of substance})}{(1.8) \times (\text{molecular weight of substance})}$$

NOTE: The factors 58.5 and 1.8 represent the molecular weight and the dissociation factor of sodium chloride, respectively.

MUST-KNOW FACTORS for SODIUM CHLORIDE
Isotonic Concentration: 0.9 grams/100 mL
Molecular Weight: 58.5 grams/mole
Dissociation Factor: 1.8

---

1. A 250-milliliter solution contains 1 gram of hydrous dextrose in water. If hydrous dextrose has an E value of 0.16, how many grams of sodium chloride must be added to make the solution isotonic?

2. A 5-milliliter ophthalmic solution contains 15 milligrams of tobramycin in sterile water. If tobramycin has an E value of 0.07, then how many milligrams of sodium chloride must be added to make the solution isotonic?

3. If sodium bicarbonate has an E value of 0.65, then how much sodium chloride must be added to a 1,000-milliliter solution of 1.26% (w/v) sodium bicarbonate to make it isotonic?

4. If procaine HCl has an E value of 0.21 and chlorobutanol has an E value of 0.24, then how much sodium chloride must be added to 500 milliliters of a solution that contains 2% (w/v) procaine HCl and 1 gram of chlorobutanol?

5. If phenylephrine HCl has an E value of 0.32, then how much sodium chloride must be added to 30 milliliters of a 1% (w/v) phenylephrine HCl nasal solution to make it isotonic?

6. If boric acid has an E value of 0.52, then how many grams of boric acid should be added to 2,000 milliliters of 0.45% (w/v) sodium chloride solution to make it isotonic?

7. If antipyrine has an E value of 0.17, boric acid has an E value of 0.52, and glycerin has an E value of 0.34, then how many milliliters of glycerin must be included to make an isotonic otic solution with a final volume of 10 milliliters that contains 54 milligrams of antipyrine and 100 milligrams of boric acid? Note: The density of glycerin is 1.26 grams/milliliter. Assume that once these three ingredients are combined, the final volume of the formulation will be adjusted as needed using sterile water.

8. If cromolyn sodium has an E value of 0.11 and benzalkonium chloride has an E value of 0.16, then how many milligrams of sodium chloride must be added to 10 milliliters of a 4% (w/v) cromolyn sodium/0.01% (w/v) benzalkonium chloride ophthalmic solution?

9. Timolol maleate has a molecular weight of 432 grams/mole and a dissociation factor of 1.8. What is the E value for timolol maleate?

10. Suppose calcium gluconate ($Ca(C_6H_{11}O_7)_2$), a compound composed of three ions, has a molecular weight of 430 grams/mole and an unknown dissociation factor. Given this information, what is the E value for calcium gluconate?

11. If phenobarbital sodium, a compound composed of two ions, has a molecular weight of 254 grams/mole and an unknown dissociation factor, what is the E value?

12. If hydrous dextrose, a nonelectrolyte, has an unknown dissociation factor and a molecular weight of 198.17 grams/mole, what is the E value for hydrous dextrose?

SOLUTIONS *for* E VALUE PROBLEMS

1. A 250-milliliter solution contains 1 gram of hydrous dextrose in water. If hydrous dextrose has an E value of 0.16, how many grams of sodium chloride must be added to make the solution isotonic?

   STEP 1: Calculate the mass of NaCl that would be present in an equal volume of normal saline solution.

   $$\frac{0.9 \text{ grams } of \text{ NaCl}}{100 \text{ mL } of \text{ solution}} \times 250 \text{ mL } of \text{ solution} = 2.25 \text{ grams } of \text{ NaCl}$$

   STEP 2: Apply the equation to determine the equivalent mass of NaCl for the substance.

   equivalent mass *of* NaCl = mass *of* substance x E value *of* substance = 1 gram *of* hydrous dextrose x 0.16 = 0.16 grams *of* NaCl

   STEP 3: Subtract the equivalent mass of NaCl (STEP 2) from the mass of NaCl required for isotonicity (STEP 1).

   2.25 grams *of* NaCl – 0.16 grams *of* NaCl = 2.09 grams *of* NaCl

2. A 5-milliliter ophthalmic solution contains 15 milligrams of tobramycin in sterile water. If tobramycin has an E value of 0.07, then how many milligrams of sodium chloride must be added to make the solution isotonic?

   STEP 1: Calculate the mass of NaCl that would be present in an equal volume of normal saline solution.

   $$\frac{0.9 \text{ grams } of \text{ NaCl}}{100 \text{ mL } of \text{ solution}} \times 5 \text{ mL } of \text{ solution} = 0.045 \text{ grams } of \text{ NaCl}$$

   STEP 2: Convert mass from grams to milligrams

   $$0.045 \text{ g } of \text{ NaCl} \times \frac{1{,}000 \text{ mg}}{\text{g}} = 45 \text{ mg } of \text{ NaCl}$$

   STEP 3: Apply the equation to determine the equivalent mass of NaCl for the substance.

   equivalent mass *of* NaCl = mass *of* substance x E value *of* substance = 15 milligrams *of* tobramycin x 0.07 = 1.05 milligrams *of* NaCl

   STEP 4: Subtract the equivalent mass of NaCl (STEP 3) from the mass of NaCl required for isotonicity (STEP 2).

   45 milligrams *of* NaCl – 1.05 milligrams *of* NaCl = 43.95 milligrams *of* NaCl

3. If sodium bicarbonate has an E value of 0.65, then how much sodium chloride must be added to a 1,000-milliliter solution of 1.26% (w/v) sodium bicarbonate to make it isotonic?

   STEP 1: Calculate the mass of NaCl that would be present in an equal volume of normal saline solution.

   $$\frac{0.9 \text{ grams } of \text{ NaCl}}{100 \text{ mL } of \text{ solution}} \times 1{,}000 \text{ mL } of \text{ solution} = 9 \text{ grams } of \text{ NaCl}$$

   STEP 2: Determine the mass of the substance present in the solution.

   $$\frac{1.26 \text{ grams } of \text{ sodium bicarbonate}}{100 \text{ mL } of \text{ solution}} \times 1{,}000 \text{ mL } of \text{ solution} = 12.6 \text{ grams } of \text{ sodium bicarbonate}$$

   STEP 3: Apply the equation to determine the equivalent mass of NaCl for the substance.

   equivalent mass *of* NaCl = mass *of* substance x E value *of* substance = 12.6 grams *of* sodium bicarbonate x 0.65 = 8.19 grams *of* NaCl

   STEP 4: Subtract the equivalent mass of NaCl (STEP 2) from the mass of NaCl required for isotonicity (STEP 1).

   9 grams *of* NaCl – 8.19 grams *of* NaCl = 0.81 grams *of* NaCl

4. If procaine HCl has an E value of 0.21 and chlorobutanol has an E value of 0.24, then how much sodium chloride must be added to 500 milliliters of a solution that contains 2% (w/v) procaine HCl and 1 gram of chlorobutanol?

   STEP 1: Calculate the mass of NaCl that would be present in an equal volume of normal saline solution.

   $$\frac{0.9 \text{ grams } of \text{ NaCl}}{100 \text{ mL } of \text{ solution}} \times 500 \text{ mL } of \text{ solution} = 4.5 \text{ grams } of \text{ NaCl}$$

   STEP 2: Determine the mass of each substance present in the solution.

   $$\frac{2 \text{ grams } of \text{ procaine HCl}}{100 \text{ mL } of \text{ solution}} \times 500 \text{ mL } of \text{ solution} = 10 \text{ grams } of \text{ procaine HCl}$$

   NOTE: The mass of chlorobutanol present in the solution is 1 gram (given in the question).

   STEP 3: Apply the equation to determine the equivalent mass of NaCl for each substance.

   equivalent mass *of* NaCl = mass *of* substance x E value *of* substance = 10 grams *of* procaine HCl x 0.21 = 2.1 grams *of* NaCl

   equivalent mass *of* NaCl = mass *of* substance x E value *of* substance = 1 gram *of* chlorobutanol x 0.24 = 0.24 grams *of* NaCl

   Total equivalent mass *of* NaCl = 2.1 grams + 0.24 grams = 2.34 grams

   STEP 4: Subtract the solute's equivalent mass of NaCl (STEP 3) from the mass of NaCl required for isotonicity (STEP 1).

   4.5 grams *of* NaCl – 2.34 grams *of* NaCl = 2.16 grams *of* NaCl

5. If phenylephrine HCl has an E value of 0.32, then how much sodium chloride must be added to 30 milliliters of a 1% (w/v) phenylephrine HCl nasal solution to make it isotonic?

   STEP 1: Calculate the mass of NaCl that would be present in an equal volume of normal saline solution.

   $$\frac{0.9 \text{ grams } of \text{ NaCl}}{100 \text{ mL } of \text{ solution}} \times 30 \text{ mL } of \text{ solution} = 0.27 \text{ grams } of \text{ NaCl}$$

   STEP 2: Determine the mass of substance present in the solution.

   $$\frac{1 \text{ gram } of \text{ phenylephrine HCl}}{100 \text{ mL } of \text{ solution}} \times 30 \text{ mL } of \text{ solution} = 0.3 \text{ grams } of \text{ phenylephrine HCl}$$

   STEP 3: Apply the equation to determine the equivalent mass of NaCl represented by the substance.

   equivalent mass *of* NaCl = mass *of* substance x E value *of* substance = 0.3 grams *of* phenylephrine HCl x 0.32 = 0.096 grams *of* NaCl

   STEP 4: Subtract the solute's equivalent mass of NaCl (STEP 3) from the mass of NaCl required for isotonicity (STEP 1).

   0.27 grams *of* NaCl – 0.096 grams *of* NaCl = 0.174 grams *of* NaCl

6. If boric acid has an E value of 0.52, then how many grams of boric acid should be added to 2,000 milliliters of 0.45% (w/v) sodium chloride solution to make it isotonic?

    STEP 1: Calculate the mass of NaCl that would be present in an equal volume of normal saline solution.

    $$\frac{0.9 \text{ grams of NaCl}}{100 \text{ mL of solution}} \times 2{,}000 \text{ mL of solution} = 18 \text{ grams of NaCl}$$

    STEP 2: Determine the mass of substance present in the solution.

    $$\frac{0.45 \text{ gram of NaCl}}{100 \text{ mL of solution}} \times 2{,}000 \text{ mL of solution} = 9 \text{ grams of NaCl}$$

    STEP 3: Subtract the mass of NaCl already present (STEP 2) from the mass of NaCl required for isotonicity (STEP 1).

    $$18 \text{ grams of NaCl} - 9 \text{ grams of NaCl} = 9 \text{ grams of NaCl}$$

    STEP 4: Rearrange the equation for the equivalent mass of NaCl to determine the mass of substance needed.

    $$\text{equivalent mass of NaCl} = \text{mass of substance} \times \text{E value of substance}$$

    $$\therefore \text{mass of substance} = \frac{\text{equivalent mass of NaCl}}{\text{E value of substance}} = \frac{9 \text{ grams of NaCl}}{0.52} = 17.3 \text{ grams of boric acid}$$

7. If antipyrine has an E value of 0.17, boric acid has an E value of 0.52, and glycerin has an E value of 0.34, then how many milliliters of glycerin must be included to make an isotonic otic solution with a final volume of 10 milliliters that contains 54 milligrams of antipyrine and 100 milligrams of boric acid? Note: The density of glycerin is 1.26 grams/milliliter. Assume that once these three ingredients are combined, the final volume of the formulation will be adjusted as needed using sterile water.

    STEP 1: Calculate the mass of NaCl that would be present in an equal volume of normal saline solution.

    $$\frac{0.9 \text{ grams of NaCl}}{100 \text{ mL of solution}} \times 10 \text{ mL of solution} = 0.09 \text{ grams of NaCl}$$

    STEP 2: Apply the equation to determine the equivalent mass of NaCl represented by each substance.

    $$\text{equivalent mass of NaCl} = \text{mass of substance} \times \text{E value of substance} = 0.054 \text{ g of antipyrine} \times 0.17 = 0.0092 \text{ g of NaCl}$$

    $$\text{equivalent mass of NaCl} = \text{mass of substance} \times \text{E value of substance} = 0.1 \text{ g of boric acid} \times 0.52 = 0.052 \text{ g of NaCl}$$

    $$\text{Total equivalent mass of NaCl} = 0.0092 \text{ g} + 0.052 \text{ g} = 0.0612 \text{ g}$$

    STEP 3: Subtract the solute's equivalent mass of NaCl (STEP 2) from the mass of NaCl required for isotonicity (STEP 1).

    $$0.09 \text{ g of NaCl} - 0.0612 \text{ g of NaCl} = 0.0288 \text{ g of NaCl}$$

    STEP 4: Rearrange the equation for the equivalent mass of NaCl to determine the mass of substance needed.

    $$\text{equivalent mass of NaCl} = \text{mass of substance} \times \text{E value of substance}$$

    $$\therefore \text{mass of substance} = \frac{\text{equivalent mass of NaCl}}{\text{E value of substance}} = \frac{0.0288 \text{ g of NaCl}}{0.34} = 0.0847 \text{ g of glycerin}$$

    STEP 5: Divide the mass of glycerin needed (STEP 4) by the density of glycerin to determine the volume needed.

    $$0.0847 \text{ g of glycerin} \times \frac{\text{mL}}{1.26 \text{ g}} = 0.0672 \text{ mL of glycerin}$$

8. If cromolyn sodium has an E value of 0.11 and benzalkonium chloride has an E value of 0.16, then how many milligrams of sodium chloride must be added to 10 milliliters of a 4% (w/v) cromolyn sodium/0.01% (w/v) benzalkonium chloride ophthalmic solution?

   STEP 1: Calculate the mass of NaCl that would be present in an equal volume of normal saline solution.

   $$\frac{0.9 \text{ grams of NaCl}}{100 \text{ mL of solution}} \times 10 \text{ mL of solution} = 0.09 \text{ grams of NaCl}$$

   NOTE: The question asks for an answer in milligrams.

   STEP 2: Convert mass from grams to milligrams

   $$0.09 \text{ g of NaCl} \times \frac{1{,}000 \text{ mg}}{\text{g}} = 90 \text{ mg of NaCl}$$

   STEP 3: Determine the mass (in milligrams) of each substance present in the solution.

   $$\frac{4 \text{ g of cromolyn sodium}}{100 \text{ mL of solution}} \times \frac{1{,}000 \text{ mg}}{\text{g}} \times 10 \text{ mL of solution} = 400 \text{ mg of cromolyn sodium}$$

   $$\frac{0.01 \text{ g of benzalkonium chloride}}{100 \text{ mL of solution}} \times \frac{1{,}000 \text{ mg}}{\text{g}} \times 10 \text{ mL of solution} = 1 \text{ mg of benzalkonium chloride}$$

   STEP 4: Apply the equation to determine the equivalent mass of NaCl represented by each substance.

   equivalent mass of NaCl = mass of substance x E value of substance = 400 mg of cromolyn sodium x 0.11 = 44 mg of NaCl

   equivalent mass of NaCl = mass of substance x E value of substance = 1 mg of benzalkonium chloride x 0.16 = 0.16 mg of NaCl

   Total equivalent mass of NaCl = 44 mg + 0.16 mg = 44.16 mg

   STEP 5: Subtract the equivalent mass of NaCl (STEP 4) from the mass of NaCl required for isotonicity (STEP 2).

   90 mg of NaCl – 44.16 mg of NaCl = 45.84 mg of NaCl

9. Timolol maleate has a molecular weight of 432 grams/mole and a dissociation factor of 1.8. What is the E value for timolol maleate?

   SOLUTION: Apply the equation to calculate the E value of a substance.

   $$\text{E value of substance} = \frac{(58.5) \times (i \text{ of substance})}{(1.8) \times (\text{molecular weight of substance})} = \frac{(58.5) \times (1.8)}{(1.8) \times (432)} = 0.14$$

10. Suppose calcium gluconate $(Ca(C_6H_{11}O_7)_2)$, a compound composed of three ions, has a molecular weight of 430 grams/mole and an unknown dissociation factor. Given this information, what is the E value for calcium gluconate?

    STEP 1: Estimate the dissociation factor (i) (see page 133).

ESTIMATE of DISSOCIATION FACTOR (i)	
Nonelectrolyte	1.0
Two ions	1.8
Three ions	2.6
Four ions	3.4
Five ions	4.2

    STEP 2: Apply the equation to calculate the E value of a substance.

    $$\text{E value of substance} = \frac{(58.5) \times (i \text{ of substance})}{(1.8) \times (\text{molecular weight of substance})} = \frac{(58.5) \times (2.6)}{(1.8) \times (430)} = 0.20$$

11. If phenobarbital sodium, a compound composed of two ions, has a molecular weight of 254 grams/mole and an unknown dissociation factor, what is the E value?

    STEP 1: Estimate the dissociation factor (i) (see page 133).

ESTIMATE *of* DISSOCIATION FACTOR (i)	
Nonelectrolyte	1.0
Two ions	1.8
Three ions	2.6
Four ions	3.4
Five ions	4.2

    STEP 2: Apply the equation to calculate the E value of a substance.

    $$\text{E value } of \text{ substance} = \frac{(58.5) \times (i \text{ } of \text{ substance})}{(1.8) \times (\text{molecular weight } of \text{ substance})} = \frac{(58.5) \times (1.8)}{(1.8) \times (254)} = 0.23$$

12. If hydrous dextrose, a nonelectrolyte, has an unknown dissociation factor and a molecular weight of 198.17 grams/mole, what is the E value for hydrous dextrose?

    STEP 1: Estimate the dissociation factor (i) (see page 133).

ESTIMATE *of* DISSOCIATION FACTOR (i)	
Nonelectrolyte	1.0
Two ions	1.8
Three ions	2.6
Four ions	3.4
Five ions	4.2

    STEP 2: Apply the equation to calculate the E value of a substance.

    $$\text{E value } of \text{ substance} = \frac{(58.5) \times (i \text{ } of \text{ substance})}{(1.8) \times (\text{molecular weight } of \text{ substance})} = \frac{(58.5) \times (1.0)}{(1.8) \times (198.17)} = 0.16$$

TEMPERATURE CONVERSION

FAHRENHEIT TO CELSIUS

$$°C = \frac{5}{9}(°F - 32)$$

CELSIUS TO FAHRENHEIT

$$°F = \left(\frac{9}{5} \times °C\right) + 32$$

TEMPERATURES TO MEMORIZE
Freezing Point of Water: 0°C = 32°F
Human Body Temperature: 37°C = 98.6°F
Boiling Point of Water: 100°C = 212°F

CONSTRUCTING THE TEMPERATURE CONVERSION EQUATION *from* SCRATCH

It is smart to memorize key temperature reference points. For instance, 0°C = 32°F, 37°C = 98.6°F, and 100°C = 212°F. If you forget the temperature conversion equation, you can use these reference points to construct the equation from scratch.

$$\text{Slope } (m) = \frac{\Delta y}{\Delta x} = \frac{212-32}{100-0} = \frac{180}{100} = \frac{9}{5} \therefore y - y_1 = m(x - x_1) \therefore y - 32 = m(x - 0) \therefore y - 32 = mx \therefore y = mx + 32 \therefore y = (9/5)x + 32$$

---

1. What is the equivalent of 0°C in degrees Fahrenheit?

2. What is the equivalent of -10°F in degrees Celsius?

3. What is the equivalent of 25°C in degrees Fahrenheit?

4. What is the equivalent of 0°F in degrees Celsius?

5. What is the equivalent of 101°F in degrees Celsius?

6. What is the equivalent of 60°C in degrees Fahrenheit?

7. According to the package insert, lisinopril-hydrochlorothiazide tablets must be stored at room temperature (20-25°C).[1] If the air conditioner in the pharmacy stops working, and the temperature in the room reaches and holds steady at 80°F, is the environment still suitable for storing the medication?

8. For a vial of Lantus® (insulin glargine) to remain stable through the expiration date printed on the label, it must be stored under refrigeration (2-8°C).[2] If the temperature inside the pharmacy refrigerator is 36.4°F, will the vial of insulin remain stable through the expiration date?

9. A patient is considered to be febrile if the oral temperature is greater than 99.5°F.[3] How would this threshold be expressed in terms of degrees Celsius?

10. Hyperpyrexia is characterized by a body temperature greater than 106°F.[3] JM, who is being hospitalized for malaria, has a body temperature of 40.6°C. Does JM have hyperpyrexia?

11. Mannitol 25% injection solution should be stored between 20-25°C; however, if mannitol crystals form within the vial, the crystals can be dissolved using a heat treatment. One option for heat treatment involves immersing the vial of mannitol in a water bath heated to 80°C for 15-20 minutes.[4] What should be the temperature of the water bath in terms of degrees Fahrenheit?

12. The pharmacy maintains an ample supply of frozen pre-mixed cefazolin 2-gram/100 mL infusions, which must be stored at or below -4°F.[5] The motor on the freezer quit working two hours ago, at which point the temperature inside the freezer was -22°F. Now, the temperature inside the freezer is -13°F. If the temperature continues to rise at the same rate, how much longer until the temperature reaches -4°F?

SOLUTIONS *for* TEMPERATURE PROBLEMS

1. What is the equivalent of 0°C in degrees Fahrenheit?

    SOLUTION: Apply the equation to convert degrees Celsius to degrees Fahrenheit.

    $$°F = \left(\frac{9}{5} \times °C\right) + 32 = \left(\frac{9}{5} \times 0\right) + 32 = 0 + 32 = 32°F$$

2. What is the equivalent of -10°F in degrees Celsius?

    SOLUTION: Apply the equation to convert degrees Fahrenheit to degrees Celsius.

    $$°C = \frac{5}{9}(°F - 32) = \frac{5}{9}(-10 - 32) = \frac{5}{9}(-42) = -23°C$$

3. What is the equivalent of 25°C in degrees Fahrenheit?

    SOLUTION: Apply the equation to convert degrees Celsius to degrees Fahrenheit.

    $$°F = \left(\frac{9}{5} \times °C\right) + 32 = \left(\frac{9}{5} \times 25\right) + 32 = 45 + 32 = 77°F$$

4. What is the equivalent of 0°F in degrees Celsius?

    SOLUTION: Apply the equation to convert degrees Fahrenheit to degrees Celsius.

    $$°C = \frac{5}{9}(°F - 32) = \frac{5}{9}(0 - 32) = \frac{5}{9}(-32) = -18°C$$

5. What is the equivalent of 101°F in degrees Celsius?

    SOLUTION: Apply the equation to convert degrees Fahrenheit to degrees Celsius.

    $$°C = \frac{5}{9}(°F - 32) = \frac{5}{9}(101 - 32) = \frac{5}{9}(69) = 38°C$$

6. What is the equivalent of 60°C in degrees Fahrenheit?

    SOLUTION: Apply the equation to convert degrees Celsius to degrees Fahrenheit.

    $$°F = \left(\frac{9}{5} \times °C\right) + 32 = \left(\frac{9}{5} \times 60\right) + 32 = 108 + 32 = 140°F$$

7. According to the package insert, lisinopril-hydrochlorothiazide tablets must be stored at room temperature (20-25°C).[1] If the air conditioner in the pharmacy stops working, and the temperature in the room reaches and holds steady at 80°F, is the environment still suitable for storing the medication?

    SOLUTION: Apply the equation to convert degrees Fahrenheit to degrees Celsius.

    $$°C = \frac{5}{9}(°F - 32) = \frac{5}{9}(80 - 32) = \frac{5}{9}(48) = 27°C \therefore \textbf{No}$$

    At 80°F (27°C), the temperature in the pharmacy exceeds the upper limit of 25°C.
    Therefore, the lisinopril-hydrochlorothiazide tablets should **not** be stored in this environment.

8. For a vial of Lantus® (insulin glargine) to remain stable through the expiration date printed on the label, it must be stored under refrigeration (2-8°C).[2] If the temperature inside the pharmacy refrigerator is 36.4°F, will the vial of insulin remain stable through the expiration date?

    SOLUTION: Apply the equation to convert degrees Fahrenheit to degrees Celsius.

    $$°C = \frac{5}{9}(°F - 32) = \frac{5}{9}(36.4 - 32) = \frac{5}{9}(4.4) = 2.4°C \therefore \text{Yes}$$

    At 36.4°F (2.4°C), the temperature in the refrigerator is within the range of 2–8°C.
    Therefore, the medication will remain stable through the expiration date if stored in this environment.

9. A patient is considered to be febrile if the oral temperature is greater than 99.5°F.[3] How would this threshold be expressed in terms of degrees Celsius?

    SOLUTION: Apply the equation to convert degrees Fahrenheit to degrees Celsius.

    $$°C = \frac{5}{9}(°F - 32) = \frac{5}{9}(99.5 - 32) = \frac{5}{9}(67.5) = 37.5°C$$

10. Hyperpyrexia is characterized by a body temperature greater than 106°F.[3] JM, who is being hospitalized for malaria, has a body temperature of 40.6°C. Does JM have hyperpyrexia?

    SOLUTION: Apply the equation to convert degrees Celsius to degrees Fahrenheit.

    $$°F = \left(\frac{9}{5} \times °C\right) + 32 = \left(\frac{9}{5} \times 40.6\right) + 32 = 73.1 + 32 = 105.1°F \therefore \text{No}$$

    At 105.1°F, JM's temperature is below the threshold for hyperpyrexia.

11. Mannitol 25% injection solution should be stored between 20-25°C; however, if mannitol crystals form within the vial, the crystals can be dissolved using a heat treatment. One option for heat treatment involves immersing the vial of mannitol in a water bath heated to 80°C for 15-20 minutes.[4] What should be the temperature of the water bath in terms of degrees Fahrenheit?

    SOLUTION: Apply the equation to convert degrees Celsius to degrees Fahrenheit.

    $$°F = \left(\frac{9}{5} \times °C\right) + 32 = \left(\frac{9}{5} \times 80\right) + 32 = 144 + 32 = 176°F$$

12. The pharmacy maintains an ample supply of frozen pre-mixed cefazolin 2-gram/100 mL infusions, which must be stored at or below negative 4°F.[5] The motor on the freezer quit working two hours ago, at which point the temperature inside the freezer was negative 30°C. Now, the temperature inside the freezer is negative 25°C. If the temperature continues to rise at the same rate, how much longer until the temperature reaches negative 4°F?

    STEP 1: Apply the equation to convert degrees Fahrenheit to degrees Celsius.

    $$°C = \frac{5}{9}(°F - 32) = \frac{5}{9}(-4 - 32) = \frac{5}{9}(-36) = -20°C$$

    STEP 2: Determine the rate of temperature increase.

    $$\frac{\Delta \text{ temperature}}{\Delta \text{ time}} = \frac{-25°C - -30°C}{2 - 0 \text{ hours}} = \frac{5°C}{2 \text{ hours}} = \frac{2.5°C}{\text{hour}}$$

    TRANSLATION: The temperature inside the freezer is rising at a rate of 2.5°C per hour.

    STEP 3: Determine the difference between the current temperature (−25°C) and −20°C (equivalent to −4°F).

    $$-20°C - -25°C = 5°C$$

    STEP 4: Using the rate of change calculated in STEP 2, determine the time required for the temperature to increase by 5°C.

    $$5°C \times \frac{\text{hour}}{2.5°C} = 2 \text{ hours}$$

REFERENCES
1. Lisinopril-hydrochlorothiazide tablets [package insert]. Parsippany, NJ: Actavis Pharma, Inc; 2017.
2. Lantus [package insert]. Bridgewater, NJ: Sanofi-Aventis US LLC; 2015.
3. Del Bene VE. Temperature. In: Walker HK, Hall WD, Hurst JW, editors. Clinical Methods: The History, Physical, and Laboratory Examinations. 3rd edition. Boston: Butterworths; 1990. Chapter 218. Available from: https://www.ncbi.nlm.nih.gov/books/NBK331/
4. Mannitol injection USP 25% [package insert]. Shirley, NY: American Regent, Inc; 2011.
5. Cefazolin sodium injection solution [package insert]. Deerfield, IL: Baxter Healthcare Corporation; 2018.

QUANTITY/DAY-SUPPLY

THE RULE *of* HAND
One gram of topical medication covers a surface area approximately equal to one side of four flat hands.

---

1. A prescription is written for the pharmacy to dispense QS prednisone 10 mg tablets with instructions for the patient to take 30 mg daily for 3 days, then 20 mg daily for 3 days, then 10 mg daily for 3 days, then 5 mg daily for 4 days, then 2.5 mg daily for 4 days, then stop. What quantity should be dispensed, and how many days will the prescription last?

2. How many days will 60 capsules of Effexor® XR (venlafaxine extended-release) 37.5 mg last with instructions to take one capsule by mouth QD x 7 days, then one capsule by mouth BID x 7 days, then two capsules by mouth QAM and one capsule QPM thereafter?

3. How many days will a 4-fluid ounce bottle of cetirizine 5 mg/5 mL solution last with instructions to administer one-half teaspoonful QHS?

4. If one bottle of Astepro® contains enough solution to deliver 200 sprays, how many days will one bottle last with instructions to instill one spray into each nostril BID?

5. Suppose the dropper is calibrated to deliver 15 drops per milliliter. How many days will one 7.5-milliliter bottle of Ciprodex® otic solution last with instructions to instill 2 gtts AS QID until gone?

6. Assuming the dropper is calibrated to deliver 20 drops per milliliter, how many days will one 15-milliliter bottle of antipyrine-benzocaine otic solution last with instructions to instill 2-4 gtts AU QID PRN?

7. How many days will a three-milliliter bottle of an ophthalmic suspension last with instructions to instill two drops into each eye three times daily until gone?

8. NovoLog® FlexPen comes in a box of five pens with each pen containing three milliliters of insulin aspart 100 units/mL solution. If a patient uses 11 units SQ with every morning meal and 9 units SQ with every evening meal, how many days will one box last?

9. A prescription for compounded magic mouthwash has instructions to swish and swallow three teaspoons four times daily for two weeks. If the quantity to dispense is "QS," how many milliliters should the pharmacist dispense?

10. Approximately how many days will a 45-gram tube of topical gel last if the patient applies the gel to the entire face once daily?

SOLUTIONS for QUANTITY/DAY-SUPPLY PROBLEMS

1. A prescription is written for the pharmacy to dispense QS prednisone 10 mg tablets with instructions for the patient to take 30 mg daily for 3 days, then 20 mg daily for 3 days, then 10 mg daily for 3 days, then 5 mg daily for 4 days, then 2.5 mg daily for 4 days, then stop. What quantity should be dispensed, and how many days will the prescription last?

   STEP 1: Calculate the number of tablets needed for each individual set of days with a fixed dose.

   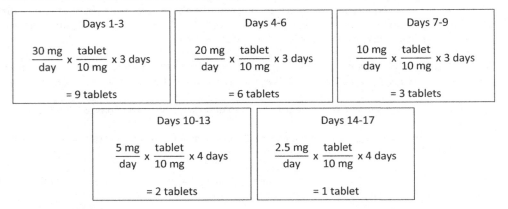

   Days 1-3: $\dfrac{30 \text{ mg}}{\text{day}} \times \dfrac{\text{tablet}}{10 \text{ mg}} \times 3 \text{ days} = 9 \text{ tablets}$

   Days 4-6: $\dfrac{20 \text{ mg}}{\text{day}} \times \dfrac{\text{tablet}}{10 \text{ mg}} \times 3 \text{ days} = 6 \text{ tablets}$

   Days 7-9: $\dfrac{10 \text{ mg}}{\text{day}} \times \dfrac{\text{tablet}}{10 \text{ mg}} \times 3 \text{ days} = 3 \text{ tablets}$

   Days 10-13: $\dfrac{5 \text{ mg}}{\text{day}} \times \dfrac{\text{tablet}}{10 \text{ mg}} \times 4 \text{ days} = 2 \text{ tablets}$

   Days 14-17: $\dfrac{2.5 \text{ mg}}{\text{day}} \times \dfrac{\text{tablet}}{10 \text{ mg}} \times 4 \text{ days} = 1 \text{ tablet}$

   STEP 2: Add together each answer from STEP 1 to determine the total number of tablets needed to fill the prescription.

   9 tablets + 6 tablets + 3 tablets + 2 tablets + 1 tablet = 21 tablets

   STEP 3: Add together the total number of days the patient will receive a dose.

   A prescription is written for the pharmacy to dispense QS prednisone 10 mg tablets with instructions for the patient to take 30 mg daily for <u>3 DAYS</u>, then 20 mg daily for <u>3 DAYS</u>, then 10 mg daily for <u>3 DAYS</u>, then 5 mg daily for <u>4 DAYS</u>, then 2.5 mg daily for <u>4 DAYS,</u> then stop.

   3 days + 3 days + 3 days + 4 days + 4 days = 17 days

2. How many days will 60 capsules of Effexor® XR (venlafaxine extended-release) 37.5 mg last with instructions to take one capsule by mouth QD x 7 days, then one capsule by mouth BID x 7 days, then two capsules by mouth QAM and one capsule QPM thereafter?

   STEP 1: Calculate the number of capsules needed for each of the first two weeks of therapy.

Days 1-7	Days 8-14
$\dfrac{1 \text{ capsule}}{\text{day}} \times 7 \text{ days} = 7 \text{ capsules}$	$\dfrac{2 \text{ capsules}}{\text{day}} \times 7 \text{ days} = 14 \text{ capsules}$

   STEP 2: Subtract the number the capsules needed for the first two weeks of therapy from the total number of capsules prescribed.

   $$60 \text{ capsules} - 21 \text{ capsules} = 39 \text{ capsules}$$

   STEP 3: Calculate how many days the remaining 39 capsules will last based on the instructions to take a total of three capsules daily.

   Day 15 & beyond

   $$39 \text{ capsules} \times \dfrac{\text{day}}{3 \text{ capsules}} = 13 \text{ days}$$

   STEP 4: Add together the total number of days the patient will receive a dose.

   $$7 \text{ days} + 7 \text{ days} + 13 \text{ days} = 27 \text{ days}$$

3. How many days will a 4-fluid ounce bottle of cetirizine 5 mg/5 mL solution last with instructions to administer one-half teaspoonful QHS?

   STEP 1: Convert the volume from fluid ounces to milliliters and the daily dose from teaspoons to milliliters.

   $$\dfrac{4 \text{ fluid ounces}}{\text{bottle}} \times \dfrac{29.57 \text{ mL}}{\text{fluid ounce}} = \dfrac{118.28 \text{ mL}}{\text{bottle}} \qquad \dfrac{0.5 \text{ teaspoon}}{\text{day}} \times \dfrac{5 \text{ mL}}{\text{teaspoon}} = \dfrac{2.5 \text{ mL}}{\text{day}}$$

   STEP 2: Divide the volume of one bottle by the daily dose to determine how many days one bottle will last.

   $$\dfrac{118.28 \text{ mL}}{\text{bottle}} \times \dfrac{\text{day}}{2.5 \text{ mL}} = 47.3 \text{ days/bottle} \therefore 47 \text{ days/bottle}$$

4. If one bottle of Astepro® contains enough solution to deliver 200 sprays, how many days will one bottle last with instructions to instill one spray into each nostril BID?

   SOLUTION: Perform dimensional analysis.

   $$200 \text{ sprays} \times \dfrac{\text{day}}{4 \text{ sprays}} = 50 \text{ days}$$

   NOTE: One spray in each nostril twice daily is equivalent to four sprays per day.

5. Suppose the dropper is calibrated to deliver 15 drops per milliliter. How many days will one 7.5-milliliter bottle of Ciprodex® otic solution last with instructions to instill 2 gtts AS QID until gone?

   SOLUTION: Perform dimensional analysis.

   $$7.5 \text{ mL} \times \dfrac{15 \text{ drops}}{\text{mL}} \times \dfrac{\text{day}}{8 \text{ drops}} = 14 \text{ days}$$

   NOTE: The instructions are to use two drops in the left ear four times daily.

6. Assuming the dropper is calibrated to deliver 20 drops per milliliter, how many days will one 15-milliliter bottle of antipyrine-benzocaine otic solution last with instructions to instill 2-4 gtts AU QID PRN?

    SOLUTION: Perform dimensional analysis.

    $$15 \text{ mL} \times \frac{20 \text{ drops}}{\text{mL}} \times \frac{\text{day}}{32 \text{ drops}} = 9 \text{ days}$$

    NOTE: The instructions are to use two to four drops into both ears four times daily. When a range is provided, always assume the patient will use the greatest amount.

7. How many days will a three-milliliter bottle of an ophthalmic suspension last with instructions to instill two drops into each eye three times daily until gone?

    SOLUTION: Perform dimensional analysis.

    $$3 \text{ mL} \times \frac{20 \text{ drops}}{\text{mL}} \times \frac{\text{day}}{12 \text{ drops}} = 5 \text{ days}$$

    NOTE: When calculating the days' supply of eye drops or ear drops, we assume there are 15-20 drops per milliliter. Unlike the previous two questions, this question does not indicate the number of drops per milliliter to be used in the calculation. It is prudent to assume **20 drops per milliliter** in such cases because this is the number referenced by the Centers for Medicare and Medicaid Services (CMS) in their Pharmacy Auditing and Dispensing Job Aid. Furthermore, the official dropper recognized by the United States Pharmacopoeia/National Formulary (USP-NF) delivers 20 drops per milliliter.

8. NovoLog® FlexPen comes in a box of five pens with each pen containing three milliliters of insulin aspart 100 units/mL solution. If a patient uses 11 units SQ with every morning meal and 9 units SQ with every evening meal, how many days will one box last?

    SOLUTION: Perform dimensional analysis.

    $$\frac{3 \text{ mL}}{\text{pen}} \times \frac{5 \text{ pens}}{\text{box}} \times \frac{100 \text{ units}}{\text{mL}} \times \frac{\text{day}}{20 \text{ units}} = 75 \text{ days}$$

9. A prescription for compounded magic mouthwash has instructions to swish and swallow three teaspoons four times daily for two weeks. If the quantity to dispense is "QS," how many milliliters should the pharmacist dispense?

    SOLUTION: Perform dimensional analysis.

    $$\frac{3 \text{ teaspoons}}{\text{dose}} \times \frac{5 \text{ mL}}{\text{teaspoon}} \times \frac{4 \text{ doses}}{\text{day}} \times 14 \text{ days} = 840 \text{ mL}$$

10. Approximately how many days will a 45-gram tube of topical gel last if the patient applies the gel to the entire face once daily?

    SOLUTION: Estimate the days' supply using the "rule of hand," which states that one gram of topical medication should cover one side of four flat hands. The surface area of the face is approximately equal to the area of two flat hands.

    $$45 \text{ grams} \times \frac{\text{day}}{1 \text{ face}} \times \frac{\text{face}}{2 \text{ flat hands}} \times \frac{4 \text{ flat hands}}{1 \text{ gram}} = 90 \text{ days}$$

    NOTE: With the "rule of hand" being relatively subjective, this type of calculation may be unlikely to appear on the NAPLEX®.

REFERENCES
1. Pharmacy Auditing and Dispensing Job Aid: Billing Other Dosage Forms. Centers for Medicare and Medicaid Services. https://www.cms.gov/Medicare-Medicaid-Coordination/Fraud-Prevention/Medicaid-Integrity-Education/pharmacy-auditing-dispensing.html/. Accessed October 23, 2018.

DENSITY

EQUATION *for* DENSITY

$$\text{Density} = \frac{\text{Mass (grams)}}{\text{Volume (milliliters)}}$$

---

1. A 0.0390-deciliter volume of simple syrup has a mass of 5,070 milligrams. What is the density of the simple syrup?

2. What is the identity of an unknown substance that weighs 33.3 grams and occupies 30 cubic centimeters of space?
    Water (Density = 1. 0 g/mL)
    Isopropyl Alcohol (Density = 0.79 g/mL)
    Glycerin (Density = 1.26 g/mL)
    Simple Syrup (Density = 1.3 g/mL)
    Ethylene Glycol (Density = 1.11 g/mL)

3. Petrolatum has a density of 0.9 grams per milliliter. How many milliliters of liquefied petrolatum are needed to compound a 60-gram formulation composed of 10% (w/w) petrolatum?

4. What is the mass of 4 milliliters of a substance with a density of 1.2 grams per milliliter?

5. What volume of simple syrup (density 1.3 g/mL) would have a mass of 2 grams?

6. If one liter of a substance weighs two pounds, then what is the density of the substance?

7. Five milliliters of ethanol weighs 3,945 milligrams. What is the density of ethanol?

8. The density of isopropyl alcohol is 0.79 g/mL. What is the expected mass of a 1,000-mL isopropyl alcohol 70% (v/v) in water solution?

SOLUTIONS for DENSITY PROBLEMS

1. A 0.0390-deciliter volume of simple syrup has a mass of 5,070 milligrams. What is the density of the simple syrup?

   STEP 1: Convert units of volume from deciliters to milliliters and mass from milligrams to grams,

   $$\text{MASS: } 5{,}070 \text{ mg} \times \frac{\text{g}}{1{,}000 \text{ mg}} = 5.07 \text{ g} \qquad \text{VOLUME: } 0.0390 \text{ dL} \times \frac{100 \text{ mL}}{\text{dL}} = 3.90 \text{ mL}$$

   STEP 2: Enter values into the equation for density.

   $$\text{Density} = \frac{\text{Mass (grams)}}{\text{Volume (milliliters)}} = \frac{5.07 \text{ g}}{3.90 \text{ mL}} = 1.3 \text{ g/mL}$$

2. What is the identity of an unknown substance that weighs 33.3 grams and occupies 30 cubic centimeters of space?
   Water (Density = 1.0 g/mL)
   Isopropyl Alcohol (Density = 0.79 g/mL)
   Glycerin (Density = 1.26 g/mL)
   Simple Syrup (Density = 1.3 g/mL)
   Ethylene Glycol (Density = 1.11 g/mL)

   STEP 1: Enter values into the equation for density.

   $$\text{Density} = \frac{\text{Mass (grams)}}{\text{Volume (milliliters)}} = \frac{33.3 \text{ g}}{30 \text{ mL}} = 1.11 \text{ g/mL}$$

   STEP 2: Match the density calculated in STEP 1 to one of the substances from the list.

   ANSWER: Ethylene Glycol (Density = 1.11 g/mL)

3. Petrolatum has a density of 0.9 grams per milliliter. How many milliliters of liquefied petrolatum are needed to compound a 60-gram formulation composed of 10% (w/w) petrolatum?

   STEP 1: Set up a proportion to determine the mass of petrolatum in 60 grams of the formulation.

   $$\frac{10 \text{ grams } of \text{ petrolatum}}{100 \text{ grams } of \text{ formulation}} = \frac{\text{UNKNOWN}}{60 \text{ g } of \text{ formulation}} \therefore \text{UNKNOWN} = \frac{10 \text{ grams } of \text{ petrolatum}}{100 \text{ grams } of \text{ formulation}} \times 60 \text{ g } of \text{ formulation} = 6 \text{ grams } of \text{ petrolatum}$$

   STEP 2: Rearrange the density equation to solve for volume.

   $$\text{Density} = \frac{\text{Mass}}{\text{Volume}} \therefore \text{Volume} = \frac{\text{Mass}}{\text{Density}} = \frac{6 \text{ g } of \text{ petrolatum}}{0.9 \text{ g/mL}} = 6.67 \text{ mL } of \text{ petrolatum}$$

4. What is the mass of 4 milliliters of a substance with a density of 1.2 grams per milliliter?

   SOLUTION: Rearrange the density equation to solve for mass.

   $$\text{Density} = \frac{\text{Mass}}{\text{Volume}} \therefore \text{Mass} = \text{Density} \times \text{Volume} = \frac{1.2 \text{ g}}{\text{mL}} \times 4 \text{ mL} = 4.8 \text{ g}$$

5. What volume of simple syrup (density 1.3 g/mL) would have a mass of 2 grams?

   SOLUTION: Rearrange the density equation to solve for volume.

   $$\text{Density} = \frac{\text{Mass}}{\text{Volume}} \therefore \text{Volume} = \frac{\text{Mass}}{\text{Density}} = \frac{2 \text{ g } of \text{ simple syrup}}{1.3 \text{ g/mL}} = 1.54 \text{ mL } of \text{ simple syrup}$$

6. If one liter of a substance weighs two pounds, then what is the density of the substance?

   STEP 1: Convert volume from liters to milliliters and mass from pounds to grams.

   $$\text{MASS: } 2 \text{ pounds} \times \frac{454 \text{ g}}{\text{pound}} = 908 \text{ g} \qquad \text{VOLUME: } 1 \text{ liter} \times \frac{1{,}000 \text{ mL}}{\text{liter}} = 1{,}000 \text{ mL}$$

   STEP 2: Enter values into the equation for density.

   $$\text{Density} = \frac{\text{Mass (grams)}}{\text{Volume (milliliters)}} = \frac{908 \text{ g}}{1{,}000 \text{ mL}} = 0.908 \text{ g/mL}$$

7. Five milliliters of ethanol weighs 3,945 milligrams. What is the density of ethanol?

   STEP 1: Convert mass from milligrams to grams.

   $$3{,}945 \text{ mg} \times \frac{\text{g}}{1{,}000 \text{ mg}} = 3.945 \text{ g}$$

   STEP 2: Enter values into the equation for density.

   $$\text{Density} = \frac{\text{Mass}}{\text{Volume}} = \frac{3.945 \text{ g } of \text{ ethanol}}{5 \text{ mL } of \text{ ethanol}} = 0.789 \text{ g/mL}$$

8. The density of isopropyl alcohol is 0.79 g/mL. What is the expected mass of a 1,000-mL isopropyl alcohol 70% (v/v) in water solution?

   STEP 1: Determine the volume of each component of the solution.

   $$\frac{70 \text{ mL } of \text{ isopropyl alcohol}}{100 \text{ mL } of \text{ solution}} \times 1{,}000 \text{ mL } of \text{ solution} = 700 \text{ mL } of \text{ isopropyl alcohol}$$

   Because the solution is aqueous, the remaining volume is water.

   $$1{,}000 \text{ mL } of \text{ solution} - 700 \text{ mL } of \text{ isopropyl alcohol} = 300 \text{ mL } of \text{ water}$$

   STEP 2: Rearrange the density equation to solve for the mass of each component.

   ISOPROPYL ALCOHOL:

   $$\text{Density} = \frac{\text{Mass}}{\text{Volume}} \therefore \text{Mass} = \text{Density} \times \text{Volume} = \frac{0.79 \text{ g}}{\text{mL}} \times 700 \text{ mL } of \text{ isopropyl alcohol} = 553 \text{ g } of \text{ isopropyl alcohol}$$

   WATER:

   $$\text{Density} = \frac{\text{Mass}}{\text{Volume}} \therefore \text{Mass} = \text{Density} \times \text{Volume} = \frac{1 \text{ g}}{\text{mL}} \times 300 \text{ mL } of \text{ water} = 300 \text{ g } of \text{ water}$$

   STEP 3: Add the mass of each component to determine the mass of the solution.

   $$553 \text{ g } of \text{ isopropyl alcohol} + 300 \text{ g } of \text{ water} = 853 \text{ g } of \text{ solution}$$

SPECIFIC GRAVITY

EQUATION *for* SPECIFIC GRAVITY

$$\text{Specific Gravity} = \frac{\text{Density } of \text{ Substance}}{\text{Density } of \text{ Reference Substance*}}$$

*Unless specified otherwise, assume the reference substance is water (1 g/mL).

1. What is the specific gravity of water?

2. If the mass of 50 milliliters of an unknown solid is 100 grams, what is the specific gravity?

3. What is the specific gravity of water if the reference substance is glycerin (density = 1.26 g/mL)?

4. What is the specific gravity of a 78-mL unknown substance with a mass of 131 grams?

5. If 12 grams of an unknown liquid occupies a volume of 15 cubic centimeters, then what is the specific gravity?

6. If glycerin had a specific gravity of 1.26, how many milliliters of liquid glycerin would be needed to compound 24 glycerin 1-gram suppositories?

SOLUTIONS for SPECIFIC GRAVITY PROBLEMS

1. What is the specific gravity of water?

    SOLUTION: Enter the density of water and the reference substance (also water) into the specific gravity equation.

    $$\text{Specific Gravity} = \frac{\text{Density of Substance}}{\text{Density of Reference Substance}} = \frac{1 \text{ g/mL}}{1 \text{ g/mL}} = 1$$

    NOTE: Unless specified otherwise, assume the reference substance is water (1 g/mL).

2. If the mass of 50 milliliters of an unknown solid is 100 grams, what is the specific gravity?

    STEP 1: Determine the density of the unknown substance.

    $$\text{Density} = \frac{\text{Mass}}{\text{Volume}} = \frac{100 \text{ g of unknown solid}}{50 \text{ mL of unknown solid}} = 2 \text{ g/mL}$$

    STEP 2: Enter the density of the unknown substance and water (reference substance) into the specific gravity equation.

    $$\text{Specific Gravity} = \frac{\text{Density of Substance}}{\text{Density of Reference Substance}} = \frac{2 \text{ g/mL}}{1 \text{ g/mL}} = 2$$

NOTE: Another viable definition for specific gravity is the quotient of the weight of the substance divided by the weight of an equal volume of water (i.e., specific gravity = weight of substance/weight of an equal volume of water). In this particular case, that equation would have been quicker; however, we prefer the equation as presented in this section because: #1 it builds on the basic concept of density from the previous section and #2 when you're dealing with density, you're automatically dealing with a standardized volume (one milliliter) for each component, thus reducing the probability of committing an error when solving more complex problems. Furthermore, if the question indicates that the reference substance is something other than water, our preferred equation is less likely to cause confusion.

3. What is the specific gravity of water if the reference substance is glycerin (density = 1.26 g/mL)?

    SOLUTION: Enter the density of water and the reference substance (glycerin) into the specific gravity equation.

    $$\text{Specific Gravity} = \frac{\text{Density of Substance}}{\text{Density of Reference Substance}} = \frac{1 \text{ g/mL}}{1.26 \text{ g/mL}} = 0.794$$

4. What is the specific gravity of a 78-mL unknown substance with a mass of 131 grams?

    STEP 1: Determine the density of the unknown substance.

    $$\text{Density} = \frac{\text{Mass}}{\text{Volume}} = \frac{131 \text{ g of unknown substance}}{78 \text{ mL of unknown substance}} = 1.68 \text{ g/mL}$$

    STEP 2: Enter the density of the unknown substance and water (reference substance) into the specific gravity equation.

    $$\text{Specific Gravity} = \frac{\text{Density of Substance}}{\text{Density of Reference Substance}} = \frac{1.68 \text{ g/mL}}{1 \text{ g/mL}} = 1.68$$

5. If 12 grams of an unknown liquid occupies a volume of 15 cubic centimeters, then what is the specific gravity?

   STEP 1: Determine the density of the unknown liquid.

   $$\text{Density} = \frac{\text{Mass}}{\text{Volume}} = \frac{12 \text{ g } of \text{ unknown liquid}}{15 \text{ mL } of \text{ unknown liquid}} = 0.8 \text{ g/mL}$$

   NOTE: Remember that 1 cubic centimeter (cc) is equivalent to one milliliter (mL).

   STEP 2: Enter the density of the unknown liquid and water (reference substance) into the specific gravity equation.

   $$\text{Specific Gravity} = \frac{\text{Density } of \text{ Substance}}{\text{Density } of \text{ Reference Substance}} = \frac{0.8 \text{ g/mL}}{1 \text{ g/mL}} = 0.8$$

6. If glycerin had a specific gravity of 1.26, how many milliliters of liquid glycerin would be needed to compound 24 glycerin 1-gram suppositories?

   STEP 1: Rearrange the specific gravity equation to solve for the density of glycerin.

   $$\text{Specific Gravity} = \frac{\text{Density } of \text{ Substance}}{\text{Density } of \text{ Reference Substance}} \therefore \text{Density } of \text{ Substance} = \text{Specific Gravity} \times \text{Density } of \text{ Reference Substance}$$

   $$= 1.26 \times \frac{1 \text{ g}}{\text{mL}} = 1.26 \text{ g/mL}$$

   STEP 2: Calculate the total mass of glycerin needed to compound a 24-count order of one-gram glycerin suppositories.

   $$\frac{1 \text{ g } of \text{ glycerin}}{\text{suppository}} \times 24 \text{ suppositories} = 24 \text{ g } of \text{ glycerin}$$

   STEP 3: Perform dimensional analysis.

   $$24 \text{ g } of \text{ glycerin} \times \frac{\text{mL}}{1.26 \text{ g}} = 19 \text{ mL } of \text{ glycerin}$$

BIOSTATISTICS

ABSOLUTE RISK REDUCTION (ARR)
ARR is the difference between the event rate in the control group (CER) and the event rate in the experimental group (EER).

$$ARR = CER - EER$$

NUMBER NEEDED TO TREAT (NNT)
The NNT is the number of patients required to receive the experimental intervention to prevent one event.

$$NNT = \frac{1}{ARR} = \frac{1}{CER - EER}$$

RELATIVE RISK (RR)
The RR compares the experimental group event rate (EER) to the control group event rate (CER).

$$RR = \frac{EER}{CER}$$

RELATIVE RISK REDUCTION (RRR)
The RRR quantifies how much the experimental intervention reduces the event rate relative to the control group.

$$RRR = \frac{ARR}{CER} = \frac{CER - EER}{CER} = 1 - RR$$

ALWAYS ROUND-UP for NNT
Always round-up NNT to the nearest whole number. For example, if NNT is 20.1, then round up to 21.

DECIMAL vs. PERCENT
Though ARR, NNT, RR, and RRR can be expressed as percentages, use the decimal form in calculations.

INTERPRETATION of RELATIVE RISK
RR < 1 means the experimental intervention (or exposure) decreased the risk of the event.
RR = 1 means that the experimental intervention (or exposure) had no effect on the risk of the event.
RR > 1 means the experimental intervention (or exposure) increased the risk of the event.

---

1. A randomized control trial was conducted to test the efficacy of bisphosphonates in reducing vertebral fractures. During the study, 11% of the bisphosphonate group developed a new vertebral fracture, and 17% of the placebo group developed a new vertebral fracture. What are the ARR, NNT, RR, and RRR?

2. A randomized control trial was conducted to test the efficacy of thienopyridines in reducing cardiovascular events. The control group received aspirin 81 mg once daily, and 81% of the patients in this group experienced a new cardiovascular event. Patients in the experimental group received a daily thienopyridine, and 33% of these patients experienced a new cardiovascular event. What are the ARR, NNT, RR, and RRR?

3. A clinical trial was conducted to determine the efficacy of factor Xa inhibitors compared to low molecular weight heparins (LMWHs) in the prevention of venous thromboembolism (VTE) within 10 days after hip fracture surgery. In the control group, 1,048 patients received a LMWH, among which 198 had a VTE within 10 days post-surgery. In the experimental group, 954 patients received a factor Xa inhibitor, among which 77 had a VTE within 10 days post-surgery. What are the ARR, NNT, RR, and RRR?

4. A clinical trial was conducted to determine whether selenium supplementation reduces the risk of developing skin cancer. In the control group, 1,652 patients received a placebo, among which 428 developed skin cancer. In the experimental group, 1,309 patients received a selenium supplement, among which 339 developed skin cancer. What are the ARR, NNT, RR, and RRR?

5. In the PROVE-IT trial, 26.6% of pravastatin recipients experienced acute cardiac events compared to 21.1% of patients in the atorvastatin group. What are the ARR, NNT, RR, and RRR?

6. A clinical trial was conducted to determine whether a new immunomodulator drug can reduce multiple sclerosis relapses within 12 months compared to beta interferon. In the control group, 356 patients received beta interferon, among which 53 experienced a relapse within the 12-month study period. In the experimental group, 340 patients received the new immunomodulator, and 37 experienced a relapse within the 12-month study period. What are the ARR, NNT, RR, and RRR?

7. A clinical trial was conducted to determine whether a 5-HT$_1$ receptor agonist can reduce the frequency of migraine recurrence within 24 hours compared to a placebo. In the control group, 188 patients received placebo at the onset of a migraine, among which 47 experienced migraine recurrence within 24 hours. In the experimental group, 189 patients received a 5-HT$_1$ receptor agonist and 19 experienced migraine recurrence within 24 hours. What are the ARR, NNT, RR, and RRR?

8. A clinical trial was conducted to determine whether benzodiazepines (BZDs) reduce the number of panic attacks within a 10-week treatment period compared to placebo. In the control group, 92 patients received a placebo once daily for 10 weeks, and 65 patients reported a panic attack within the 10-week treatment period. In the experimental group, 96 patients received a BZD once daily for 10 weeks, and 38 reported a panic attack within the treatment period. What are the ARR, NNT, RR, and RRR?

9. A clinical trial was conducted to determine whether a selective estrogen receptor modulator (SERM) reduces the number of vertebral fractures over four years compared to placebo. In the control group, 919 postmenopausal female patients were treated with placebo once daily, among which 49 sustained at least one new vertebral fracture during the four-year treatment period. In the experimental group, 923 postmenopausal female patients were treated with a SERM once daily, and only 23 sustained at least one new vertebral fracture over the same four years. What are the ARR, NNT, RR, and RRR?

10. A clinical trial was conducted to determine whether a proton pump inhibitor (PPI) is more effective than placebo at eliminating gastroesophageal reflux disease (GERD) symptoms in seven days. In the experimental group, 200 patients received a PPI once daily for seven days, among which 50 reported continued GERD symptoms at the end of the treatment period. In the placebo group, 200 patients received a placebo once daily for seven days, among which 170 reported continued GERD symptoms at the end of the treatment period. What are the ARR, NNT, RR, and RRR?

11. In a clinical trial, 40% of the control group died, and 10% of the experimental group died. What are the ARR, NNT, RR, and RRR?

12. A clinical trial was undertaken to determine whether a parathyroid hormone (PTH) analog reduces vertebral fractures in postmenopausal women. In the experimental group, 434 postmenopausal females received once-daily injections of the PTH analog, 22 of which sustained a vertebral fracture. In the control group, 449 postmenopausal female patients received once-daily placebo injections, among which 63 suffered a vertebral fracture. What are the ARR, NNT, RR, and RRR?

13. A clinical trial was conducted to determine whether an antiviral is more effective than a placebo for influenza post-exposure prophylaxis. In the control group, 207 household contacts received a placebo for influenza post-exposure prophylaxis, and 25 contracted influenza. In the experimental group, 226 household contacts received an antiviral for influenza post-exposure prophylaxis, among which three contracted influenza. What are the ARR, NNT, RR, and RRR?

14. A clinical trial was conducted in patients with unstable angina to determine whether the combination of a glycoprotein (GP) IIb/IIIa inhibitor and low molecular weight heparin (LMWH) results in fewer cases of cutaneous bleeding compared to the combination of a GP IIb/IIIa and unfractionated heparin (UFH). In the experimental group, 661 patients received a GP IIb/IIIa inhibitor and LMWH, among which 125 experienced cutaneous bleeding. In the control group, 639 patients received the GP IIb/IIIa inhibitor and UFH, and 142 experienced cutaneous bleeding. What are the ARR, NNT, RR, and RRR?

15. A clinical trial was conducted in patients experiencing a chronic obstructive pulmonary disease (COPD) exacerbation to determine whether the combination of albuterol, antibiotics, and prednisone is more effective than albuterol, antibiotics, and placebo at reducing recurrent COPD exacerbations within 30 days. In the control group, 100 patients were treated with albuterol, antibiotics, and placebo, among which 45 experienced a COPD exacerbation within 30 days. In the experimental group, 100 patients were treated with albuterol, antibiotics, and prednisone, and 30 experienced a COPD exacerbation within 30 days. What are the ARR, NNT, RR, and RRR?

SOLUTIONS for BIOSTATISTICS PROBLEMS

1. A randomized control trial was conducted to test the efficacy of bisphosphonates in reducing vertebral fractures. During the study, 11% of the bisphosphonate group developed a new vertebral fracture, and 17% of the placebo group developed a new vertebral fracture. What are the ARR, NNT, RR, and RRR?

ABSOLUTE RISK REDUCTION (ARR)

ARR = CER − EER = 0.17 − 0.11 = 0.06

INTERPRETATION: The probability of a new vertebral fracture in the bisphosphonate group is 0.06 (or 6%) lower than the probability of a new vertebral fracture in the placebo group.

NUMBER NEEDED TO TREAT (NNT)

$NNT = \frac{1}{ARR} = \frac{1}{0.06} = 16.67$ ∴ 17 patients

INTERPRETATION: 17 patients must receive the bisphosphonate instead of a placebo to prevent one patient from experiencing a new vertebral fracture.

RELATIVE RISK (RR)

$RR = \frac{EER}{CER} = \frac{0.11}{0.17} = 0.647$

INTERPRETATION: The probability of a new vertebral fracture in the bisphosphonate group is 0.647 times that of the probability of a new vertebral fracture in the placebo group.

RELATIVE RISK REDUCTION (RRR)

RRR = 1 − RR = 1 − 0.647 = 0.353

INTERPRETATION: Patients in the bisphosphonate group have a 0.353 (or 35.3%) lower probability of a new vertebral fracture than patients in the placebo group.

2. A randomized control trial was conducted to test the efficacy of thienopyridines in reducing cardiovascular events. The control group received aspirin 81 mg once daily, and 81% of the patients in this group experienced a new cardiovascular event. Patients in the experimental group received a daily thienopyridine, and 33% of these patients experienced a new cardiovascular event. What are the ARR, NNT, RR, and RRR?

ABSOLUTE RISK REDUCTION (ARR)

ARR = CER − EER = 0.81 − 0.33 = 0.48

INTERPRETATION: The probability that a patient in the thienopyridine group will have a new cardiovascular event is 0.48 (or 48%) lower than a patient in the aspirin group.

NUMBER NEEDED TO TREAT (NNT)

$NNT = \frac{1}{ARR} = \frac{1}{0.48} = 2.083$ ∴ 3 patients

INTERPRETATION: 3 patients must receive the thienopyridine instead of the 81-mg aspirin to prevent one patient from experiencing a new cardiovascular event.

RELATIVE RISK (RR)

$RR = \frac{EER}{CER} = \frac{0.33}{0.81} = 0.407$

INTERPRETATION: The probability of a new cardiovascular event in the thienopyridine group is 0.407 times that of the probability of a new cardiovascular event in the aspirin group.

RELATIVE RISK REDUCTION (RRR)

RRR = 1 − RR = 1 − 0.407 = 0.593

INTERPRETATION: Patients in the thienopyridine group have a 0.593 (or 59.3%) lower probability of experiencing a new cardiovascular event compared to patients in the aspirin group.

3. A clinical trial was conducted to determine the efficacy of factor Xa inhibitors compared to low molecular weight heparins (LMWHs) in the prevention of venous thromboembolism (VTE) within 10 days after hip fracture surgery. In the control group, 1,048 patients received a LMWH, among which 198 had a VTE within 10 days post-surgery. In the experimental group, 954 patients received a factor Xa inhibitor, among which 77 had a VTE within 10 days post-surgery. What are the ARR, NNT, RR, and RRR?

ABSOLUTE RISK REDUCTION (ARR)

ARR = CER − EER = (198/1,048) − (77/954) = 0.1082

INTERPRETATION: The probability of VTE within 10 days post-surgery in the factor Xa inhibitor group is 0.1082 (or 10.82%) lower than the probability in the LMWH group.

NUMBER NEEDED TO TREAT (NNT)

$$NNT = \frac{1}{ARR} = \frac{1}{0.1082} = 9.24 \therefore 10 \text{ patients}$$

INTERPRETATION: 10 patients must receive the factor Xa inhibitor instead of LMWH to prevent one patient from experiencing a VTE within 10 days post-surgery.

RELATIVE RISK (RR)

$$RR = \frac{EER}{CER} = \frac{77/954}{198/1,048} = 0.427$$

INTERPRETATION: The probability of a VTE within 10 days post-surgery in the factor Xa inhibitor group is 0.427 times that of the probability of a VTE in the LMWH group.

RELATIVE RISK REDUCTION (RRR)

RRR = 1 − RR = 1 − 0.427 = 0.573

INTERPRETATION: Patients in the factor Xa inhibitor group have a 0.573 (or 57.3%) lower probability of a VTE within 10 days post-surgery compared to patients in the LMWH group.

4. A clinical trial was conducted to determine whether selenium supplementation reduces the risk of developing skin cancer. In the control group, 1,652 patients received a placebo, among which 428 developed skin cancer. In the experimental group, 1,309 patients received a selenium supplement, among which 339 developed skin cancer. What are the ARR, NNT, RR, and RRR?

ABSOLUTE RISK REDUCTION (ARR)

ARR = CER − EER = (428/1,652) − (339/1,309) = 0.0001

INTERPRETATION: The probability that a patient in the selenium group will experience skin cancer is 0.0001 (or 0.01%) lower than a patient in the placebo group.

NUMBER NEEDED TO TREAT (NNT)

$$NNT = \frac{1}{ARR} = \frac{1}{0.0001} = 10,000 \text{ patients}$$

INTERPRETATION: 10,000 patients must receive the selenium instead of placebo to prevent one patient from developing skin cancer.

RELATIVE RISK (RR)

$$RR = \frac{EER}{CER} = \frac{339/1,309}{428/1,652} = 0.9996$$

INTERPRETATION: The probability of skin cancer in the selenium group is 0.9996 times that of the probability of skin cancer in the placebo group.

RELATIVE RISK REDUCTION (RRR)

RRR = 1 − RR = 1 − 0.9996 = 0.0004

INTERPRETATION: Patients in the selenium group have a 0.0004 (or 0.04%) lower probability of developing skin cancer compared to patients in the placebo group.

5. In the PROVE-IT trial, 26.6% of pravastatin recipients experienced acute cardiac events compared to 21.1% of patients in the atorvastatin group. What are the ARR, NNT, RR, and RRR?

ABSOLUTE RISK REDUCTION (ARR)

ARR = CER − EER = 0.266 − 0.211 = 0.055

INTERPRETATION: The probability that a patient in the atorvastatin group experienced an acute cardiac event was 0.055 (or 5.5%) lower than a patient in the pravastatin group.

NUMBER NEEDED TO TREAT (NNT)

$$NNT = \frac{1}{ARR} = \frac{1}{0.055} = 18.2 \therefore 19 \text{ patients}$$

INTERPRETATION: 19 patients must receive atorvastatin instead of pravastatin to prevent one patient from experiencing an acute cardiac event.

RELATIVE RISK (RR)

$$RR = \frac{EER}{CER} = \frac{0.211}{0.266} = 0.793$$

INTERPRETATION: The probability of an acute cardiac event in the atorvastatin group is 0.793 times that of the probability of an acute cardiac event in the pravastatin group.

RELATIVE RISK REDUCTION (RRR)

RRR = 1 − RR = 1 − 0.793 = 0.207

INTERPRETATION: Patients in the atorvastatin group have a 0.207 (or 20.7%) lower probability of an acute cardiac event compared to patients in the pravastatin group.

---

6. A clinical trial was conducted to determine whether a new immunomodulator drug can reduce multiple sclerosis relapses within 12 months compared to beta interferon. In the control group, 356 patients received beta interferon, among which 53 experienced a relapse within the 12-month study period. In the experimental group, 340 patients received the new immunomodulator, and 37 experienced a relapse within the 12-month study period. What are the ARR, NNT, RR, and RRR?

ABSOLUTE RISK REDUCTION (ARR)

ARR = CER − EER = (53/356) − (37/340) = 0.04

INTERPRETATION: The probability that a patient in the immunomodulator group will experience a relapse is 0.04 (or 4%) lower than a patient in the beta interferon group.

NUMBER NEEDED TO TREAT (NNT)

$$NNT = \frac{1}{ARR} = \frac{1}{0.04} = 25 \text{ patients}$$

INTERPRETATION: 25 patients must receive the new immunomodulator instead of beta interferon for 12 months to prevent one patient from experiencing a relapse.

RELATIVE RISK (RR)

$$RR = \frac{EER}{CER} = \frac{37/340}{53/356} = 0.731$$

INTERPRETATION: The probability of a relapse in the immunomodulator group is 0.731 times that of the probability of a relapse in the beta interferon group.

RELATIVE RISK REDUCTION (RRR)

RRR = 1 − RR = 1 − 0.731 = 0.269

INTERPRETATION: Patients in the immunomodulator group have a 0.269 (or 26.9%) lower probability of a relapse compared to patients in the beta interferon group.

7. A clinical trial was conducted to determine whether a 5-HT$_1$ receptor agonist can reduce the frequency of migraine recurrence within 24 hours compared to a placebo. In the control group, 188 patients received placebo at the onset of a migraine, among which 47 experienced migraine recurrence within 24 hours. In the experimental group, 189 patients received a 5-HT$_1$ receptor agonist and 19 experienced migraine recurrence within 24 hours. What are the ARR, NNT, RR, and RRR?

ABSOLUTE RISK REDUCTION (ARR)

ARR = CER − EER = (47/188) − (19/189) = 0.15

INTERPRETATION: The probability that a patient in the 5-HT$_1$ agonist group will have a recurrent migraine within 24 hours is 0.15 (or 15%) lower than a patient in the placebo group.

NUMBER NEEDED TO TREAT (NNT)

$$\text{NNT} = \frac{1}{\text{ARR}} = \frac{1}{0.15} = 6.7 \therefore 7 \text{ patients}$$

INTERPRETATION: 7 patients must receive the 5-HT$_1$ agonist instead of the placebo to prevent one patient from having a recurrent migraine within 24 hours.

RELATIVE RISK (RR)

$$\text{RR} = \frac{\text{EER}}{\text{CER}} = \frac{19/189}{47/188} = 0.40$$

INTERPRETATION: The probability of a recurrent migraine within 24 hours in the 5-HT$_1$ agonist group is 0.40 times that of the probability in the placebo group.

RELATIVE RISK REDUCTION (RRR)

RRR = 1 − RR = 1 − 0.40 = 0.60

INTERPRETATION: Patients in the 5-HT$_1$ agonist group have a 0.60 (or 60%) lower probability of a recurrent migraine within 24 hours compared to patients in the placebo group.

8. A clinical trial was conducted to determine whether benzodiazepines (BZDs) reduce the number of panic attacks within a 10-week treatment period compared to placebo. In the control group, 92 patients received a placebo once daily for 10 weeks, and 65 patients reported a panic attack within the 10-week treatment period. In the experimental group, 96 patients received a BZD once daily for 10 weeks, and 38 reported a panic attack within the treatment period. What are the ARR, NNT, RR, and RRR?

ABSOLUTE RISK REDUCTION (ARR)

ARR = CER − EER = (65/92) − (38/96) = 0.31

INTERPRETATION: The probability that a patient in the BZD group will have a panic attack within 10 weeks is 0.31 (or 31%) lower than a patient in the placebo group.

NUMBER NEEDED TO TREAT (NNT)

$$\text{NNT} = \frac{1}{\text{ARR}} = \frac{1}{0.31} = 3.2 \therefore 4 \text{ patients}$$

INTERPRETATION: 4 patients must receive the BZD instead of placebo to prevent one patient from having a panic attack within 10 weeks.

RELATIVE RISK (RR)

$$\text{RR} = \frac{\text{EER}}{\text{CER}} = \frac{38/96}{65/92} = 0.56$$

INTERPRETATION: The probability of a panic attack within 10 weeks in the BZD group is 0.56 times that of the probability in the placebo group.

RELATIVE RISK REDUCTION (RRR)

RRR = 1 − RR = 1 − 0.56 = 0.44

INTERPRETATION: Patients in the BZD group have a 0.44 (or 44%) lower probability of a panic attack within 10 weeks compared to patients in the placebo group.

9. A clinical trial was conducted to determine whether a selective estrogen receptor modulator (SERM) reduces the number of vertebral fractures over four years compared to placebo. In the control group, 919 postmenopausal female patients were treated with placebo once daily, among which 49 sustained at least one new vertebral fracture during the four-year treatment period. In the experimental group, 923 postmenopausal female patients were treated with a SERM once daily, and only 23 sustained at least one new vertebral fracture over the same four years. What are the ARR, NNT, RR, and RRR?

ABSOLUTE RISK REDUCTION (ARR)

ARR = CER − EER = (49/919) − (23/923) = 0.0284

INTERPRETATION: The probability that a patient in the SERM group will have at least one new vertebral fracture in four years is 0.0284 (or 2.84%%) lower than a patient in the placebo group.

NUMBER NEEDED TO TREAT (NNT)

$$\text{NNT} = \frac{1}{\text{ARR}} = \frac{1}{0.0284} = 35.2 \therefore 36 \text{ patients}$$

INTERPRETATION: 36 patients must receive the SERM instead of placebo to prevent one patient from having at least one new vertebral fracture in four years.

RELATIVE RISK (RR)

$$\text{RR} = \frac{\text{EER}}{\text{CER}} = \frac{23/923}{49/919} = 0.467$$

INTERPRETATION: The probability of at least one new vertebral fracture over four years in the SERM group is 0.467 times that of the probability in the placebo group.

RELATIVE RISK REDUCTION (RRR)

RRR = 1 − RR = 1 − 0.467 = 0.533

INTERPRETATION: Patients in the SERM group have a 0.533 (or 53.3%) lower probability of at least one new vertebral fracture over four years compared to patients in the placebo group.

---

10. A clinical trial was conducted to determine whether a proton pump inhibitor (PPI) is more effective than placebo at eliminating gastroesophageal reflux disease (GERD) symptoms in seven days. In the experimental group, 200 patients received a PPI once daily for seven days, among which 50 reported continued GERD symptoms at the end of the treatment period. In the placebo group, 200 patients received a placebo once daily for seven days, among which 170 reported continued GERD symptoms at the end of the treatment period. What are the ARR, NNT, RR, and RRR?

ABSOLUTE RISK REDUCTION (ARR)

ARR = CER − EER = (170/200) − (50/200) = 0.60

INTERPRETATION: The probability that a patient in the PPI group will have GERD symptoms in seven days is 0.60 (or 60%) lower than a patient in the placebo group.

NUMBER NEEDED TO TREAT (NNT)

$$\text{NNT} = \frac{1}{\text{ARR}} = \frac{1}{0.60} = 1.67 \therefore 2 \text{ patients}$$

INTERPRETATION: 2 patients must receive the PPI instead of placebo to prevent one patient from experiencing continued GERD symptoms in seven days.

RELATIVE RISK (RR)

$$\text{RR} = \frac{\text{EER}}{\text{CER}} = \frac{50/200}{170/200} = 0.294$$

INTERPRETATION: The probability that a patient in the PPI group experiences continued GERD symptoms in seven days is 0.294 times that of the probability in the placebo group.

RELATIVE RISK REDUCTION (RRR)

RRR = 1 − RR = 1 − 0.294 = 0.706

INTERPRETATION: Patients in the PPI group have a 0.706 (or 70.6%) lower probability of continued GERD symptoms in seven days compared to patients in the placebo group.

11. In a clinical trial, 40% of the control group died, and 10% of the experimental group died. What are the ARR, NNT, RR, and RRR?

ABSOLUTE RISK REDUCTION (ARR)

ARR = CER − EER = 0.40 − 0.10 = 0.30

INTERPRETATION: The probability that a patient in the control group will die is 0.30 (or 30%) lower than the probability of death for a patient in the placebo group.

NUMBER NEEDED TO TREAT (NNT)

$$NNT = \frac{1}{ARR} = \frac{1}{0.30} = 3.33 \therefore 4 \text{ patients}$$

INTERPRETATION: 4 patients must receive the experimental treatment instead of the control treatment to prevent one patient from dying.

RELATIVE RISK (RR)

$$RR = \frac{EER}{CER} = \frac{0.10}{0.40} = 0.25$$

INTERPRETATION: The probability that a patient in the experimental group will die is 0.25 times that of the probability of death for a patient in the control group.

RELATIVE RISK REDUCTION (RRR)

RRR = 1 − RR = 1 − 0.25 = 0.75

INTERPRETATION: Patients in the experimental group have a 0.75 (or 75%) lower probability of death compared to patients in the control group.

12. A clinical trial was undertaken to determine whether a parathyroid hormone (PTH) analog reduces vertebral fractures in postmenopausal women. In the experimental group, 434 postmenopausal females received once-daily injections of the PTH analog, 22 of which sustained a vertebral fracture. In the control group, 449 postmenopausal female patients received once-daily placebo injections, among which 63 suffered a vertebral fracture. What are the ARR, NNT, RR, and RRR?

ABSOLUTE RISK REDUCTION (ARR)

ARR = CER − EER = (63/449) − (22/434) = 0.09

INTERPRETATION: The probability that a patient in the PTH analog group will sustain a vertebral fracture is 0.09 (or 9%) lower than the probability in the placebo group.

NUMBER NEEDED TO TREAT (NNT)

$$NNT = \frac{1}{ARR} = \frac{1}{0.09} = 11.11 \therefore 12 \text{ patients}$$

INTERPRETATION: 12 patients must receive the PTH analog instead of placebo to prevent one patient from sustaining a vertebral fracture.

RELATIVE RISK (RR)

$$RR = \frac{EER}{CER} = \frac{22/434}{63/449} = 0.36$$

INTERPRETATION: The probability that a patient in the PTH analog group will sustain a vertebral fracture is 0.36 times that of the probability in the placebo group.

RELATIVE RISK REDUCTION (RRR)

RRR = 1 − RR = 1 − 0.36 = 0.64

INTERPRETATION: Patients in the PTH analog group have a 0.64 (or 64%) lower probability of sustaining a vertebral fracture compared to patients in the placebo group.

13. A clinical trial was conducted to determine whether an antiviral is more effective than a placebo for influenza post-exposure prophylaxis. In the control group, 207 household contacts received a placebo for influenza post-exposure prophylaxis, and 25 contracted influenza. In the experimental group, 226 household contacts received an antiviral for influenza post-exposure prophylaxis, among which three contracted influenza. What are the ARR, NNT, RR, and RRR?

ABSOLUTE RISK REDUCTION (ARR)

ARR = CER − EER = (25/207) − (3/226) = 0.1075

INTERPRETATION: The probability that a patient in the antiviral group will contract influenza is 0.1075 (or 10.75%) lower than the probability in the placebo group.

NUMBER NEEDED TO TREAT (NNT)

$$\text{NNT} = \frac{1}{\text{ARR}} = \frac{1}{0.1075} = 9.3 \therefore 10 \text{ patients}$$

INTERPRETATION: 10 patients must receive the antiviral drug instead of placebo to prevent one patient from contracting influenza.

RELATIVE RISK (RR)

$$\text{RR} = \frac{\text{EER}}{\text{CER}} = \frac{3/226}{25/207} = 0.11$$

INTERPRETATION: The probability that a patient in the antiviral group will contract influenza is 0.11 times that of the probability in the placebo group.

RELATIVE RISK REDUCTION (RRR)

RRR = 1 − RR = 1 − 0.11 = 0.89

INTERPRETATION: Patients in the antiviral group have a 0.89 (or 89%) lower probability of contracting influenza compared to patients in the placebo group.

---

14. A clinical trial was conducted in patients with unstable angina to determine whether the combination of a glycoprotein (GP) IIb/IIIa inhibitor and low molecular weight heparin (LMWH) results in fewer cases of cutaneous bleeding compared to the combination of a GP IIb/IIIa and unfractionated heparin (UFH). In the experimental group, 661 patients received a GP IIb/IIIa inhibitor and LMWH, among which 125 experienced cutaneous bleeding. In the control group, 639 patients received the GP IIb/IIIa inhibitor and UFH, and 142 experienced cutaneous bleeding. What are the ARR, NNT, RR, and RRR?

ABSOLUTE RISK REDUCTION (ARR)

ARR = CER − EER = (142/639) − (125/661) = 0.033

INTERPRETATION: The probability that a patient in the LMWH group will experience cutaneous bleeding is 0.033 (or 3.3%) lower than the probability in the UFH group.

NUMBER NEEDED TO TREAT (NNT)

$$\text{NNT} = \frac{1}{\text{ARR}} = \frac{1}{0.033} = 30.3 \therefore 31 \text{ patients}$$

INTERPRETATION: 31 patients must receive the LMWH instead of UFH (in combination with the GP IIb/IIIa inhibitor) to prevent one patient from experiencing cutaneous bleeding.

RELATIVE RISK (RR)

$$\text{RR} = \frac{\text{EER}}{\text{CER}} = \frac{125/661}{142/639} = 0.851$$

INTERPRETATION: The probability that a patient in the LMWH group will experience cutaneous bleeding is 0.851 times that of the probability in the UFH group.

RELATIVE RISK REDUCTION (RRR)

RRR = 1 − RR = 1 − 0.851 = 0.149

INTERPRETATION: Patients in the LMWH group have a 0.149 (or 14.9%) lower probability of cutaneous bleeding compared to patients in the UFH group.

15. A clinical trial was conducted in patients experiencing a chronic obstructive pulmonary disease (COPD) exacerbation to determine whether the combination of albuterol, antibiotics, and prednisone is more effective than albuterol, antibiotics, and placebo at reducing recurrent COPD exacerbations within 30 days. In the control group, 100 patients were treated with albuterol, antibiotics, and placebo, among which 45 experienced a COPD exacerbation within 30 days. In the experimental group, 100 patients were treated with albuterol, antibiotics, and prednisone, and 30 experienced a COPD exacerbation within 30 days. What are the ARR, NNT, RR, and RRR?

ABSOLUTE RISK REDUCTION (ARR)

ARR = CER − EER = (45/100) − (30/100) = 0.15

INTERPRETATION: The probability that a patient in the prednisone group will have another exacerbation within 30 days is 0.15 (or 15%) lower than the probability in the placebo group.

NUMBER NEEDED TO TREAT (NNT)

$$NNT = \frac{1}{ARR} = \frac{1}{0.15} = 6.67 \therefore 7 \text{ patients}$$

INTERPRETATION: 7 patients must receive the prednisone instead of placebo (with albuterol and antibiotics) to prevent one patient from having another exacerbation within 30 days.

RELATIVE RISK (RR)

$$RR = \frac{EER}{CER} = \frac{30/100}{45/100} = 0.67$$

INTERPRETATION: The probability that a patient in the prednisone group will have another exacerbation is 0.67 times that of the probability in the placebo group.

RELATIVE RISK REDUCTION (RRR)

RRR = 1 − RR = 1 − 0.67 = 0.33

INTERPRETATION: Patients in the prednisone group have a 0.33 (or 33%) lower probability of another exacerbation compared to patients in the placebo group.

TIPS for SUCCESS

THE 48-HOUR RULE

Never underestimate how much you can forget in a few days. It may be tempting to work through this book one time and never look back. Despite any level of confidence you may feel, I strongly recommend reviewing as many math problems as possible during the 48 hours leading up to the exam. You'll likely bring to mind many important nuances that might otherwise have been forgotten.

2X

MINIMUM
DO EVERY PROBLEM AT LEAST TWO TIMES

℥
29.57 mL
1 FLUID OUNCE (VOLUME)

1 pint
16 FLUID OUNCES

1 quart
32 FLUID OUNCES

1 gallon
128 FLUID OUNCES

28.35 g
1 OUNCE (MASS)

454 g
1 POUND

64.8 mg
1 GRAIN

aa

SIG CODE *for* "OF EACH"

ss

SIG CODE *for* "ONE-HALF"

SID

VETERINARY SIG CODE *for* "ONCE DAILY"

Made in the USA
Las Vegas, NV
01 May 2024

89307958R00096